AF505744

A GUIDE FOR THE PROTECTION OF THE PUBLIC IN PEACETIME

by

ARCHIVE OF MODERN CONFLICT

NOT FOR THE GENERAL PUBLIC

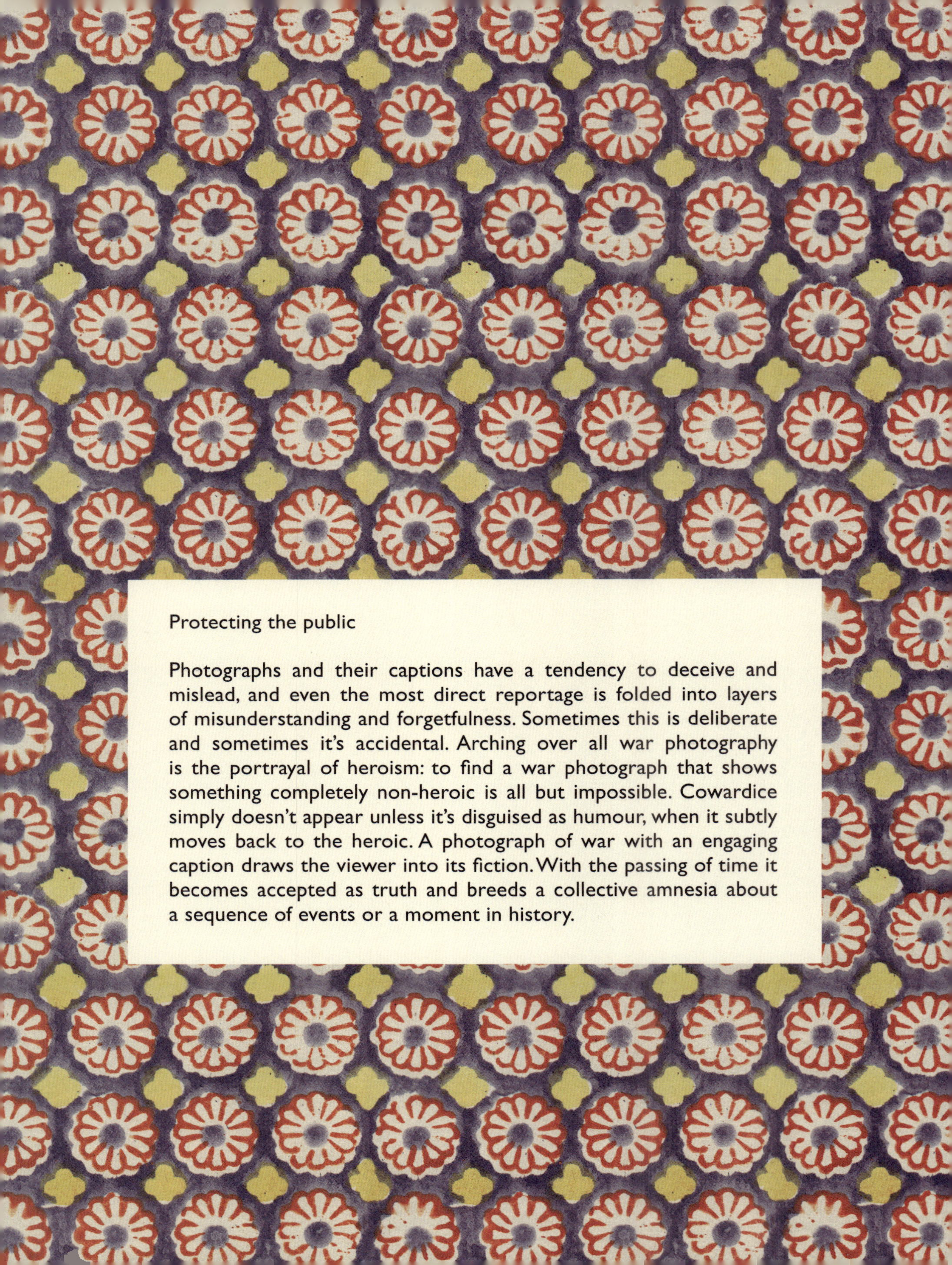

Protecting the public

Photographs and their captions have a tendency to deceive and mislead, and even the most direct reportage is folded into layers of misunderstanding and forgetfulness. Sometimes this is deliberate and sometimes it's accidental. Arching over all war photography is the portrayal of heroism: to find a war photograph that shows something completely non-heroic is all but impossible. Cowardice simply doesn't appear unless it's disguised as humour, when it subtly moves back to the heroic. A photograph of war with an engaging caption draws the viewer into its fiction. With the passing of time it becomes accepted as truth and breeds a collective amnesia about a sequence of events or a moment in history.

pour des expériences de gaz

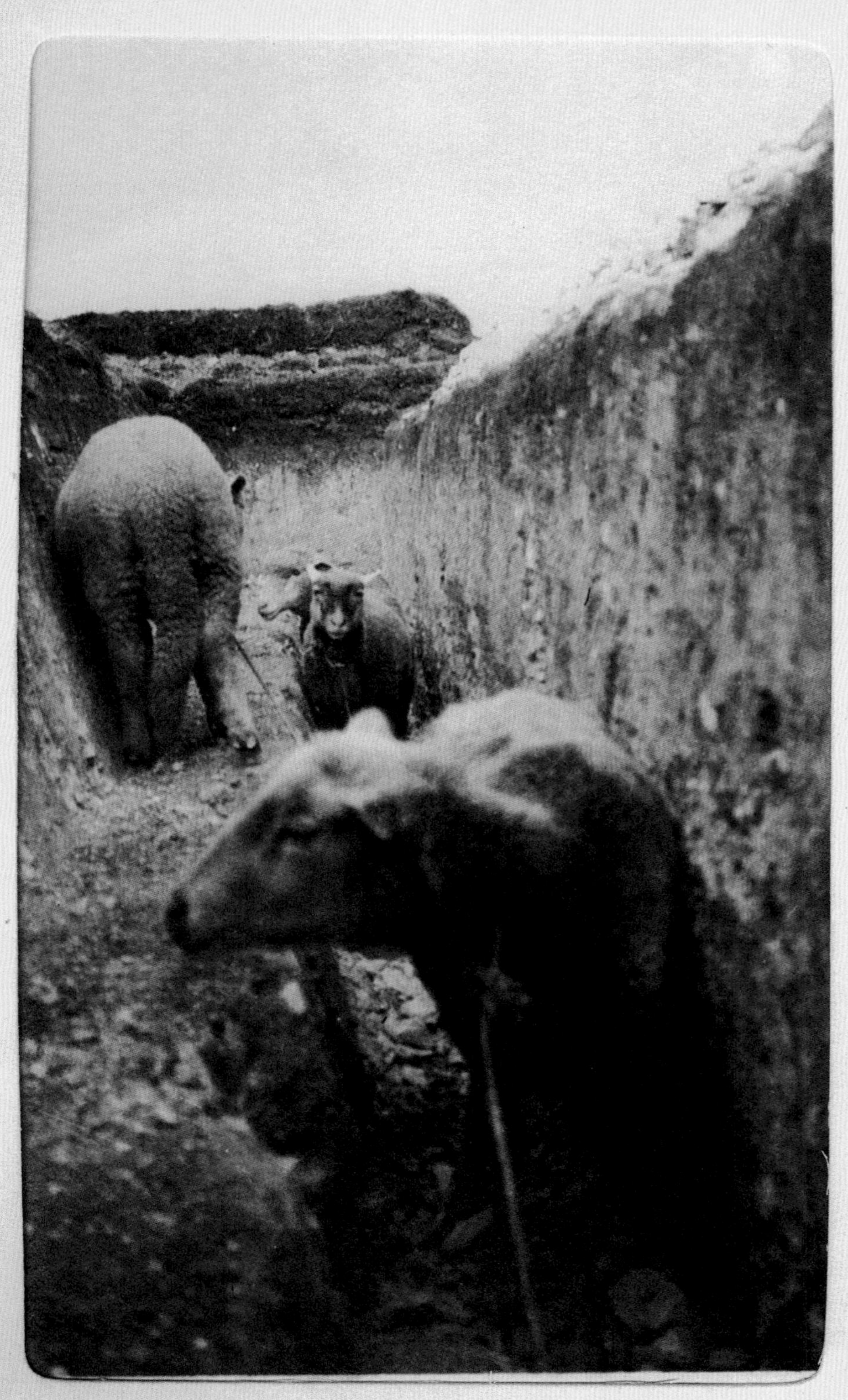

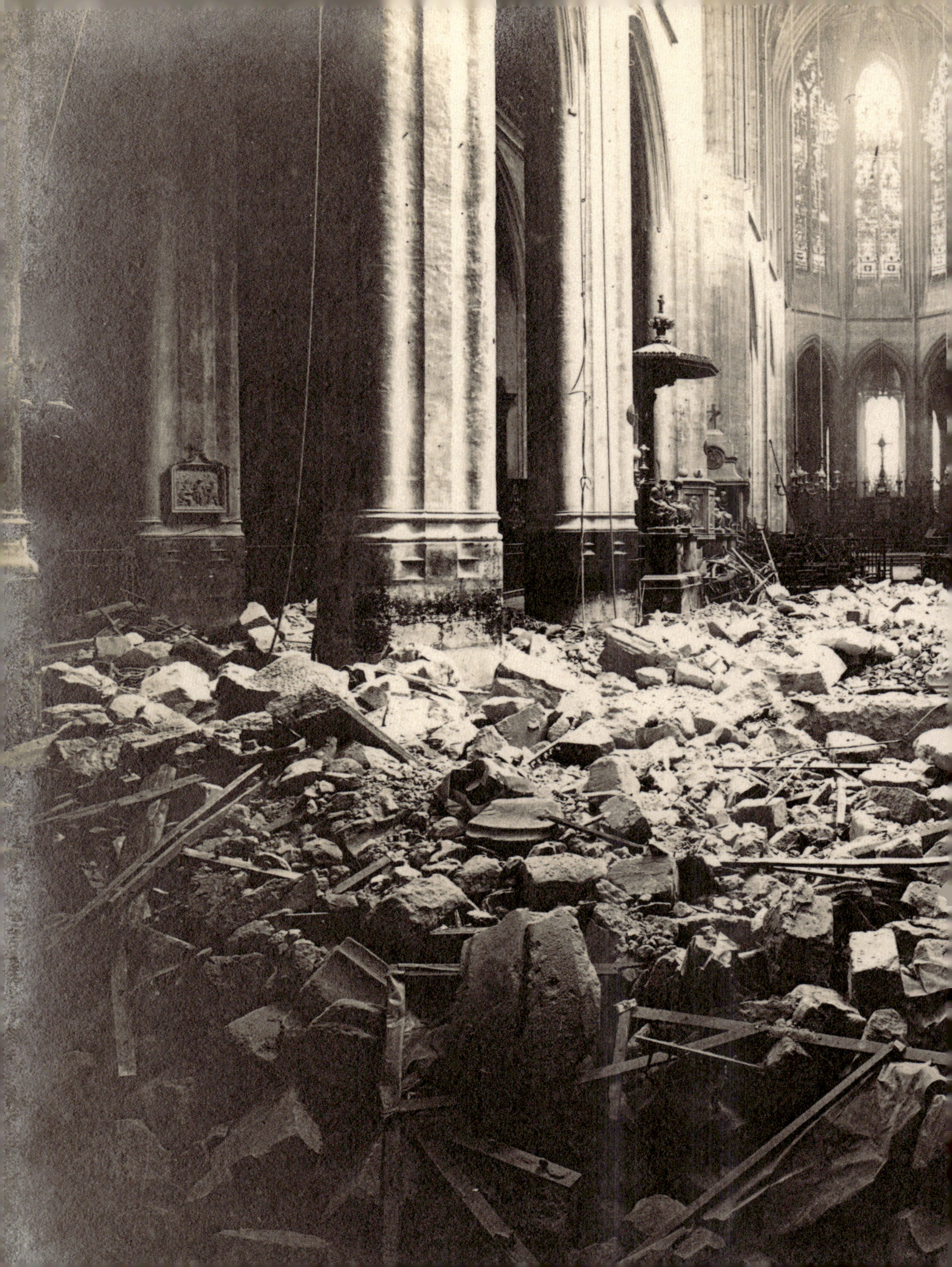

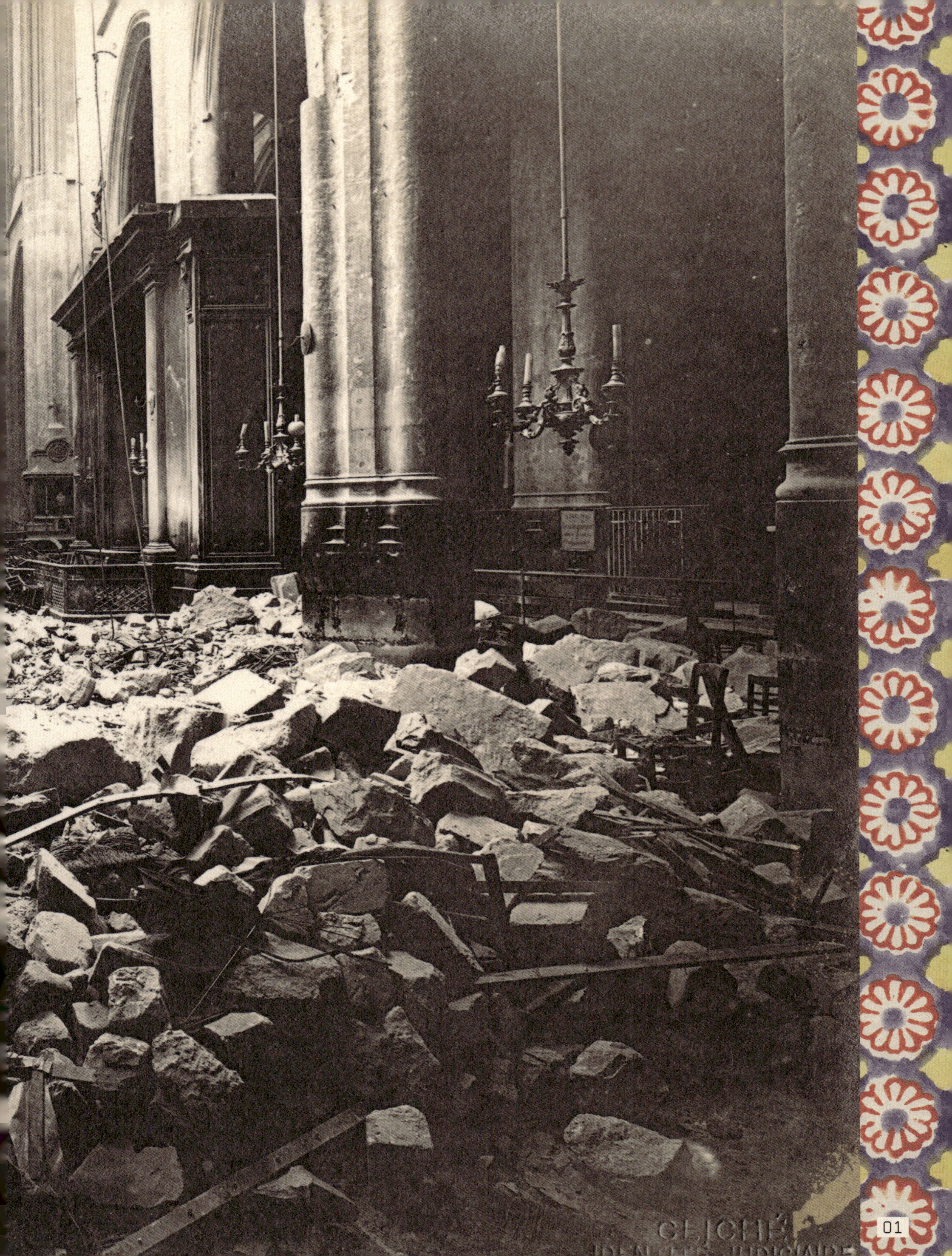
CLICHÉ
IDENTITÉS JUDICIAIRE

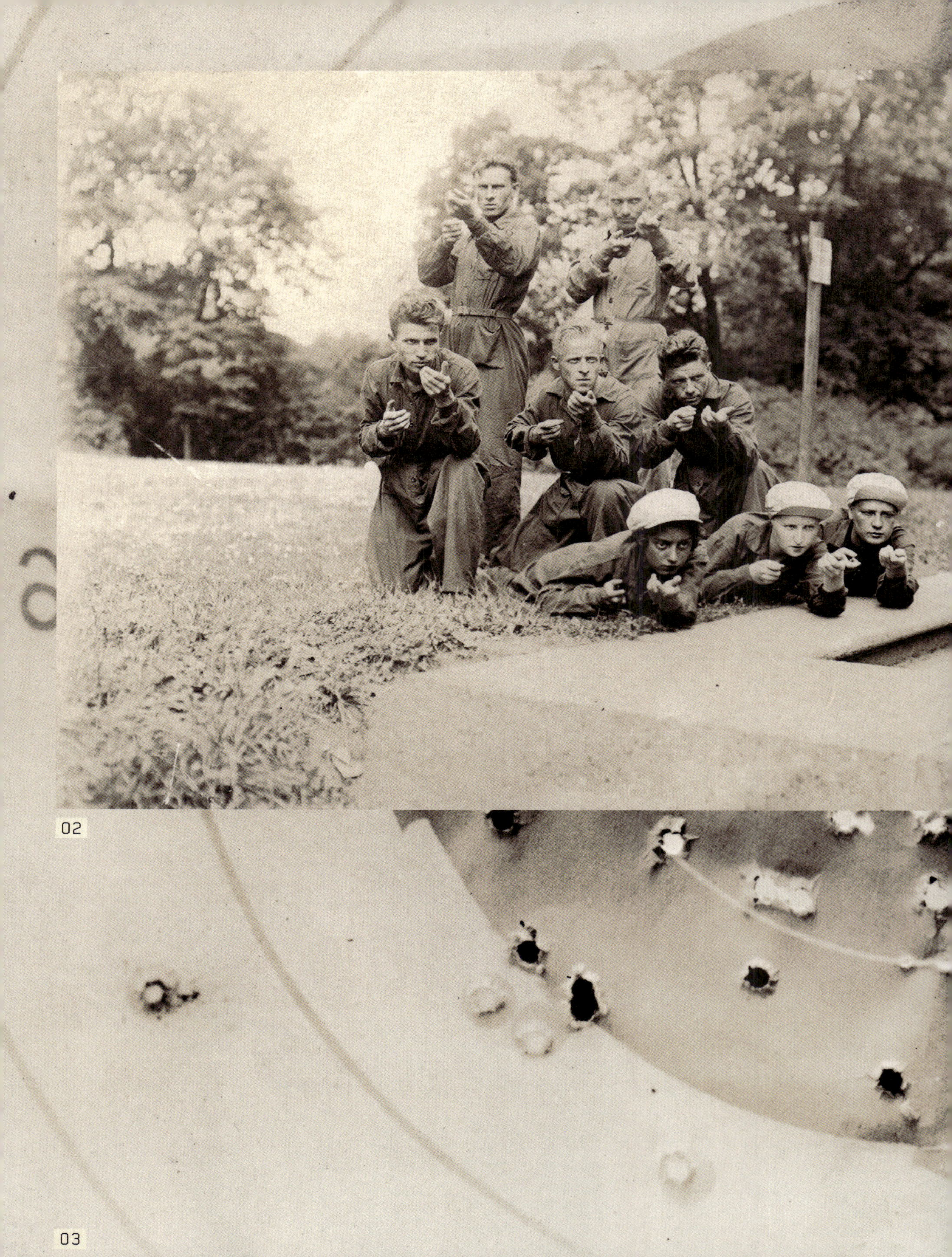

02

03

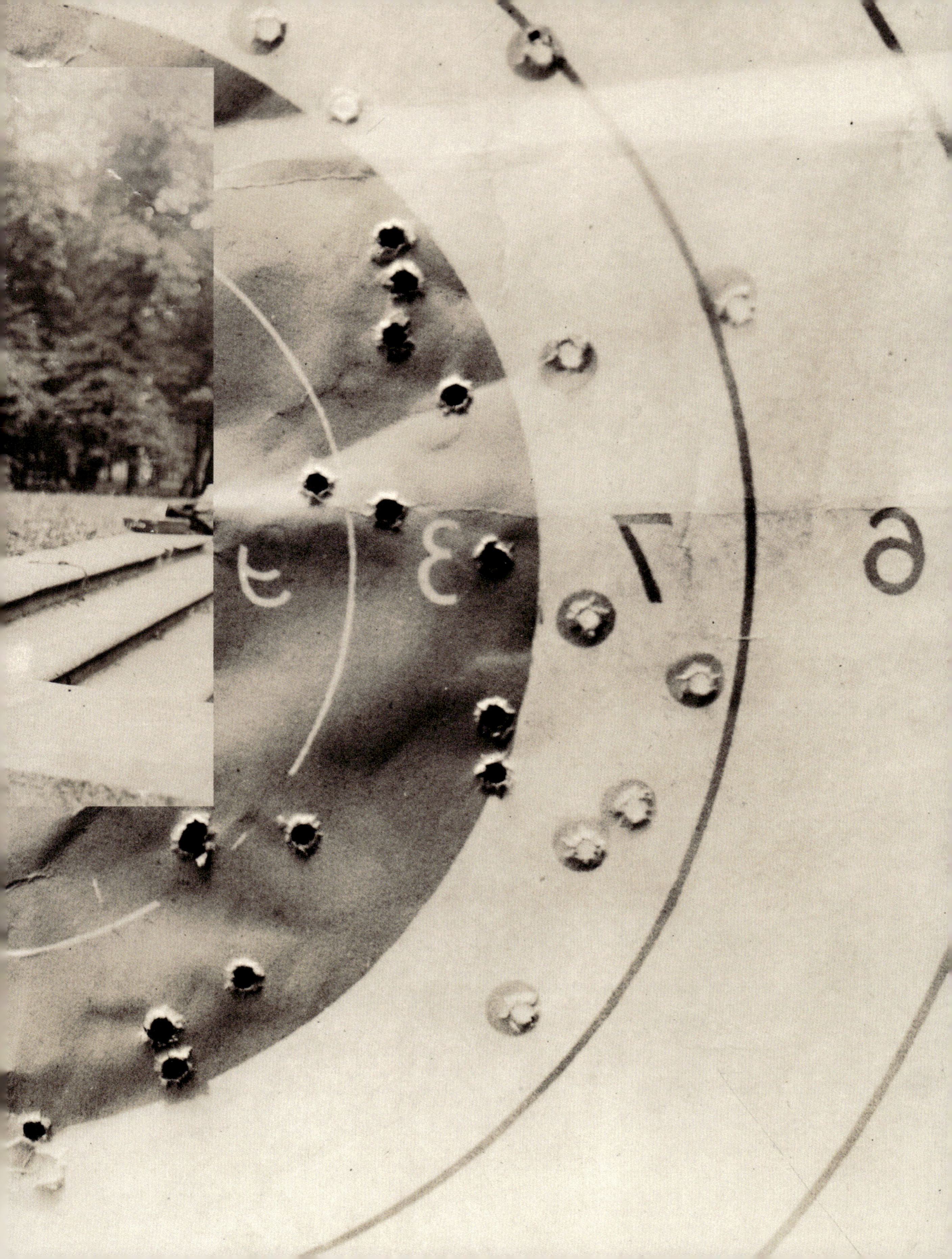

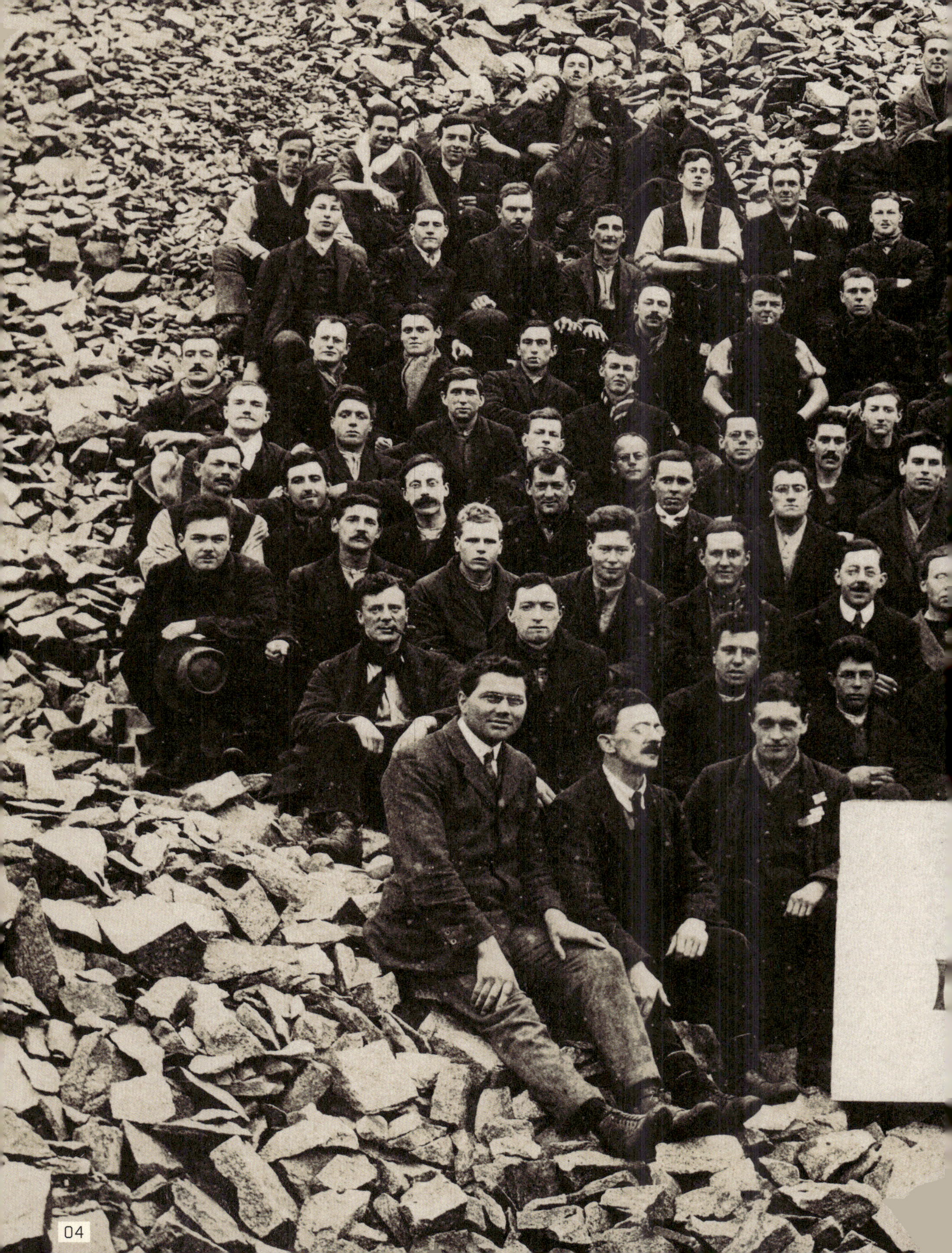

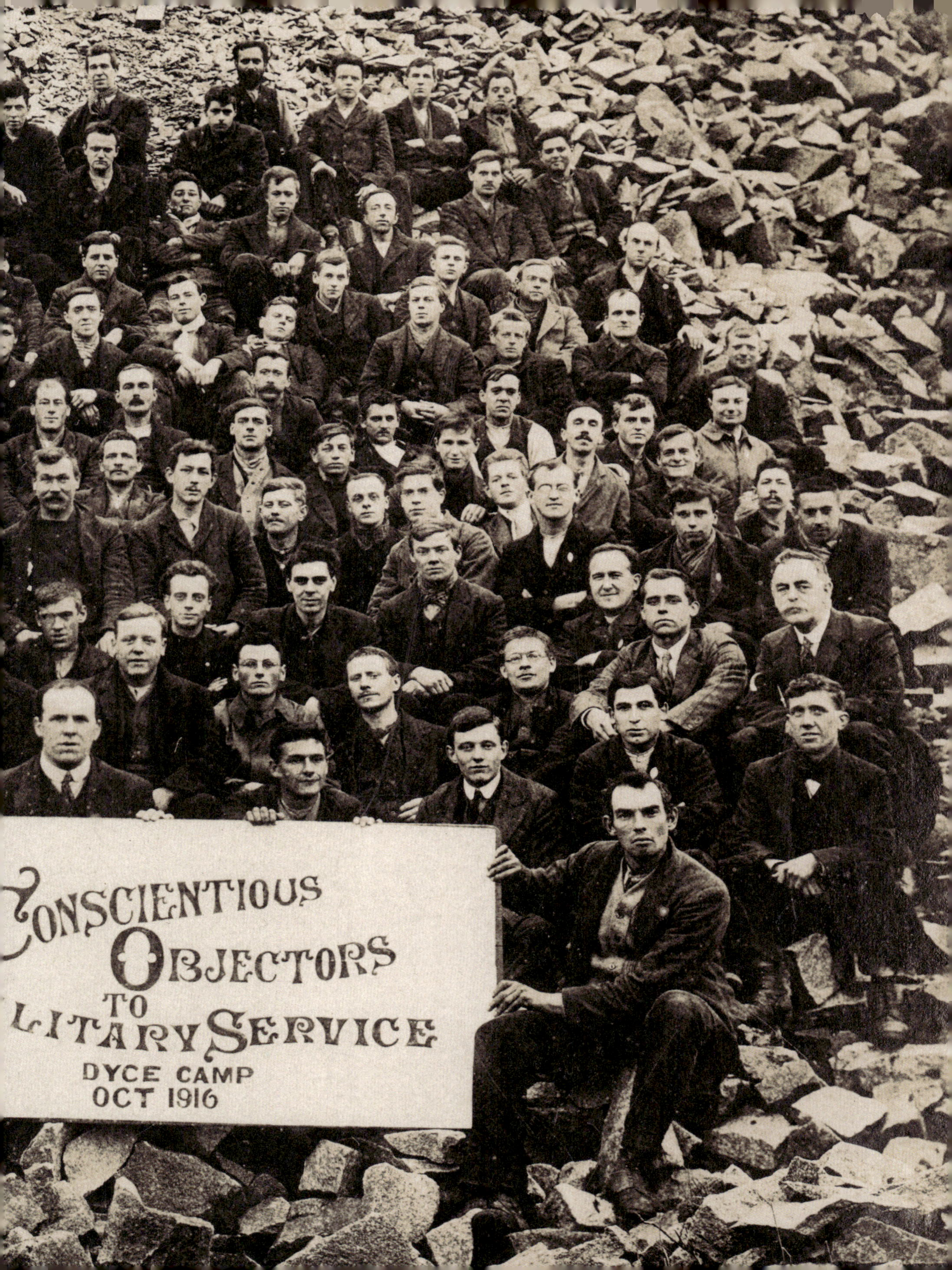

CONSCIENTIOUS
OBJECTORS
TO
MILITARY SERVICE
DYCE CAMP
OCT 1916

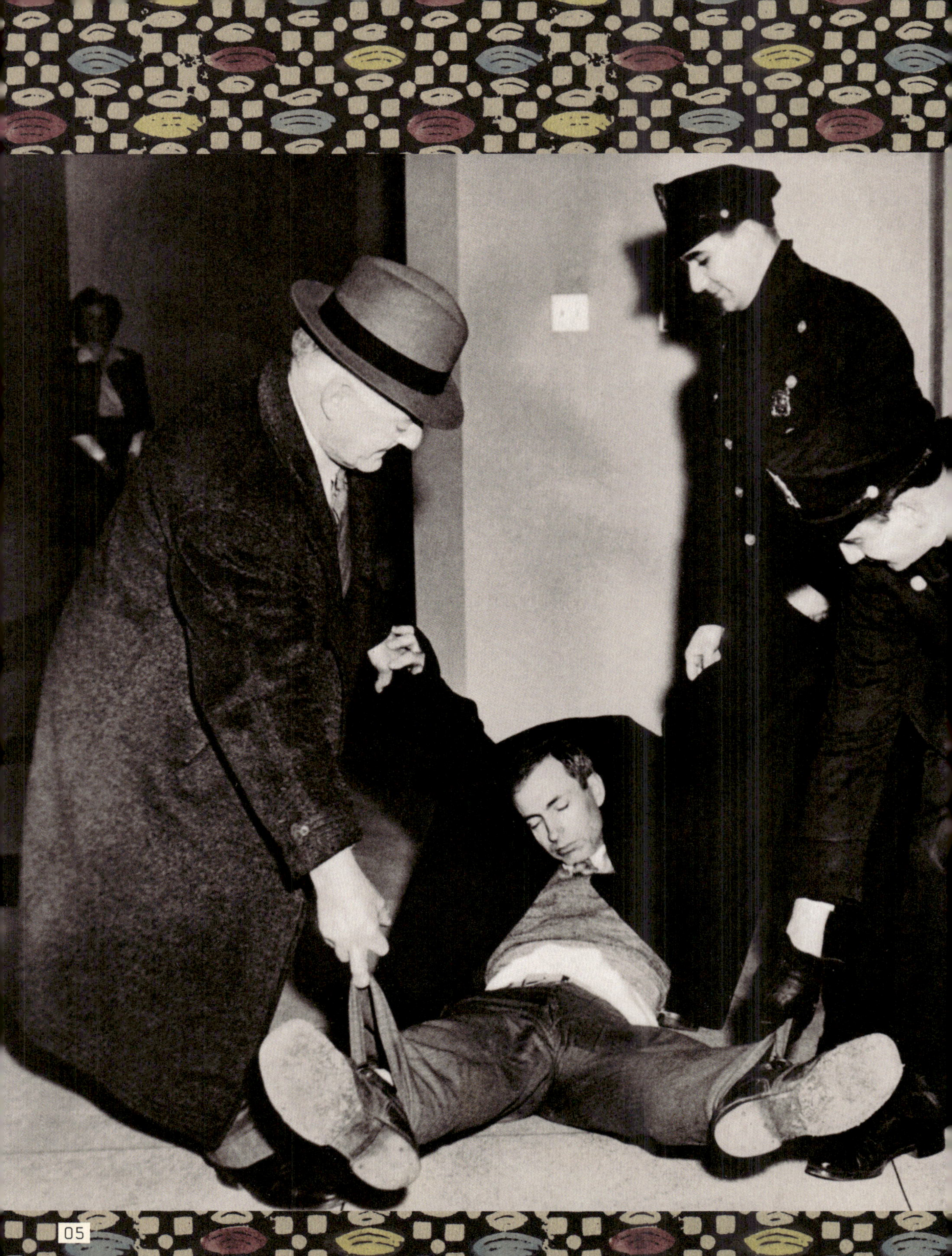

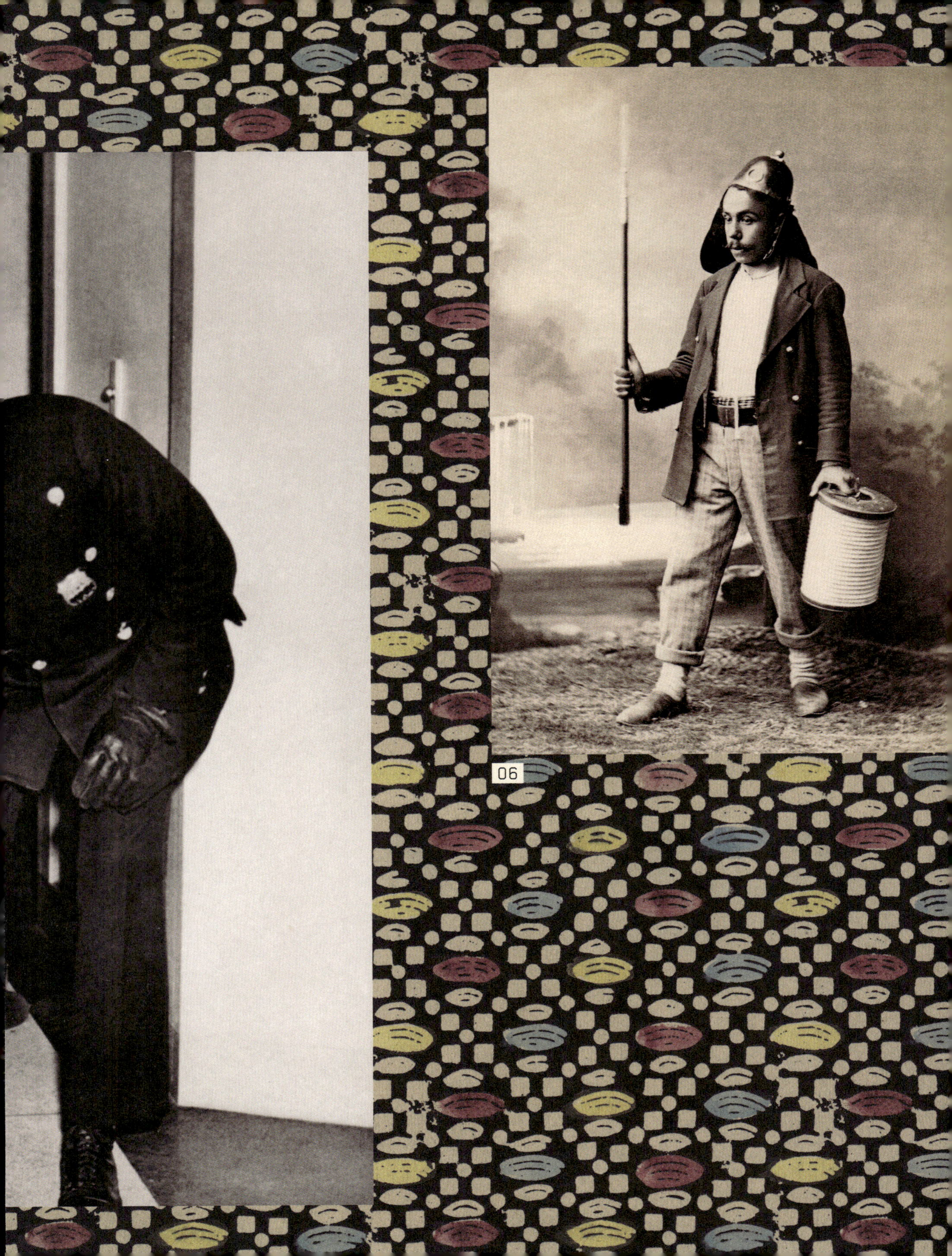
06

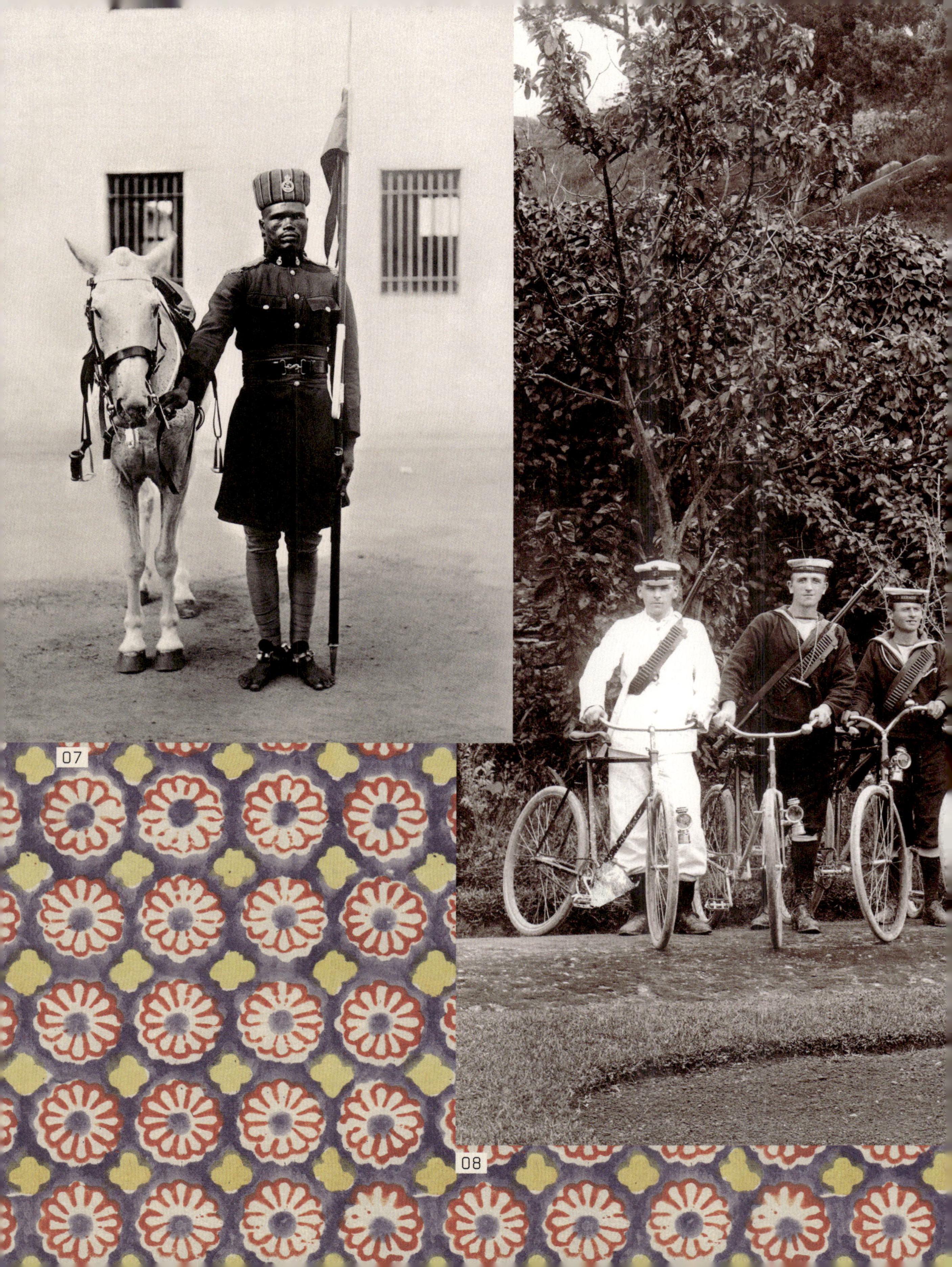
07
08

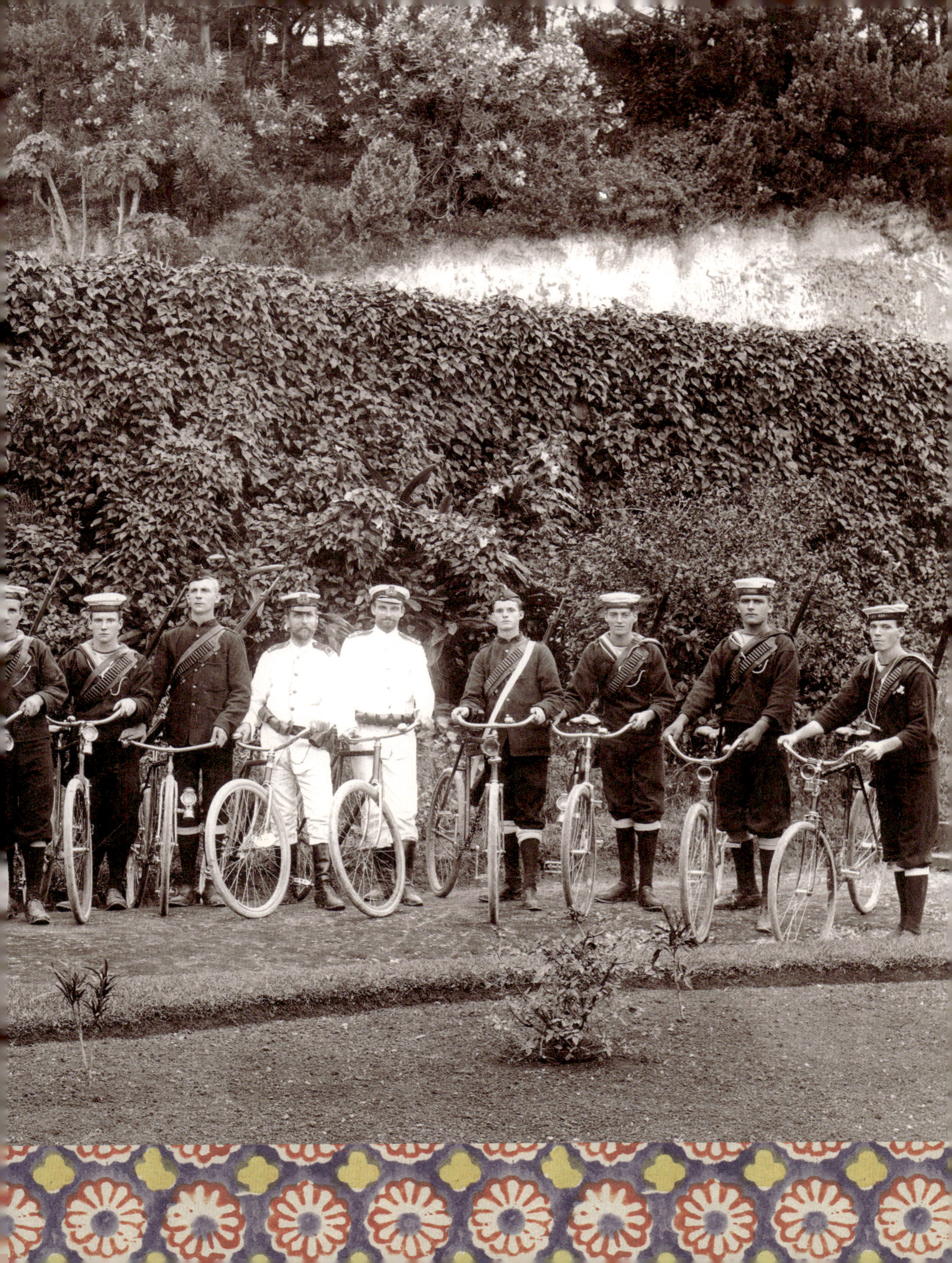

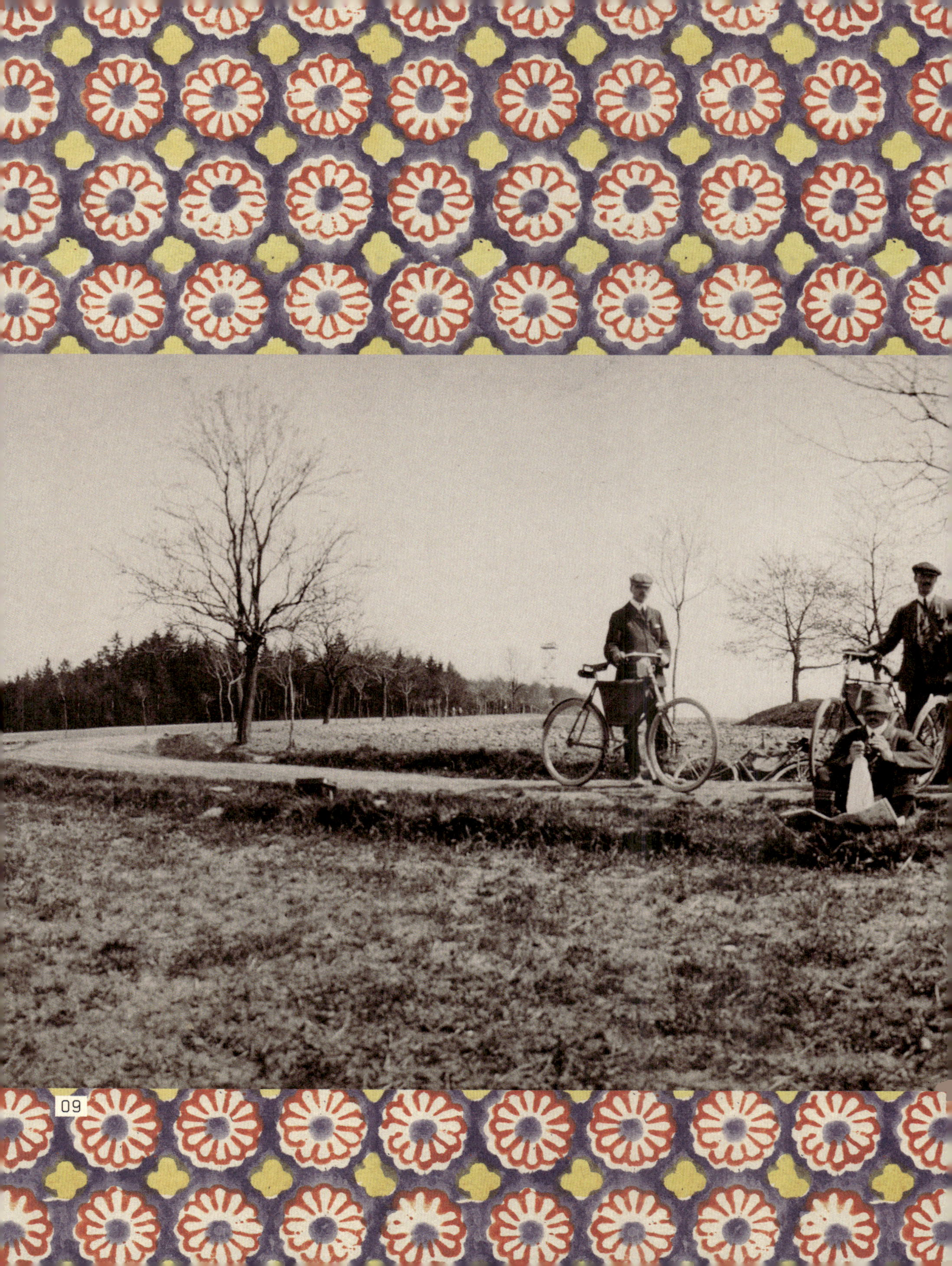

09

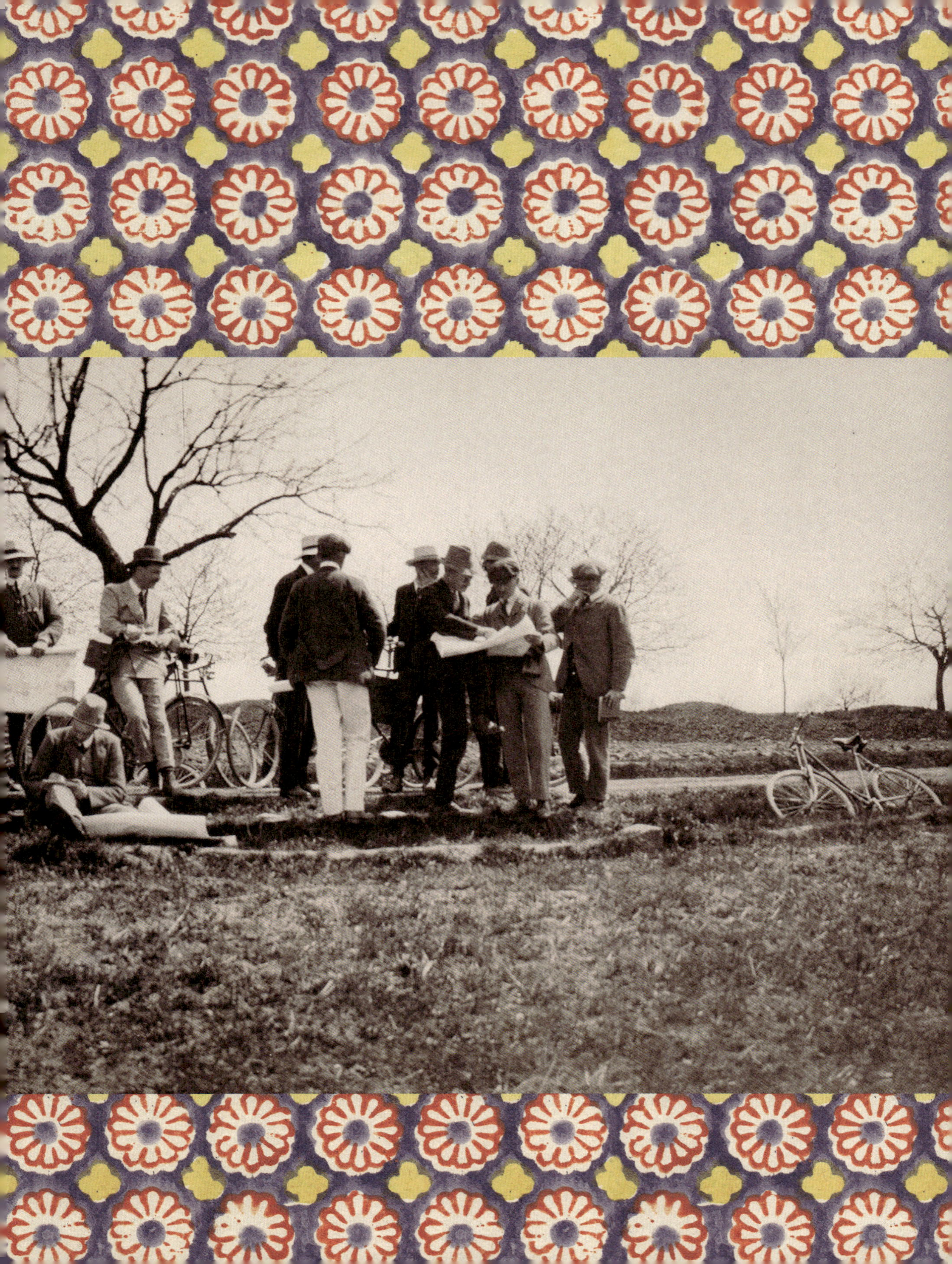

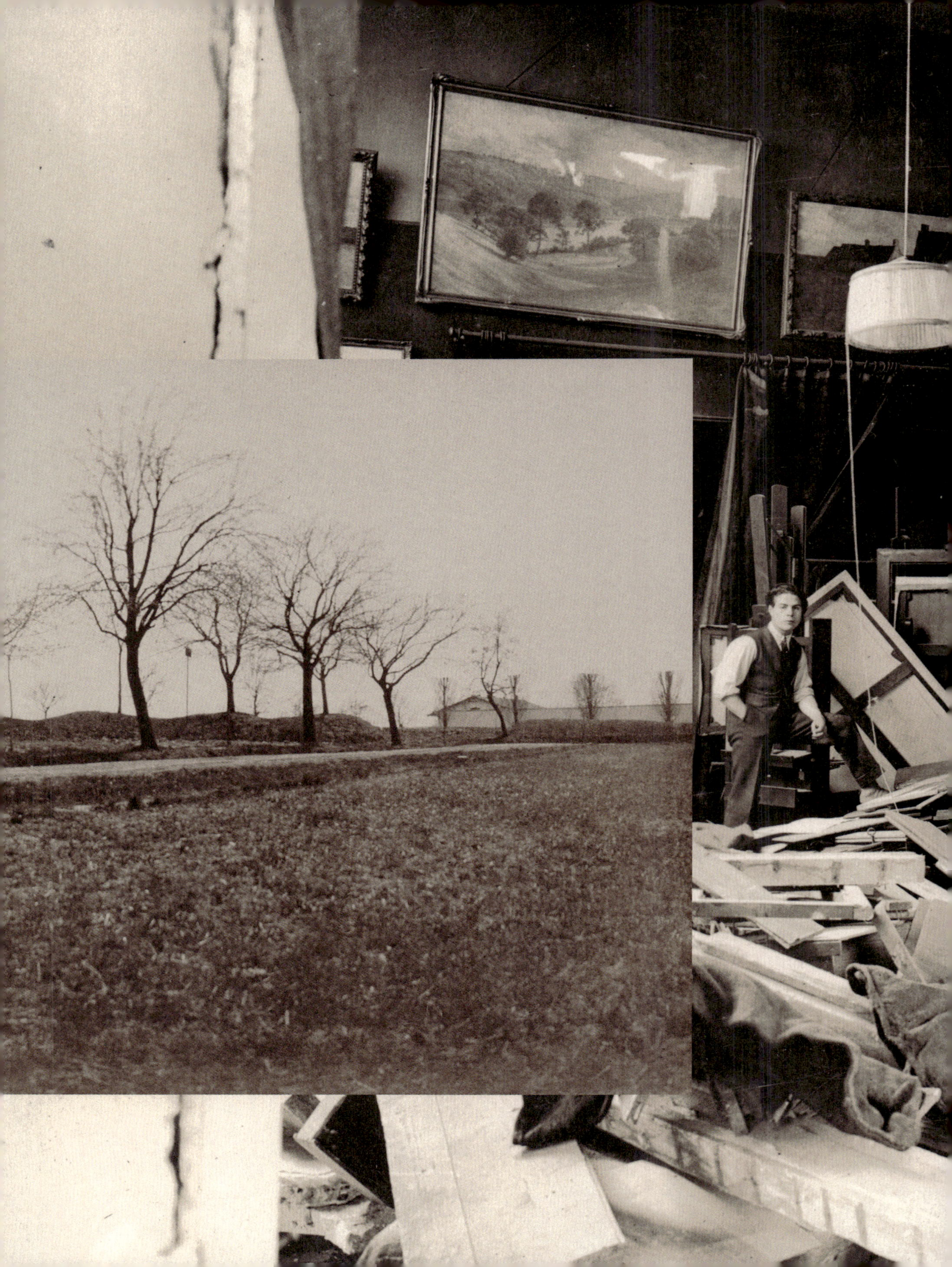

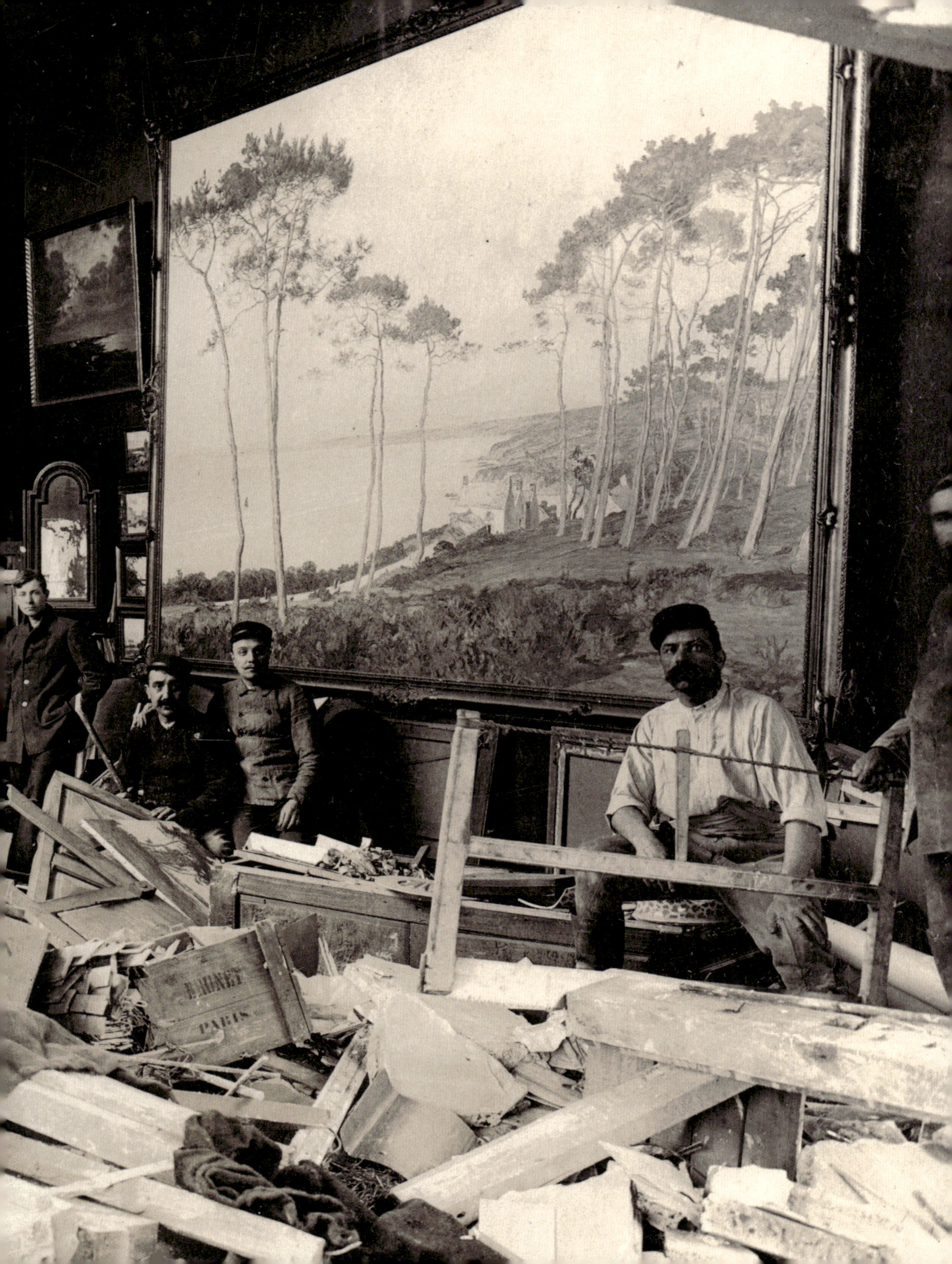
BRUNET
PARIS

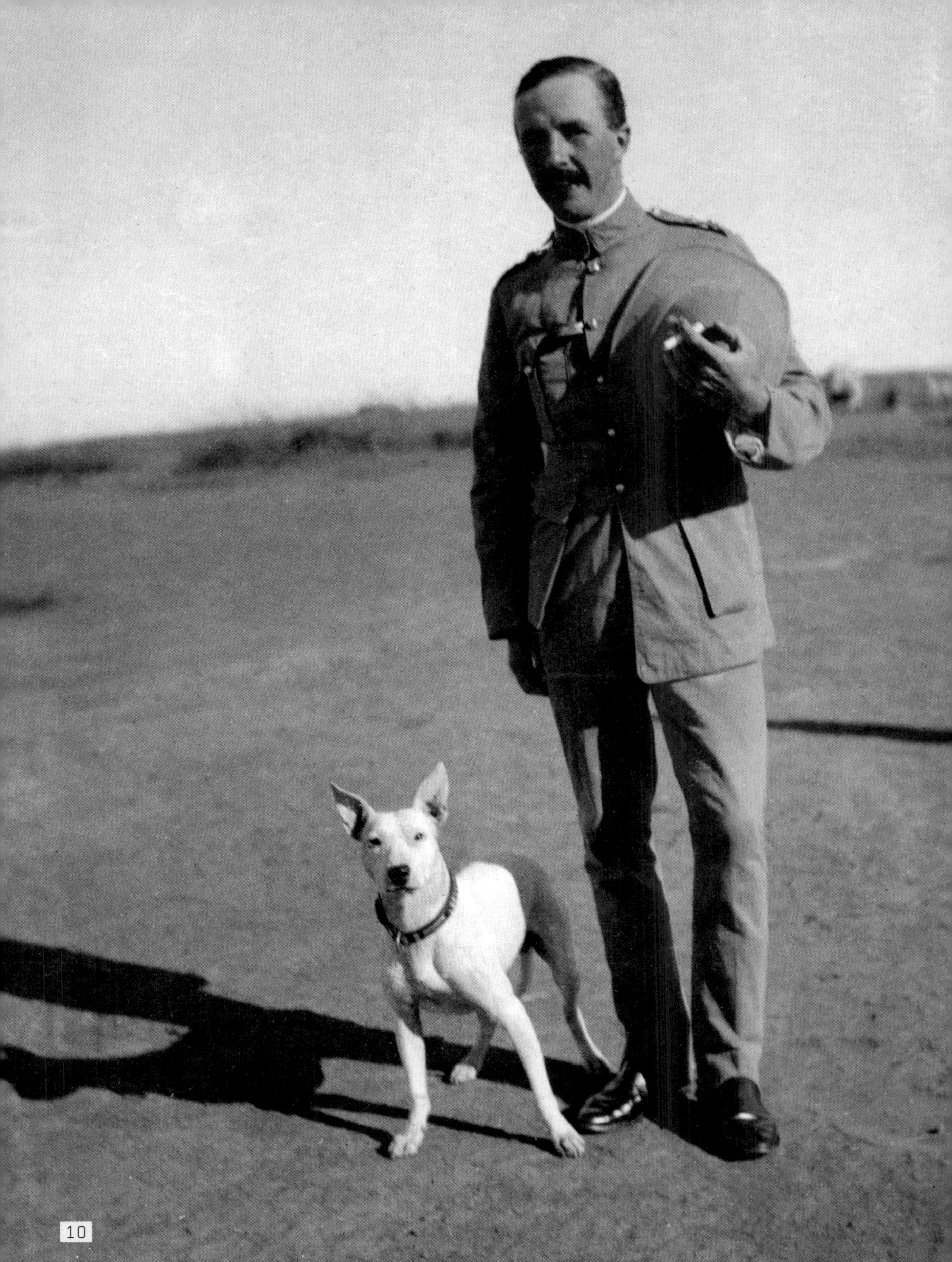

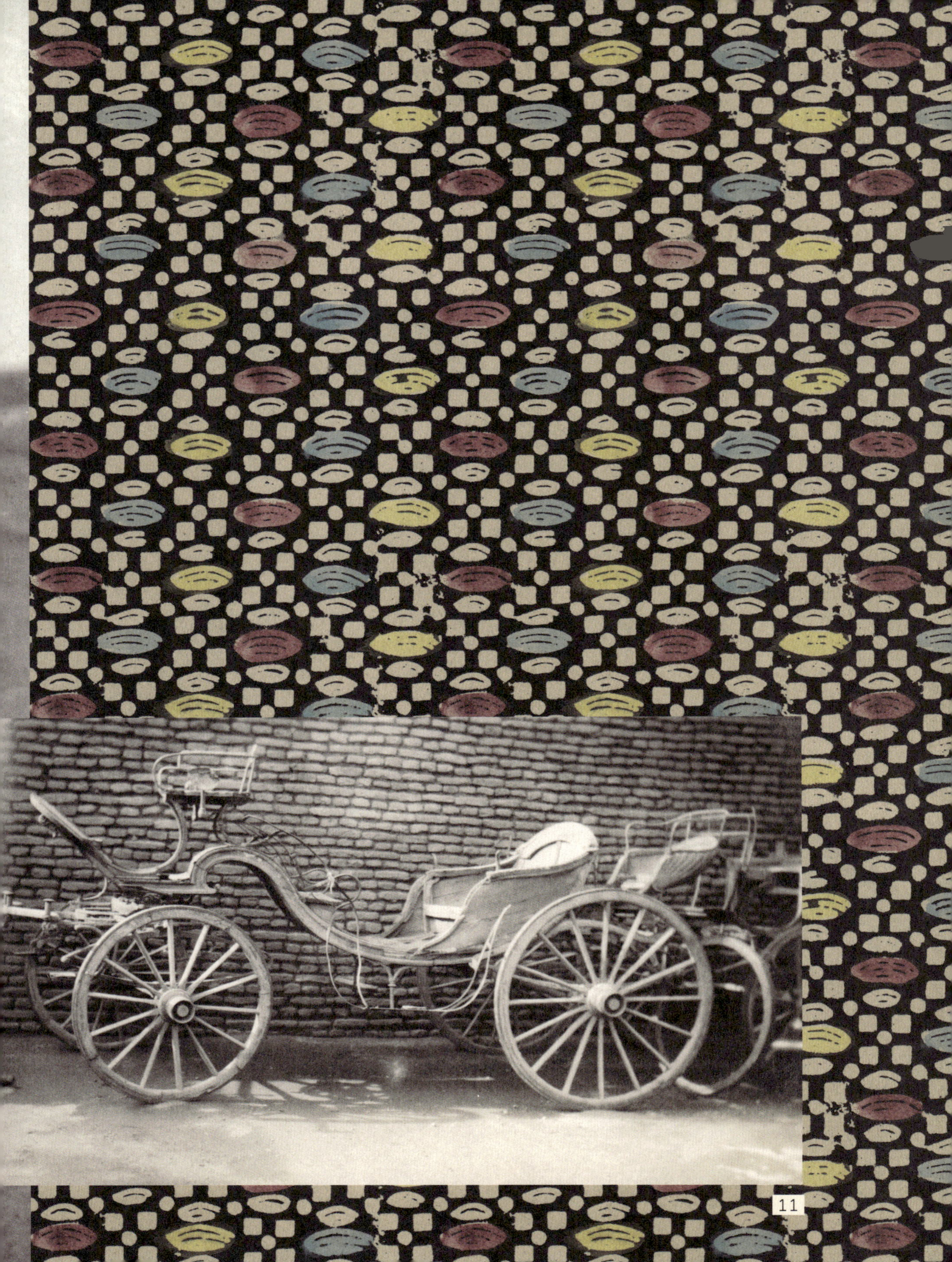

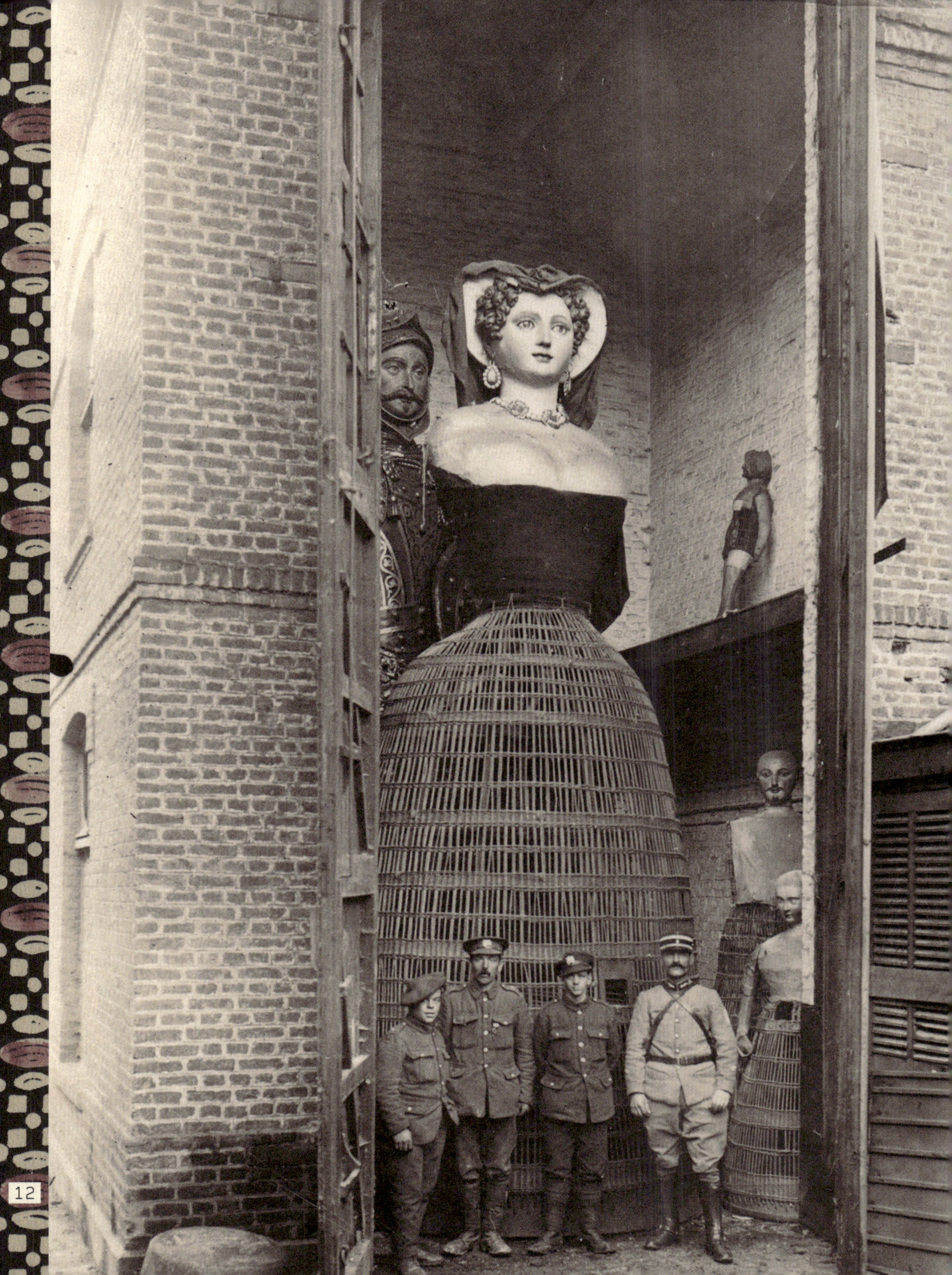
12

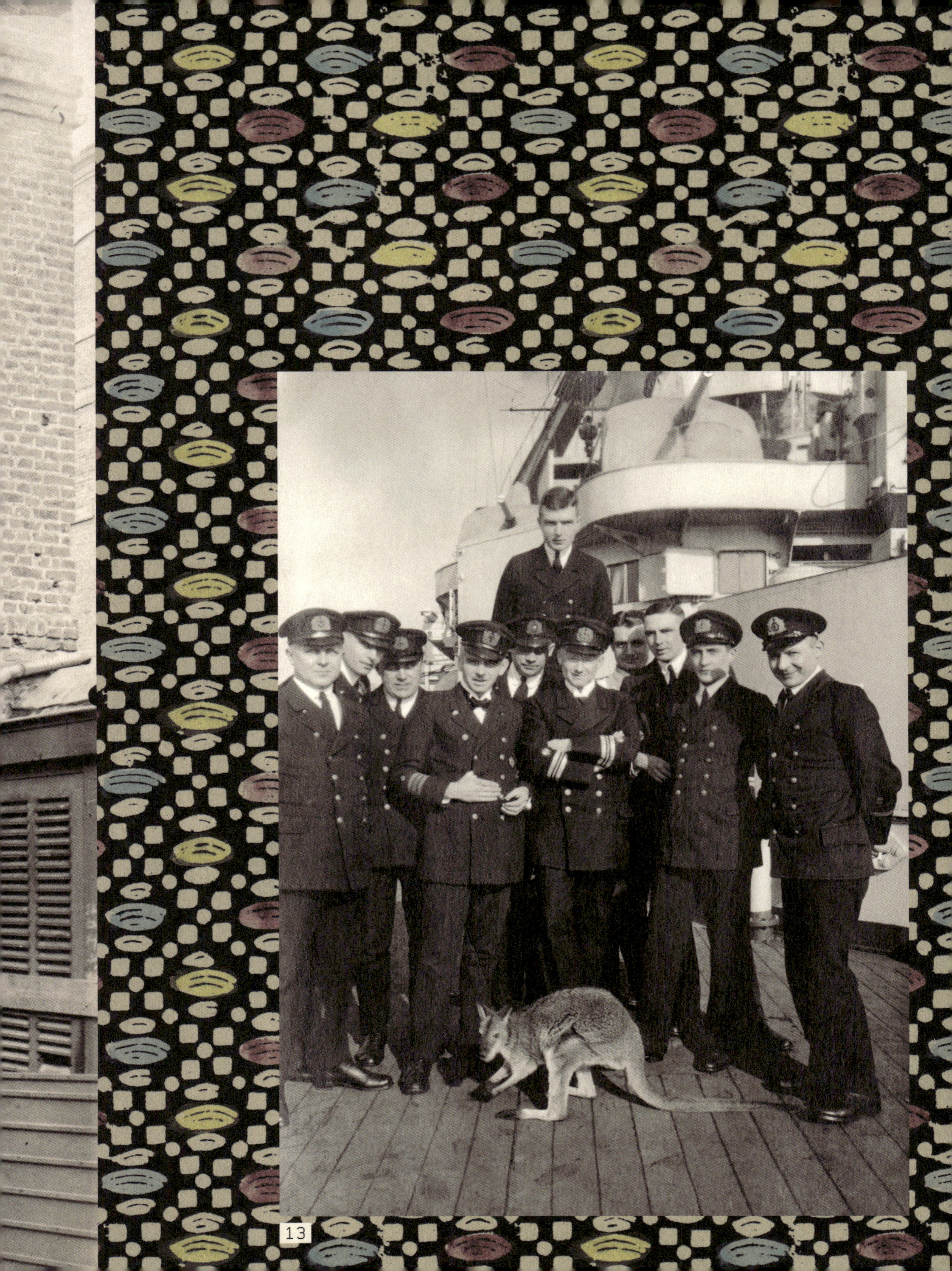

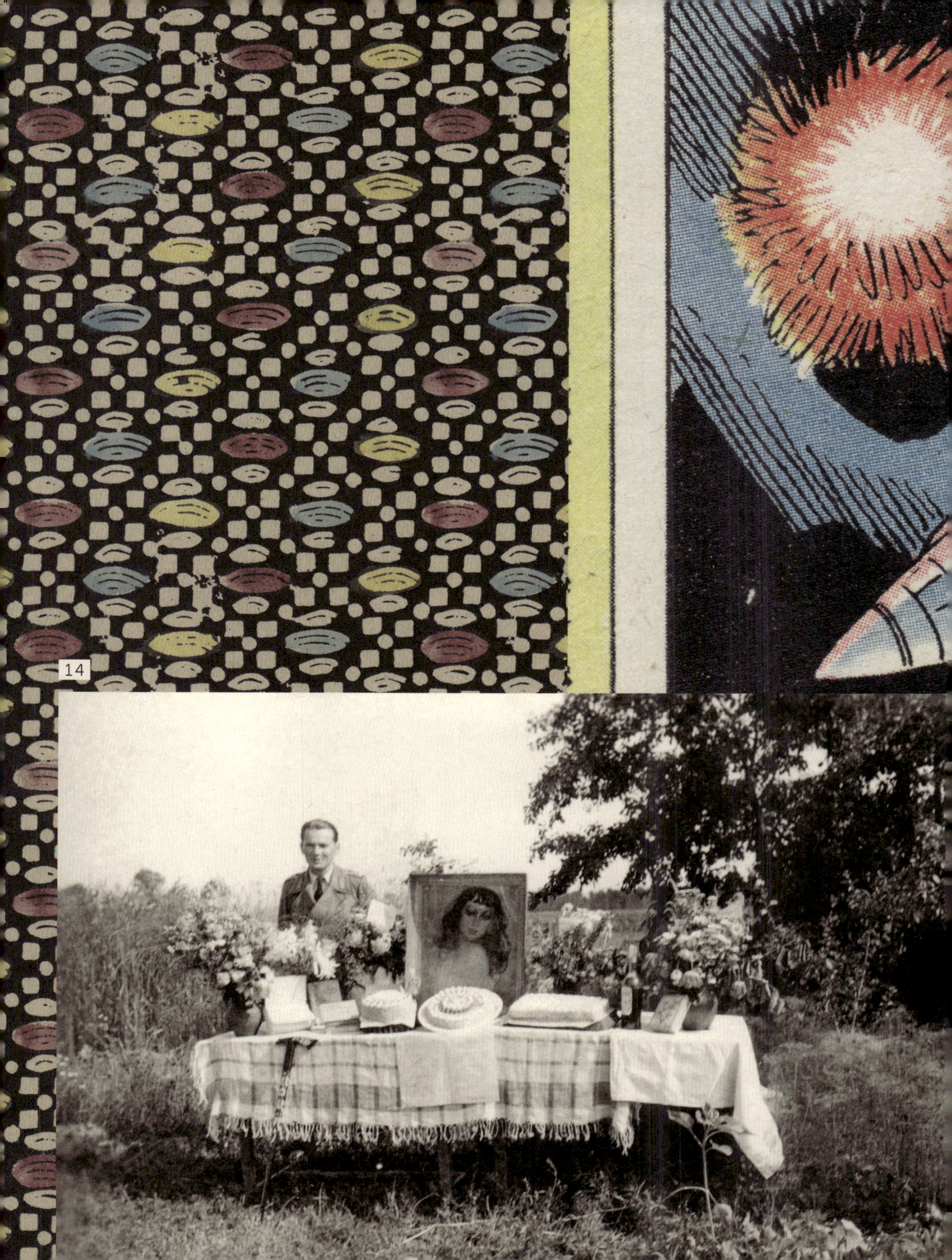

14

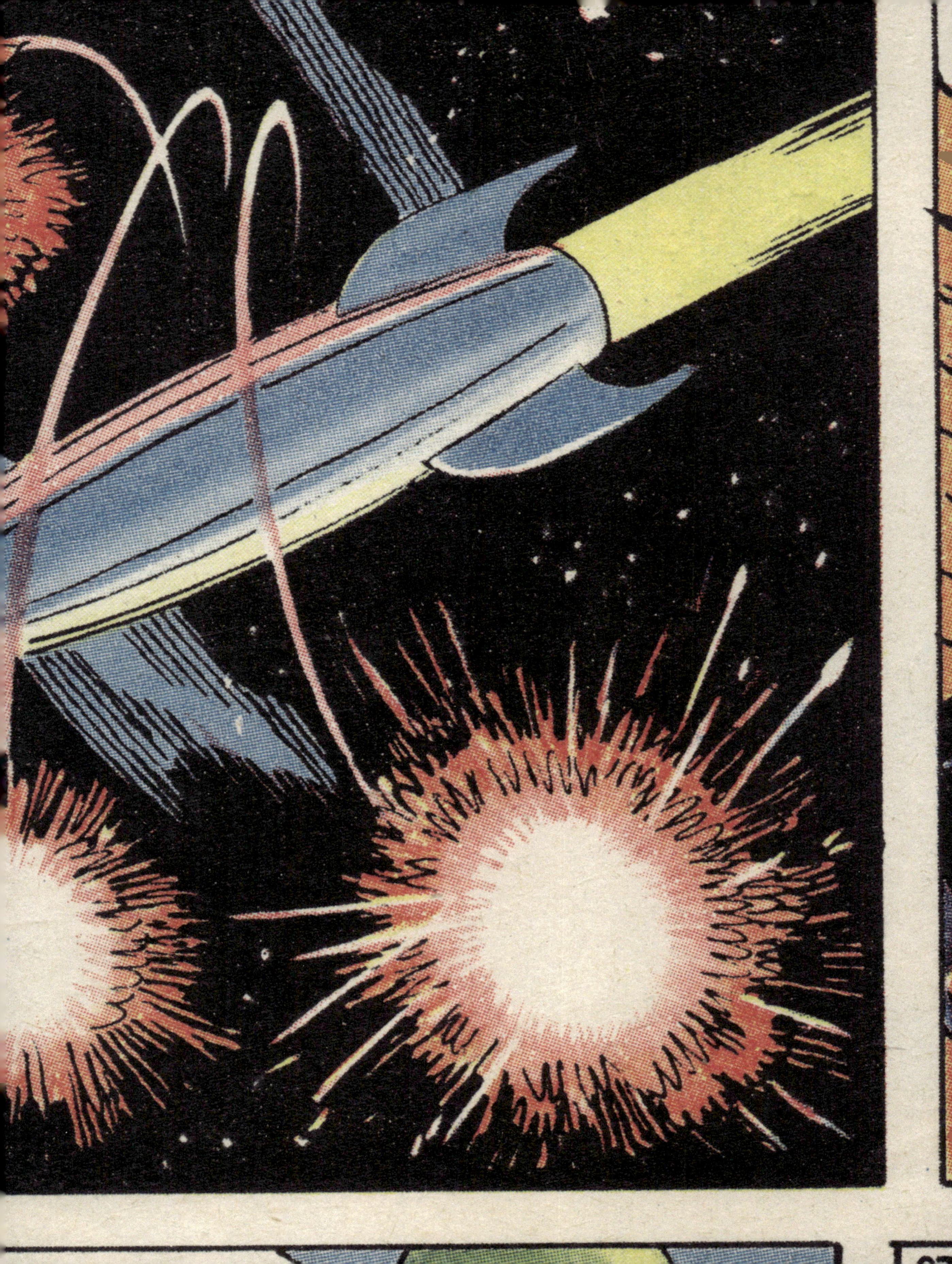

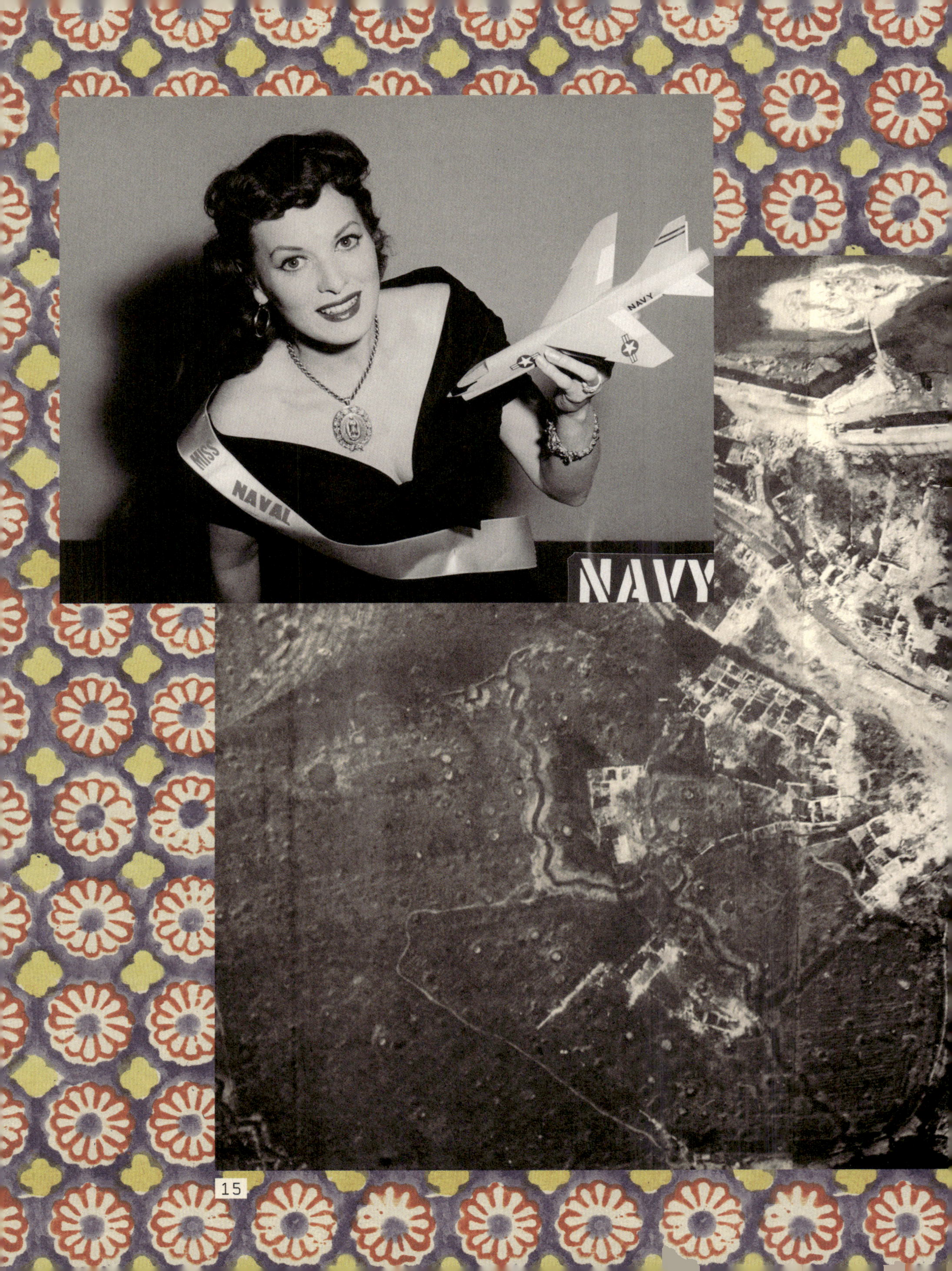
MISS
NAVAL
NAVY

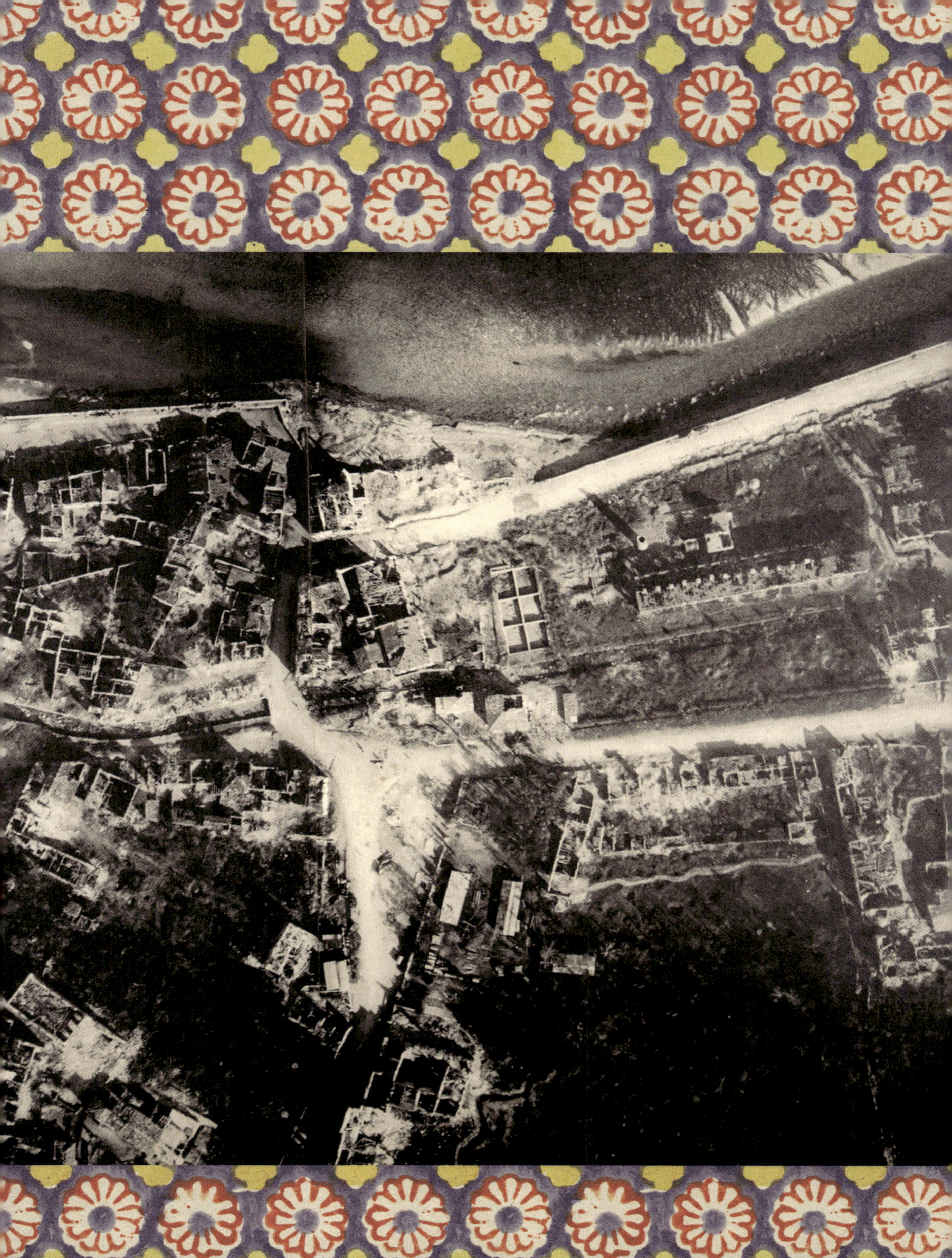

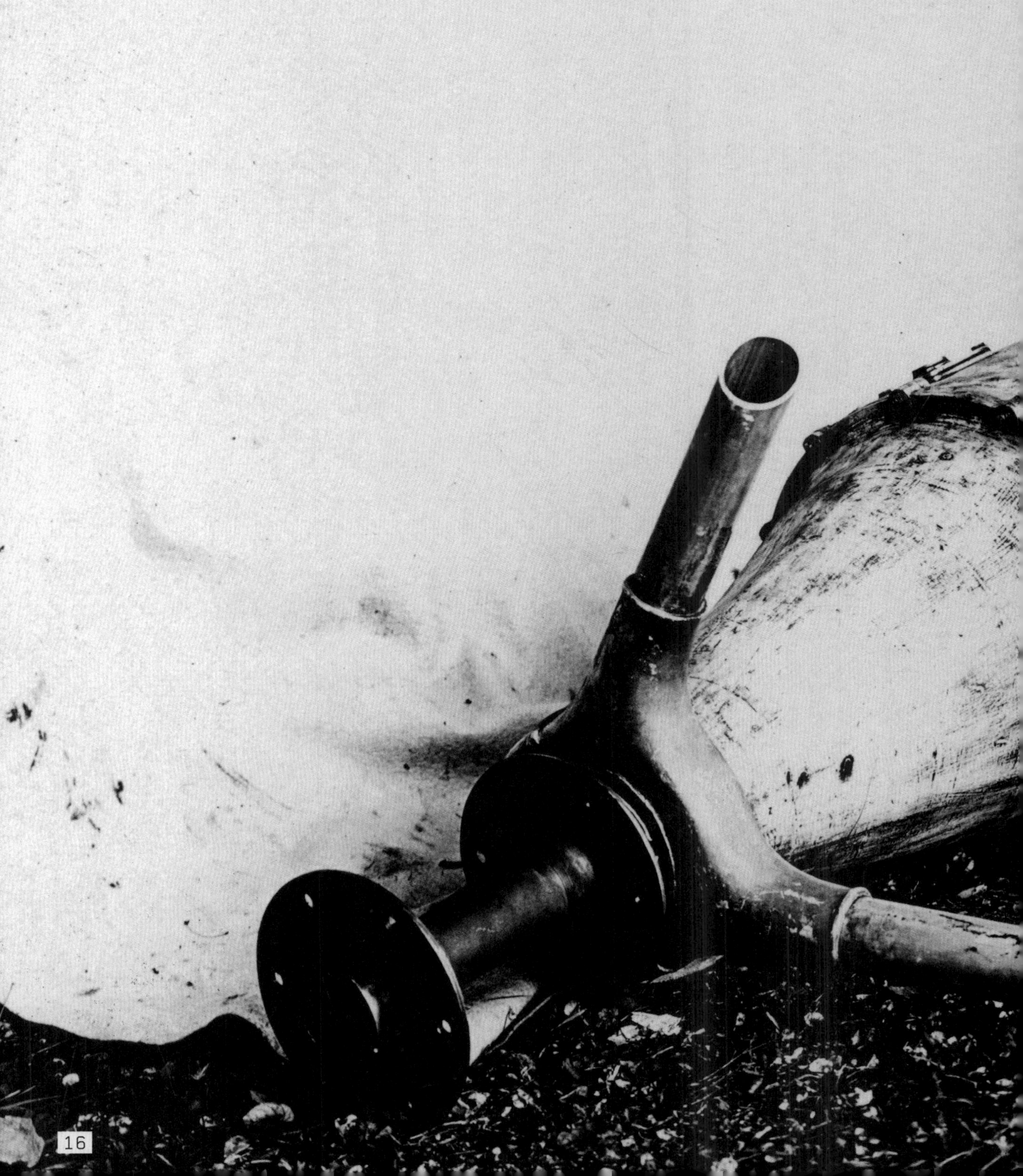

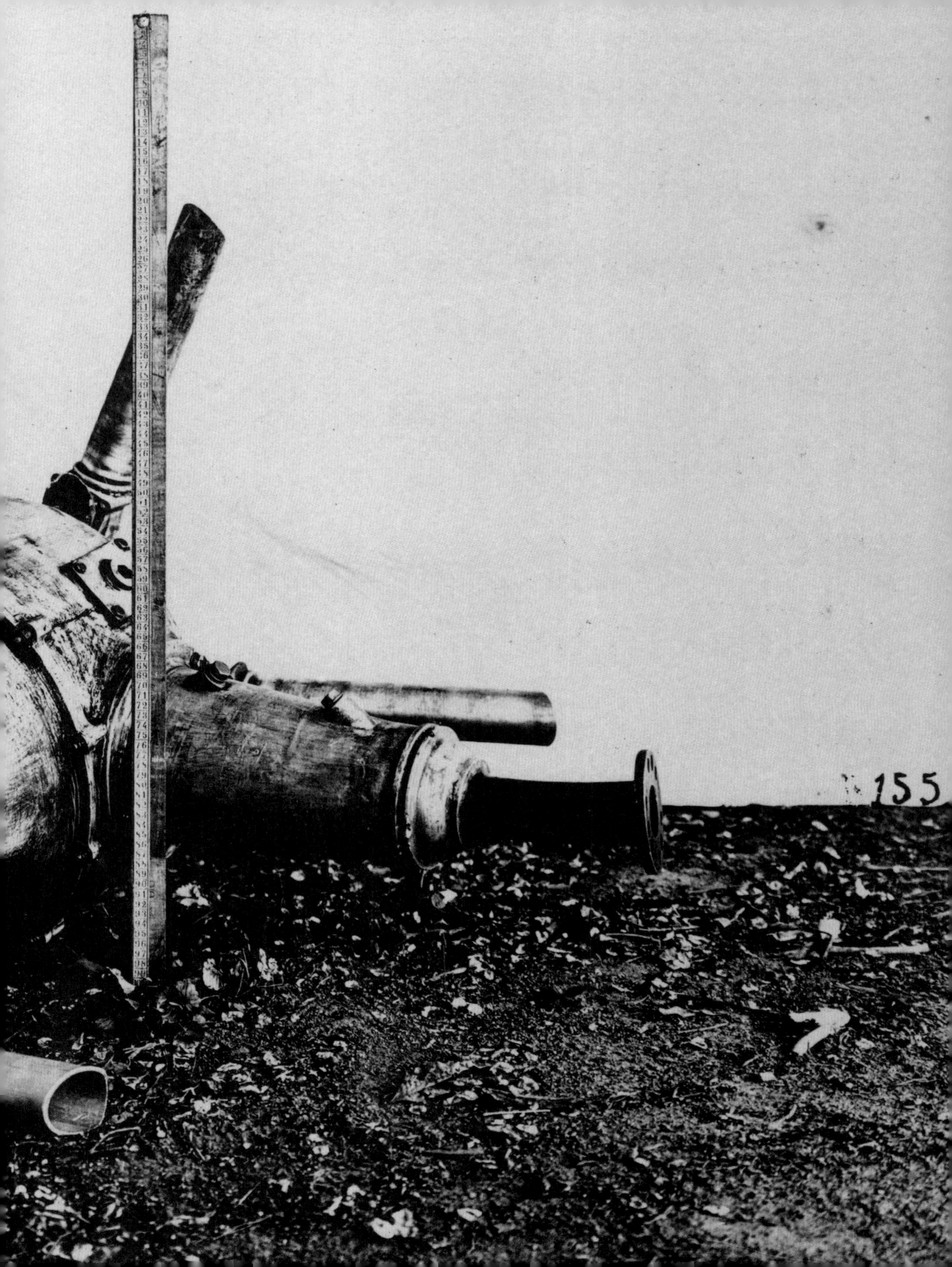
155

There is plenty of evidence t 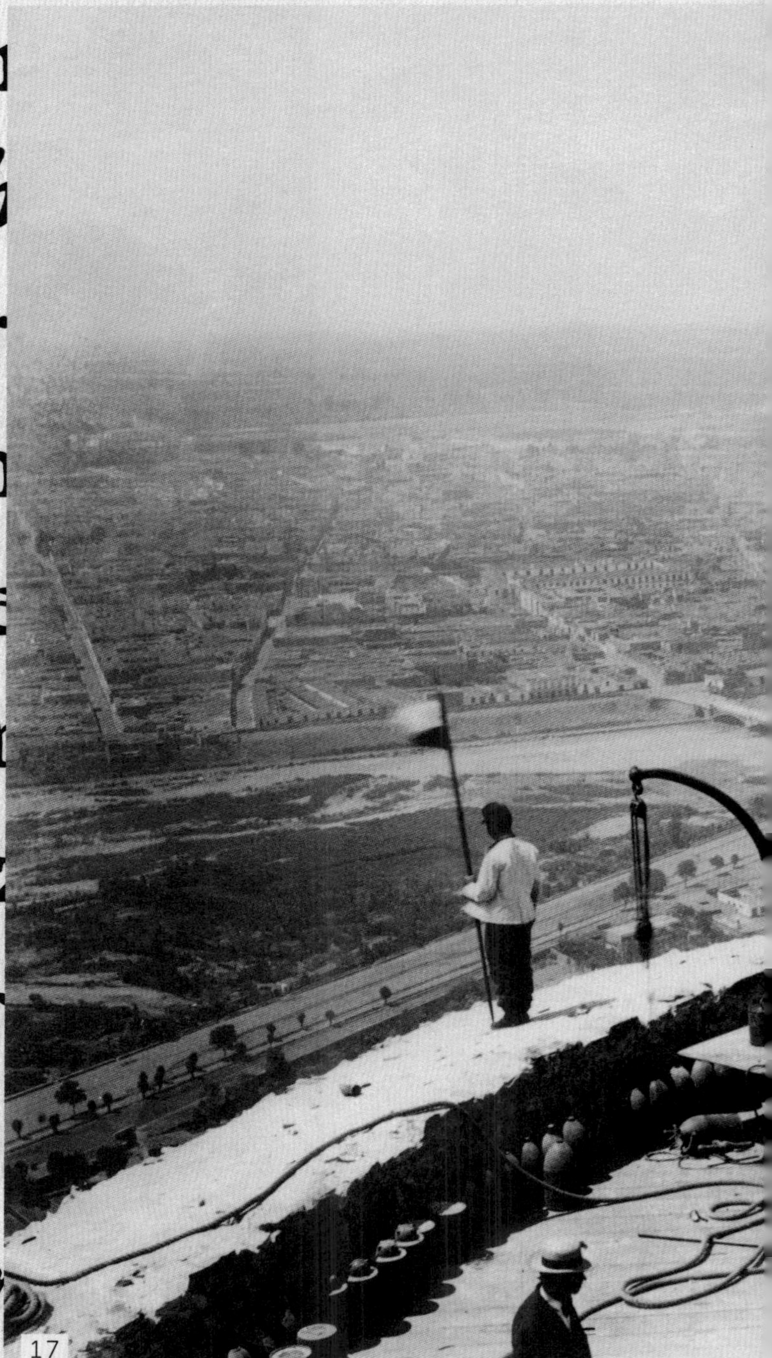
system is ve
recognition of th
causes a *remar*
that in patien
quickly as the
of life is to for
without realiz
When the gr
on the other
record *the wor*
word. When that's done we can
That's work enough for a lifetir

indicate that the hippocampal

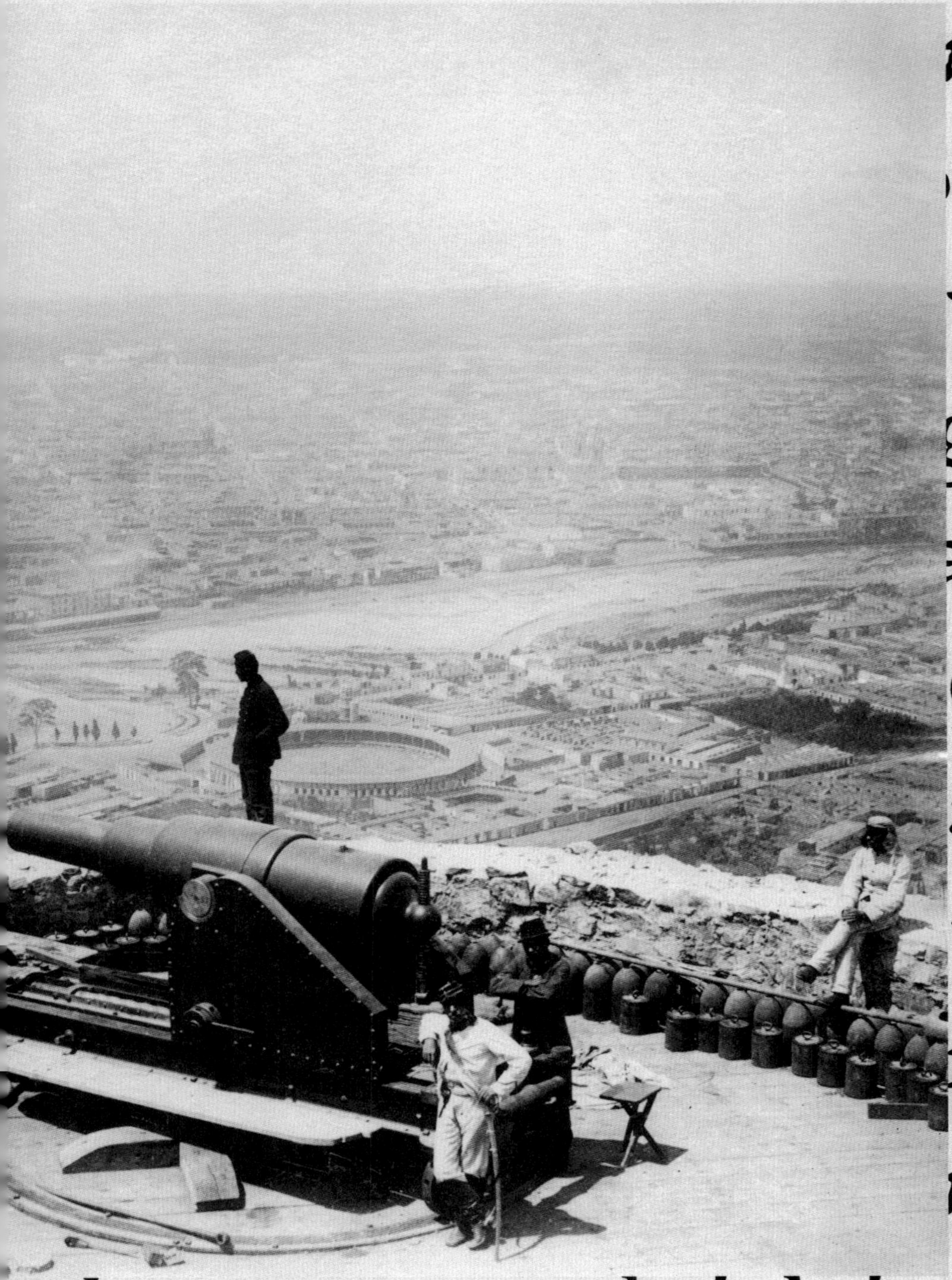

nory and

th sides

y found

gotten as

artment

d to die

mminess.

tty, but

iness to

ging one

url up our toes and sink in the pit.

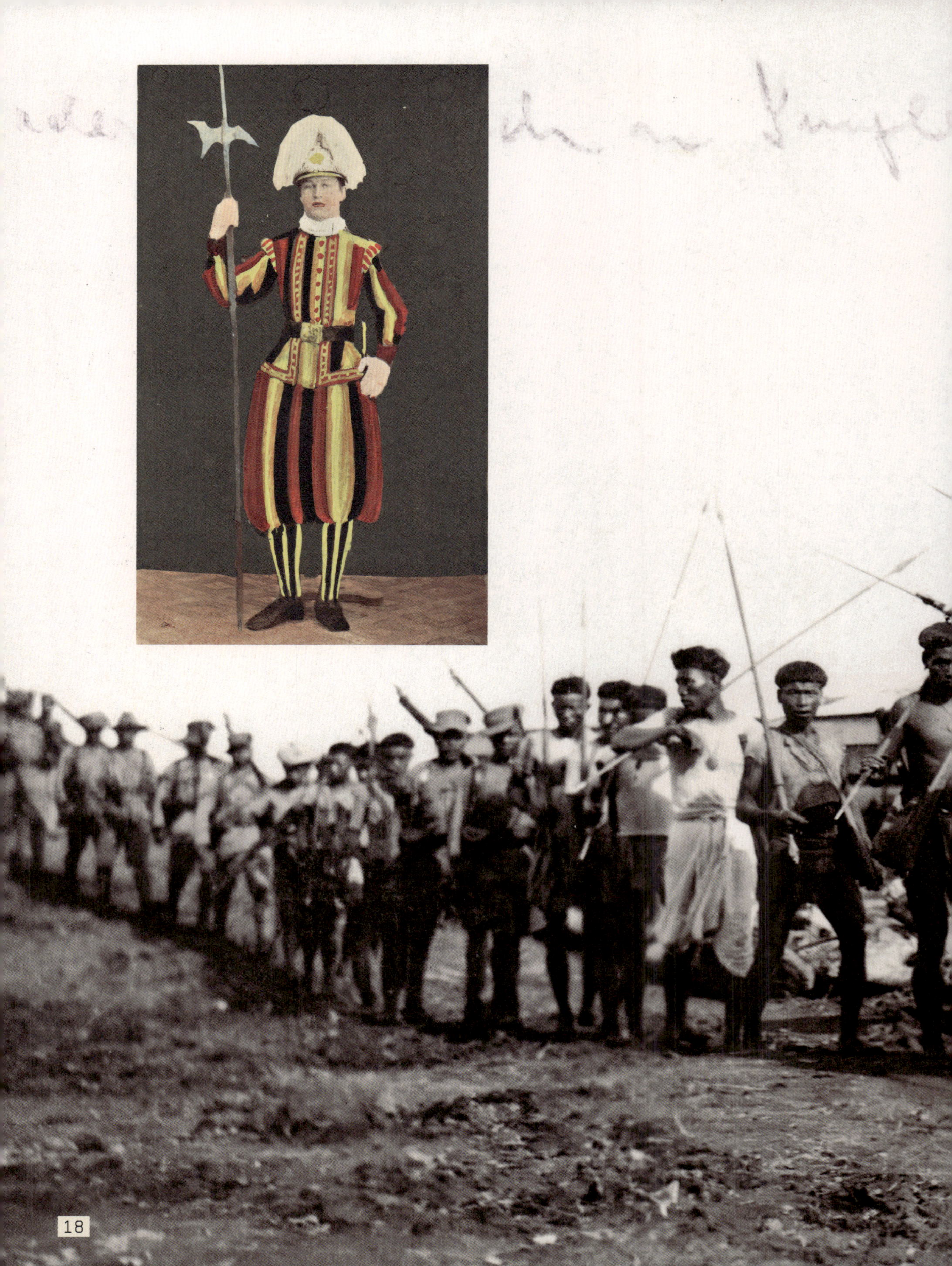

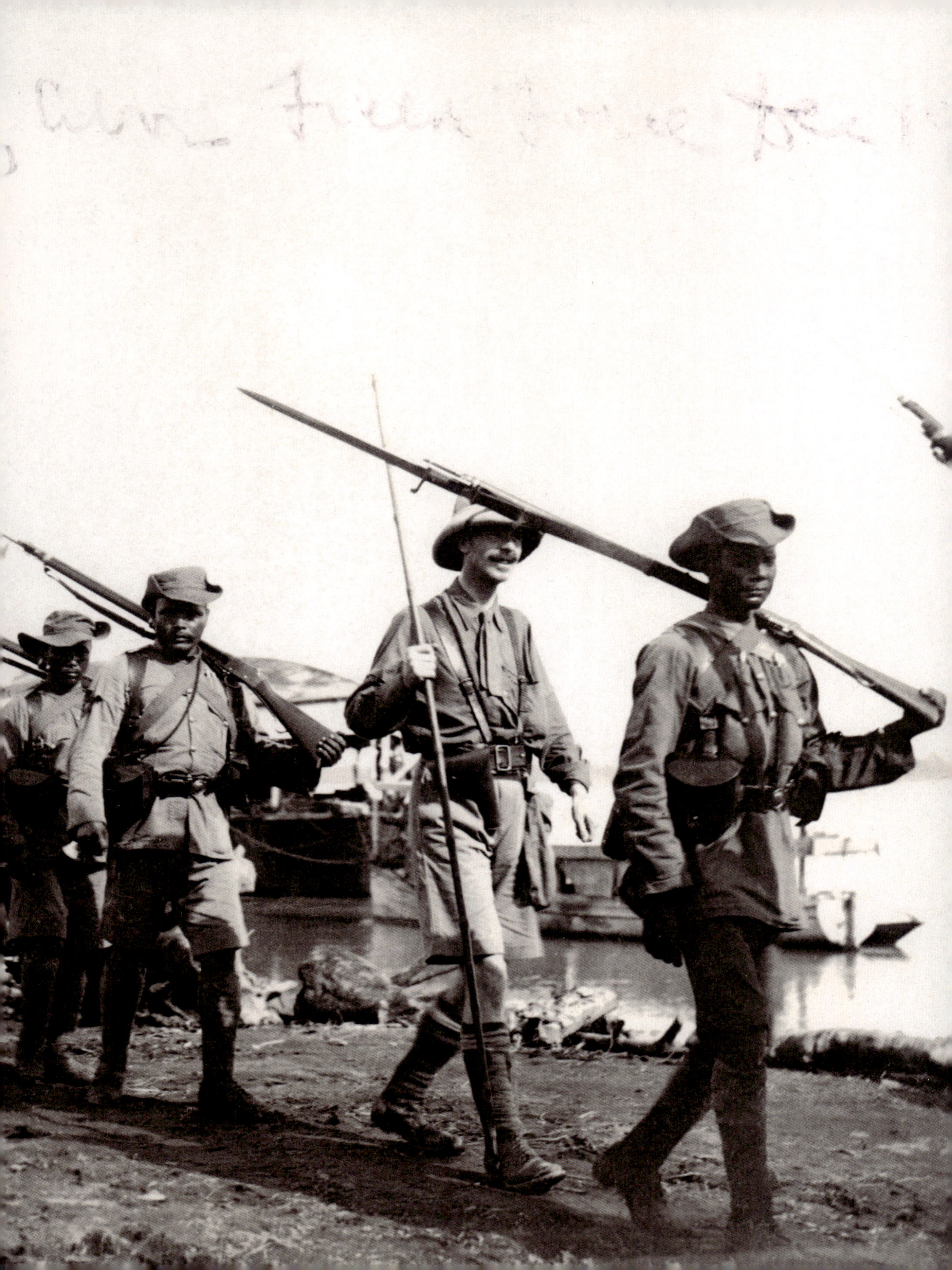

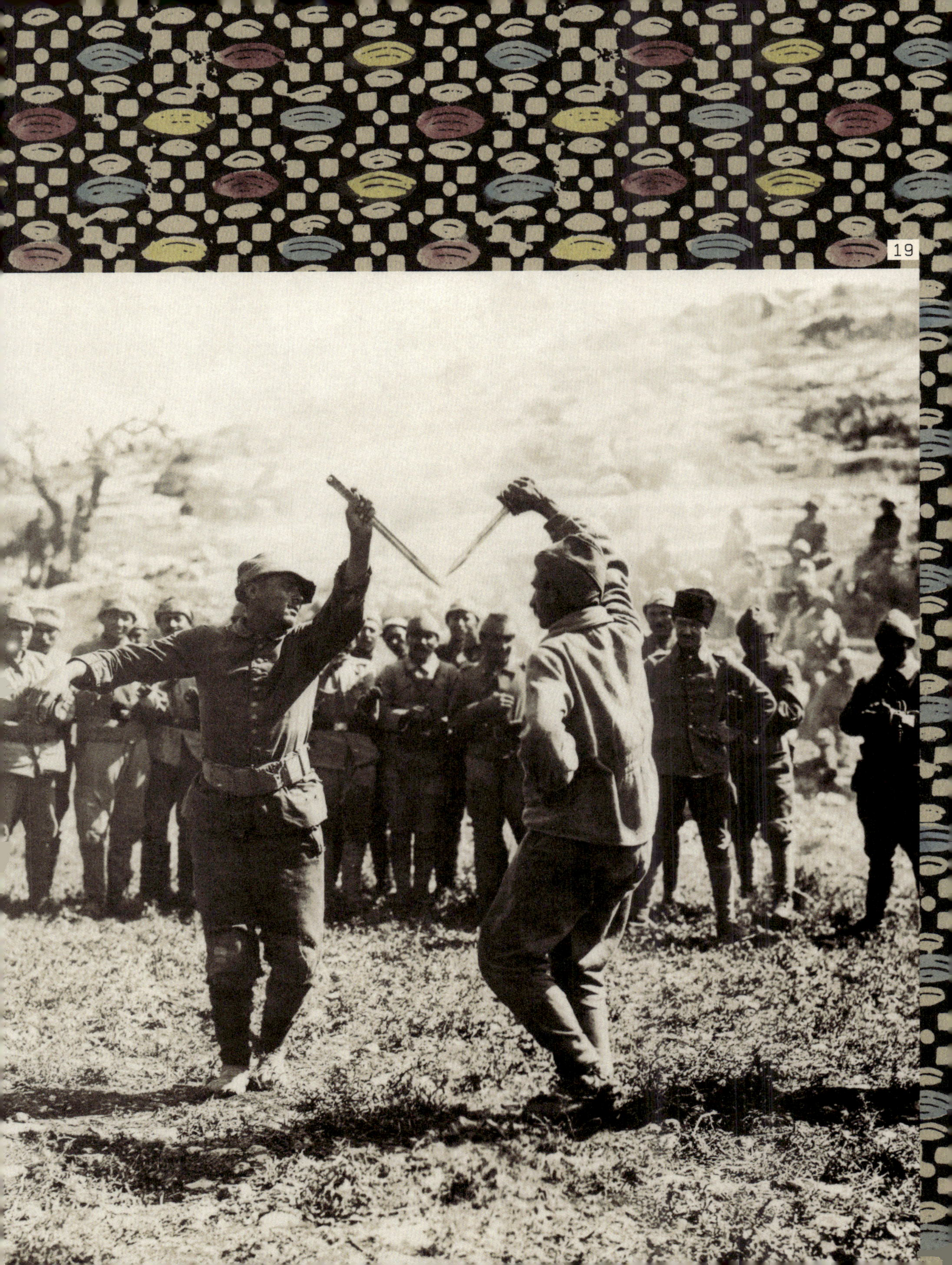

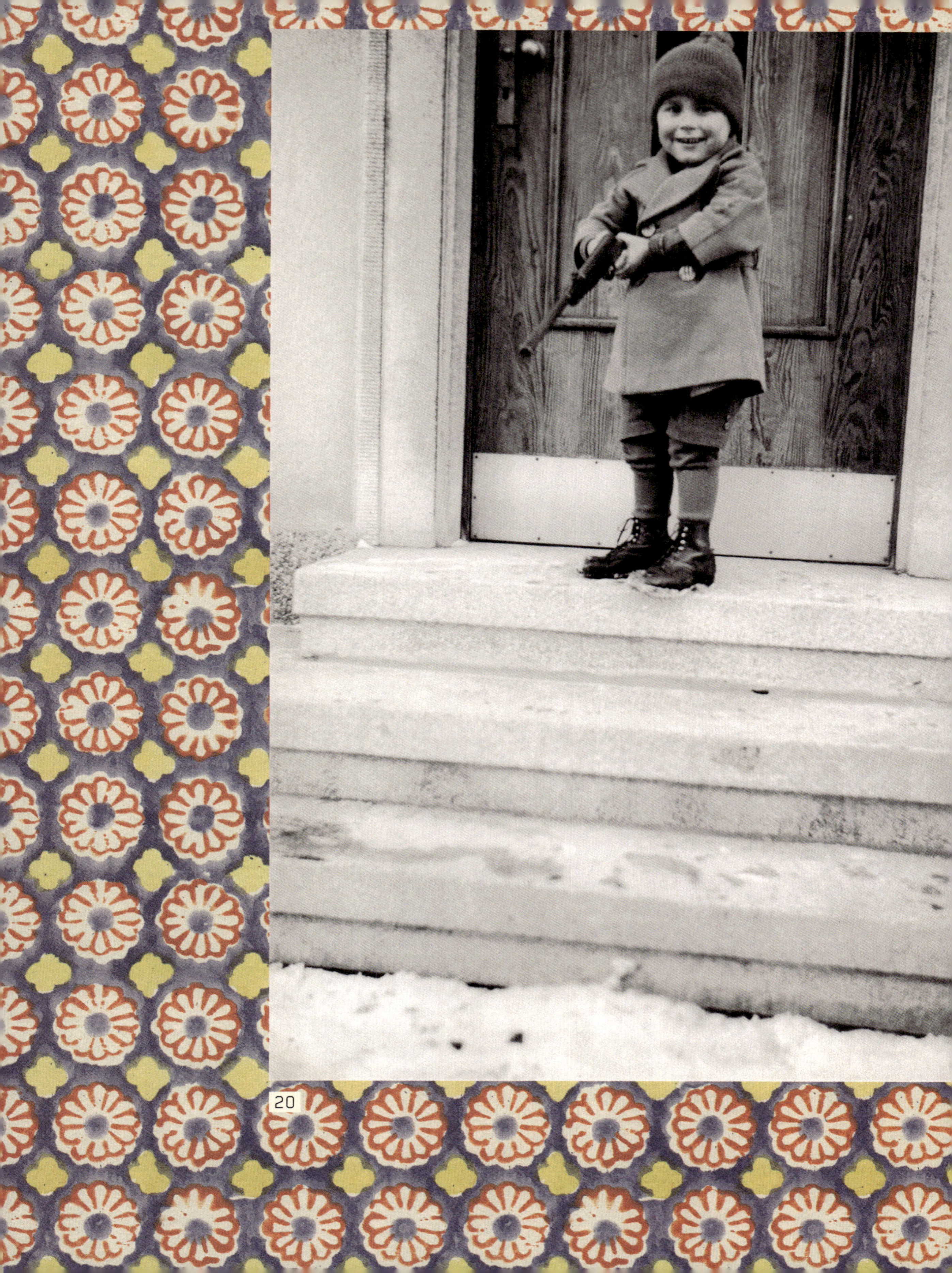

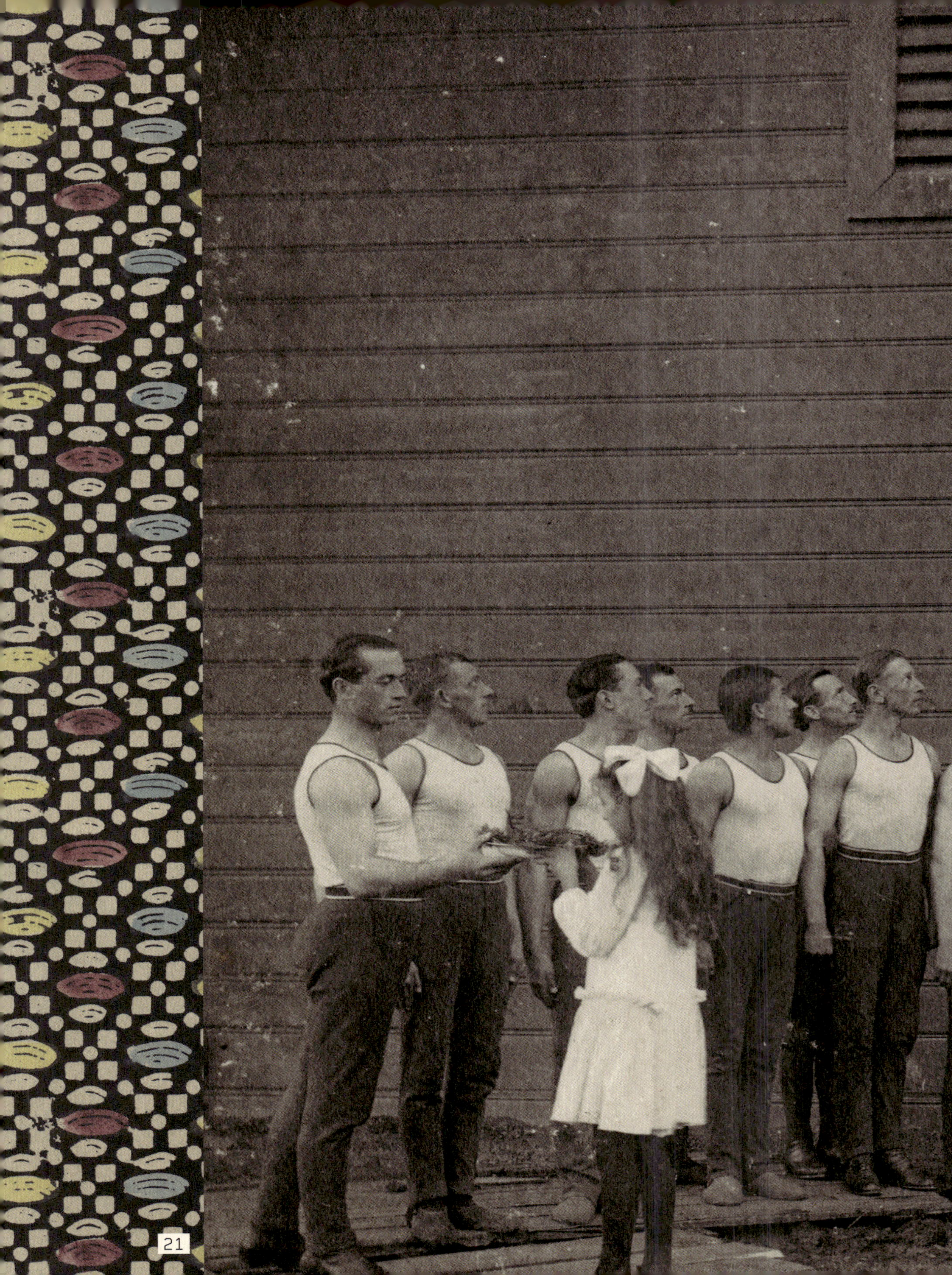

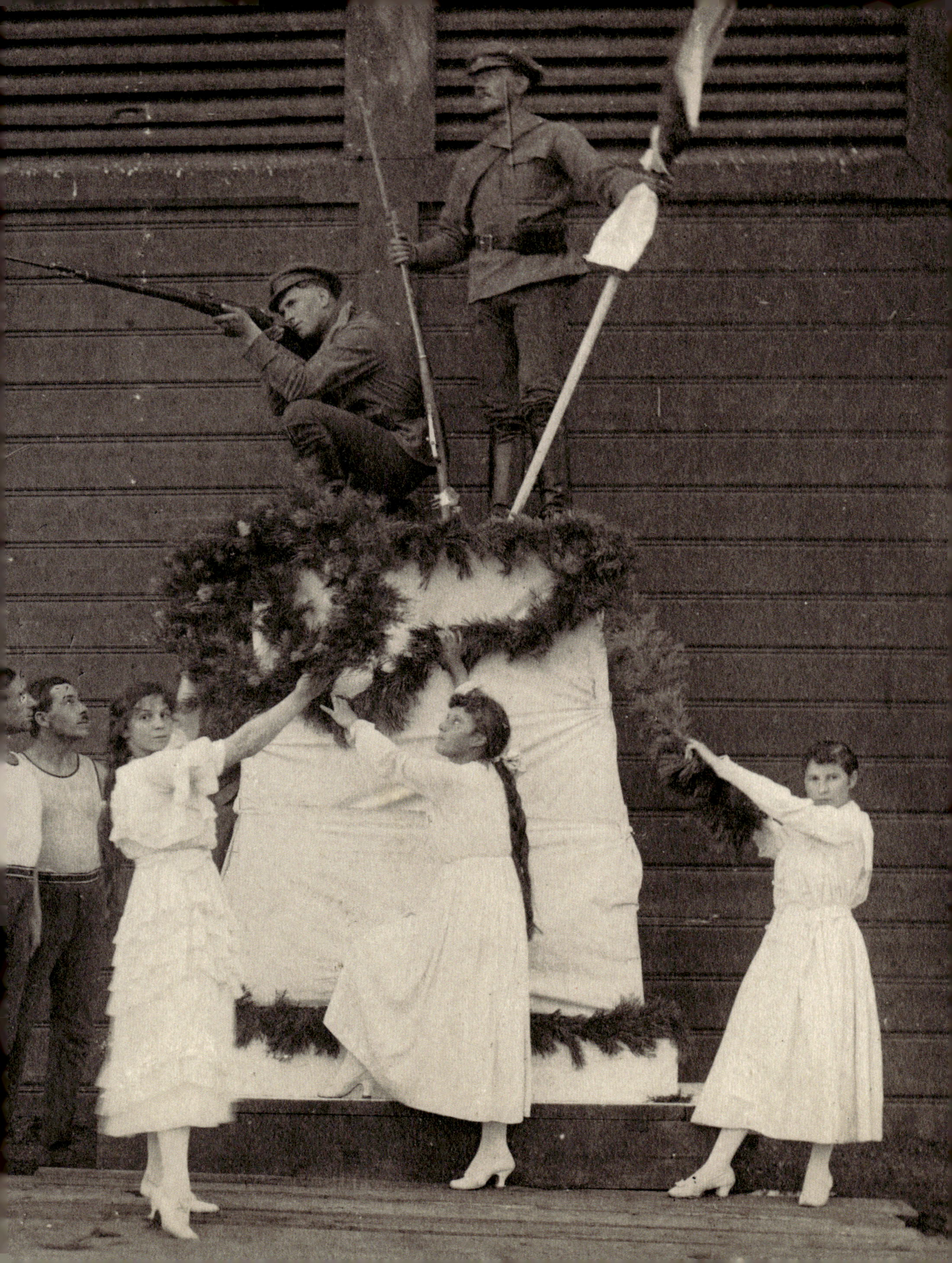

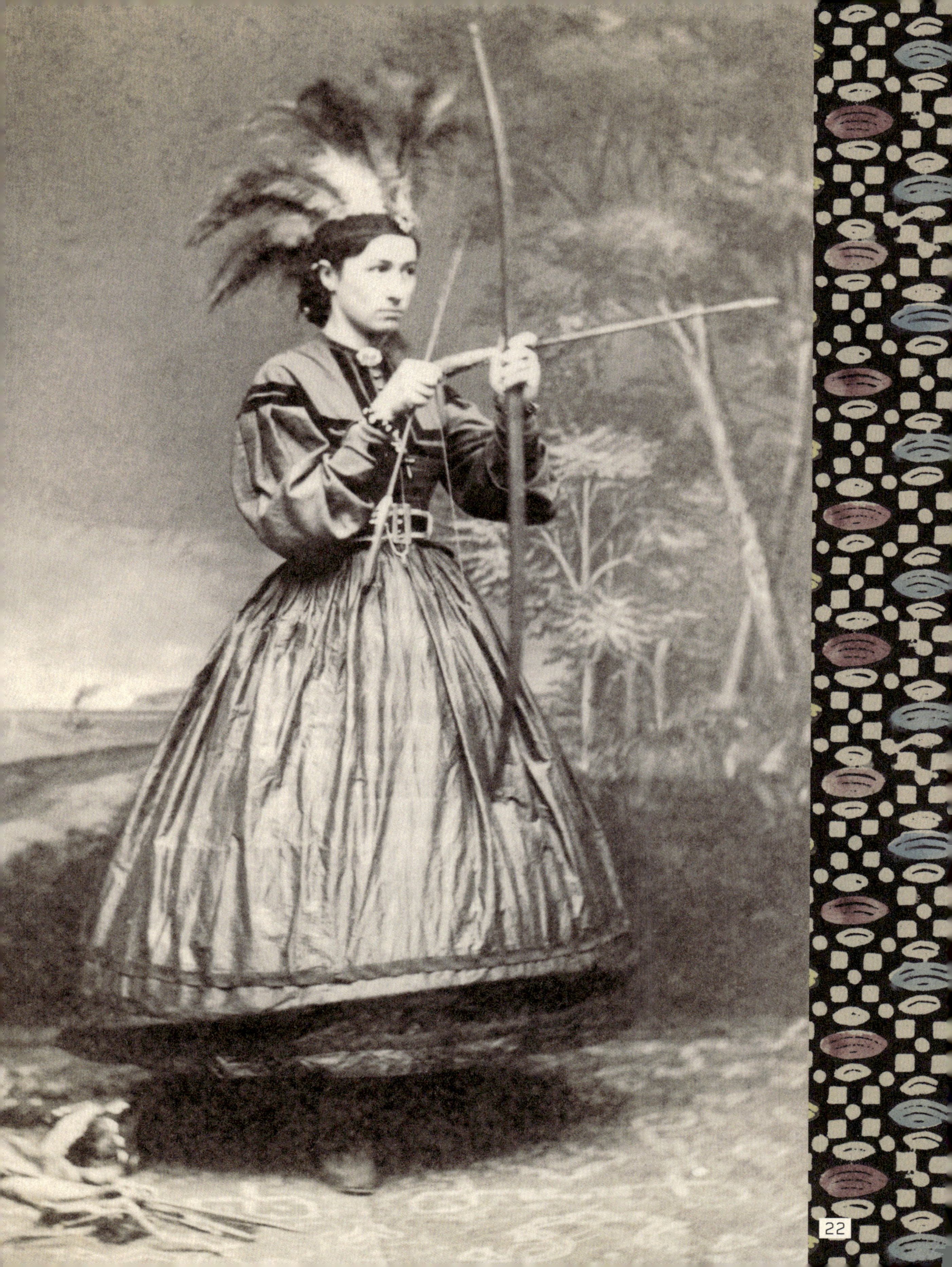

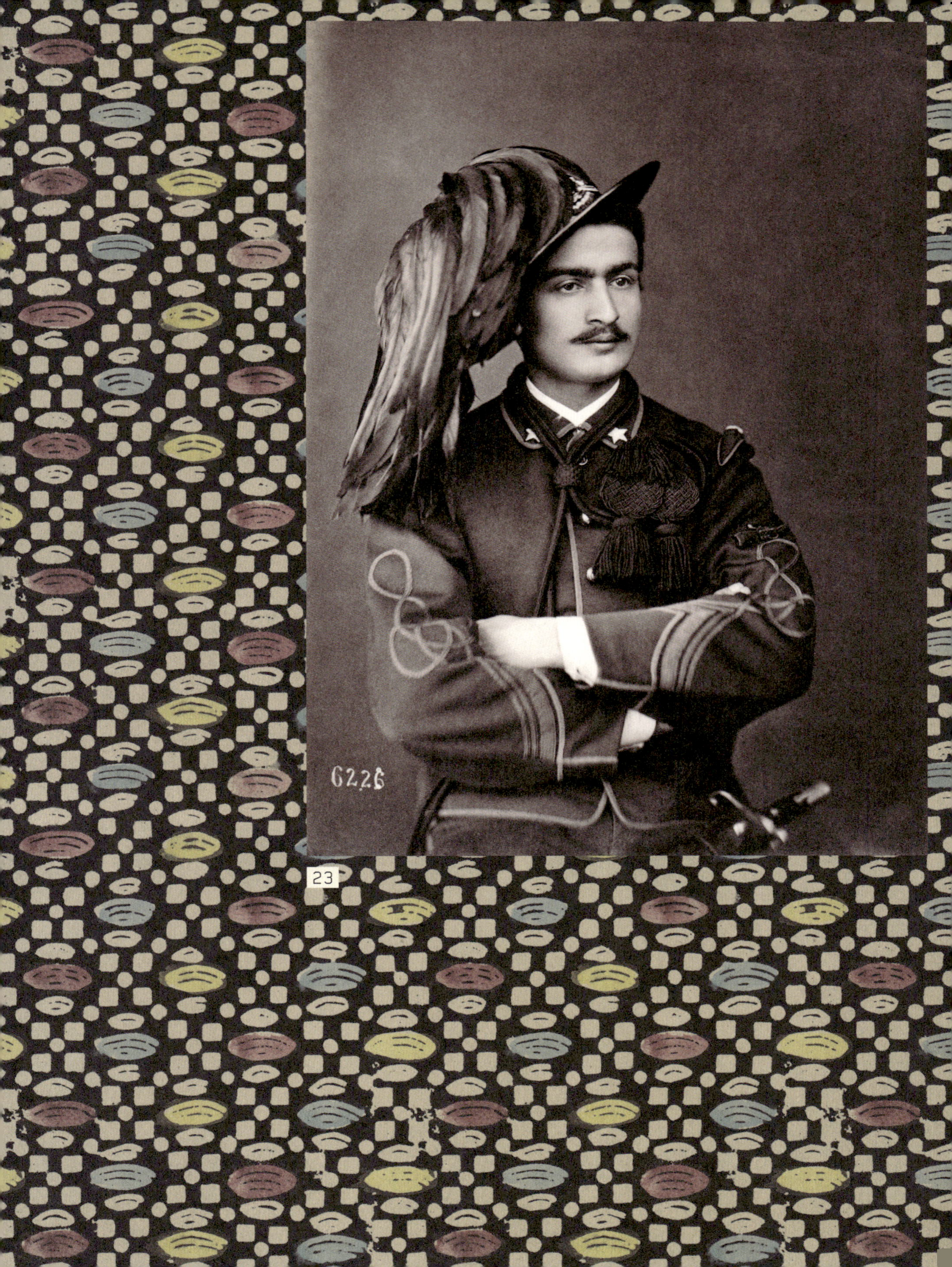

23

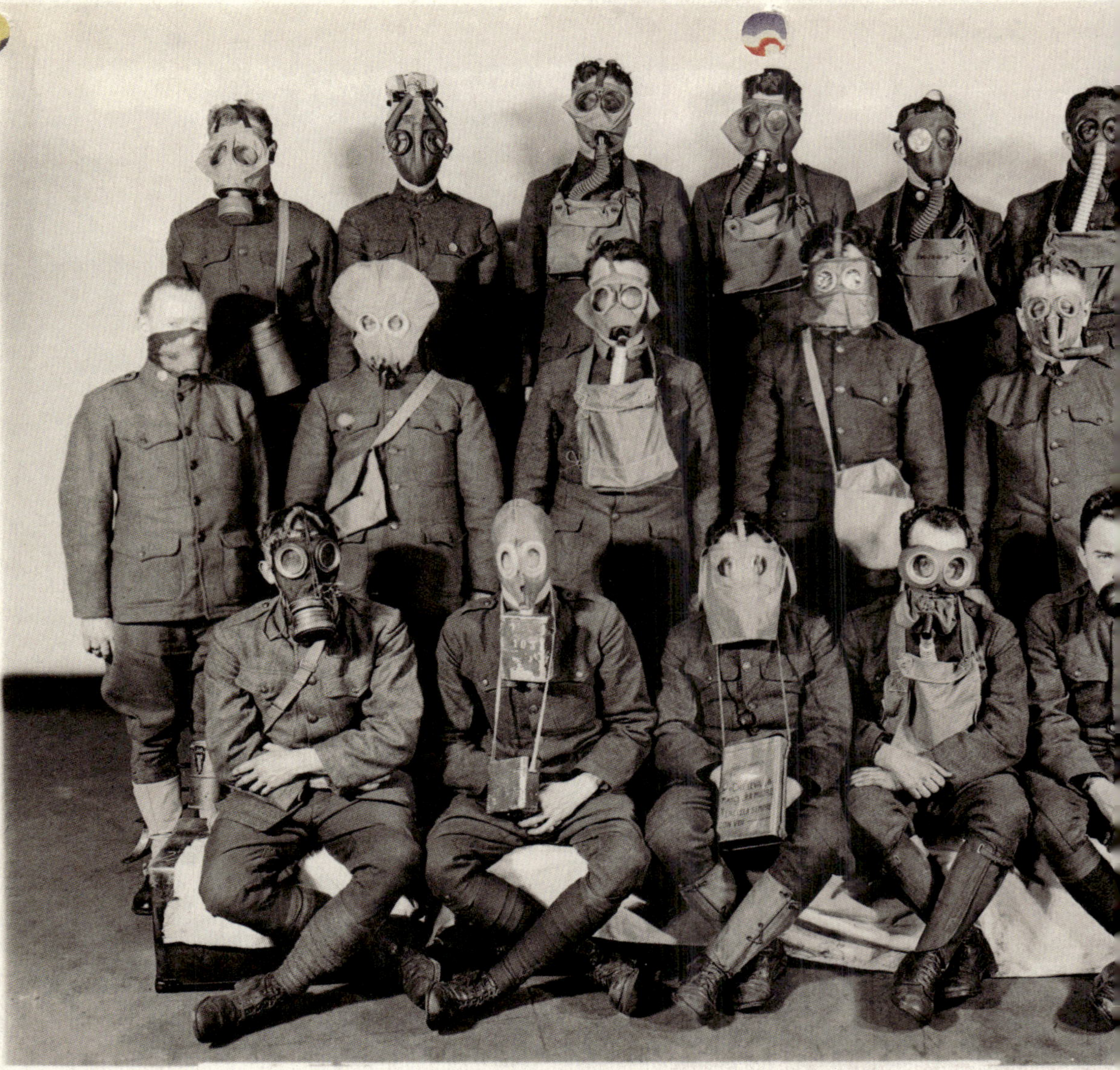

39 –

U.S. Navy Mask (Obsolete)	U.S. Navy Mask.	U.S. C.E. Respirator.	U.S. R.F.K. Respirator.	U.S. A.T. Respirator.
British Black Veil Mask.	British P. H. Helmet.	British Box Respirator.	French M2 Mask.	French T Artillery
Late type German Mask.	Russian Mask.	Italian Mask.	British Motor Corps Mask	Em

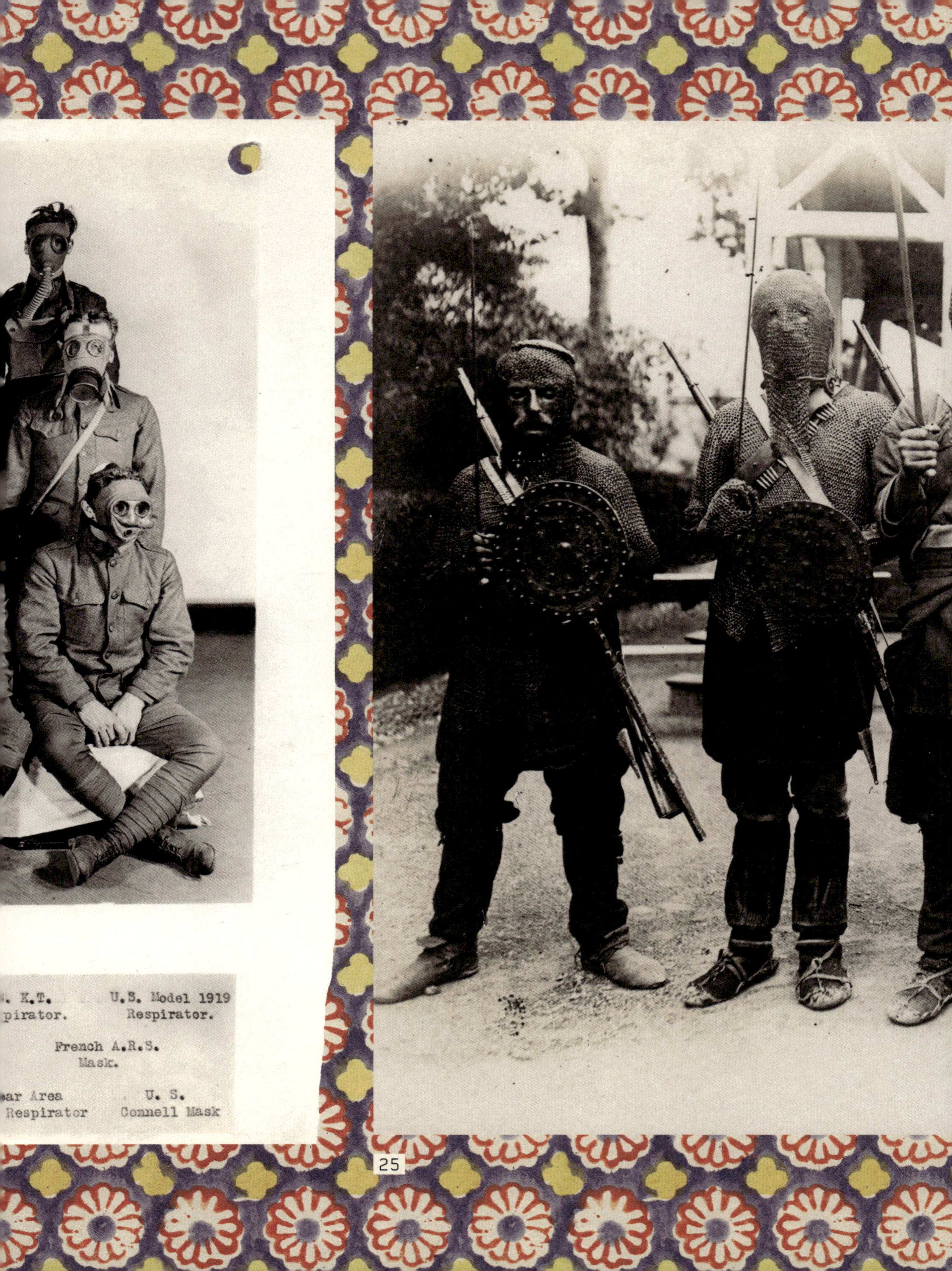

. K.T.   U.S. Model 1919
pirator.   Respirator.

          French A.R.S.
             Mask.

ear Area   U. S.
Respirator   Connell Mask

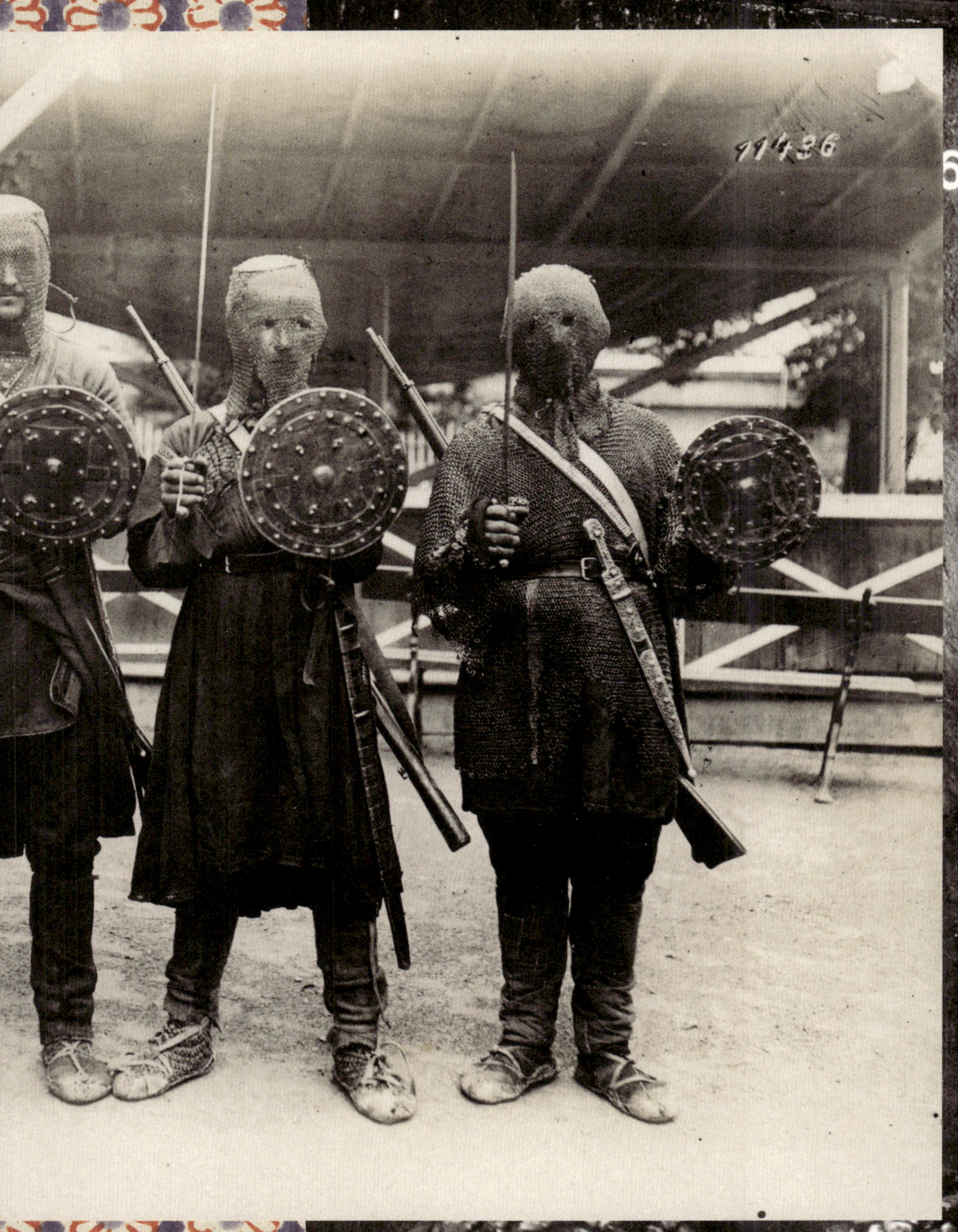

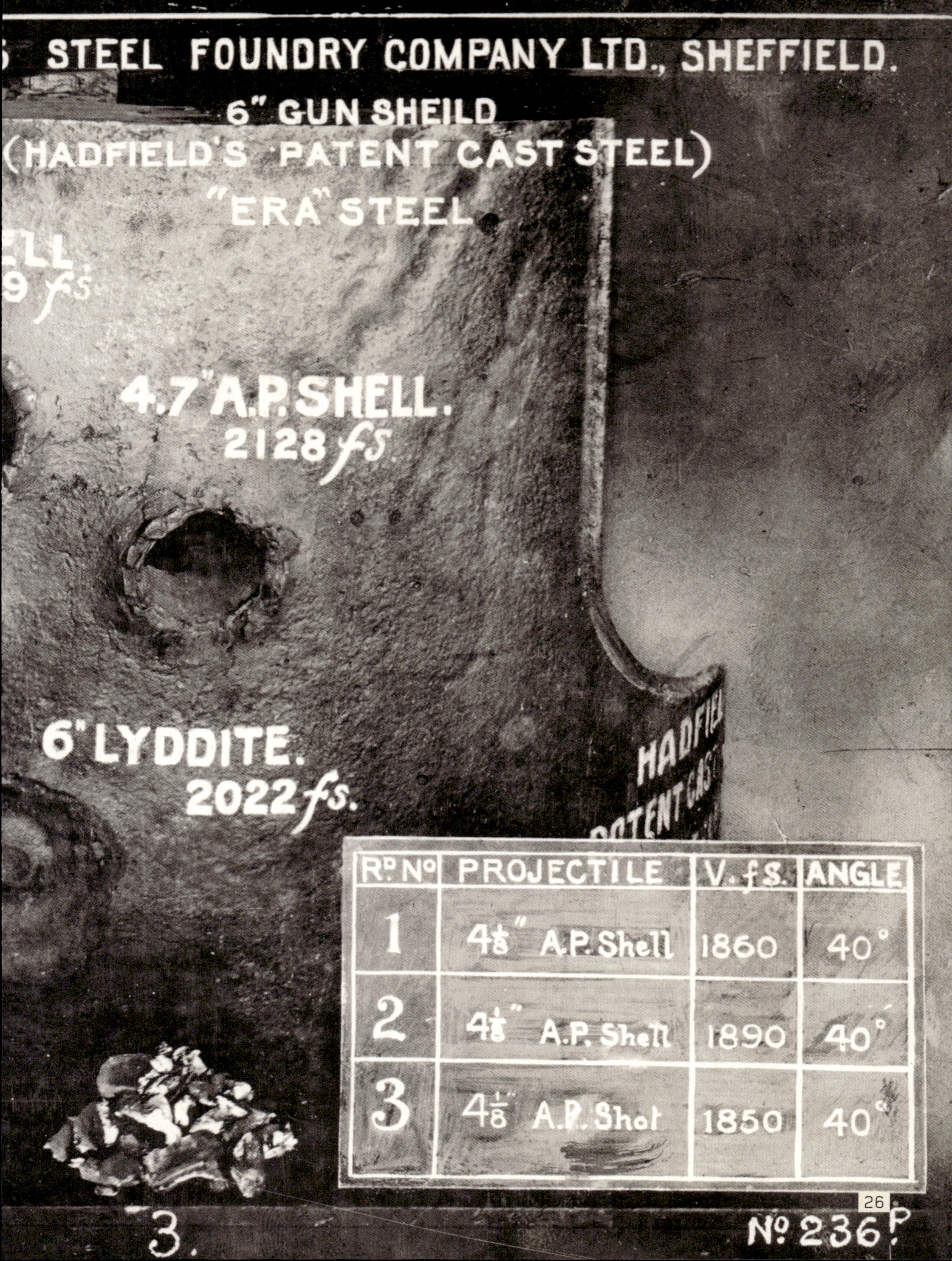

STEEL FOUNDRY COMPANY LTD., SHEFFIELD.

6" GUN SHEILD

(HADFIELD'S PATENT CAST STEEL)

"ERA" STEEL

4.7" A.P. SHELL.
2128 fs.

6" LYDDITE.
2022 fs.

Rᵈ Nº	PROJECTILE	V. fs.	ANGLE
1	4⅛" A.P. Shell	1860	40°
2	4⅛" A.P. Shell	1890	40°
3	4⅛" A.P. Shot	1850	40°

3.

Nº 236 P

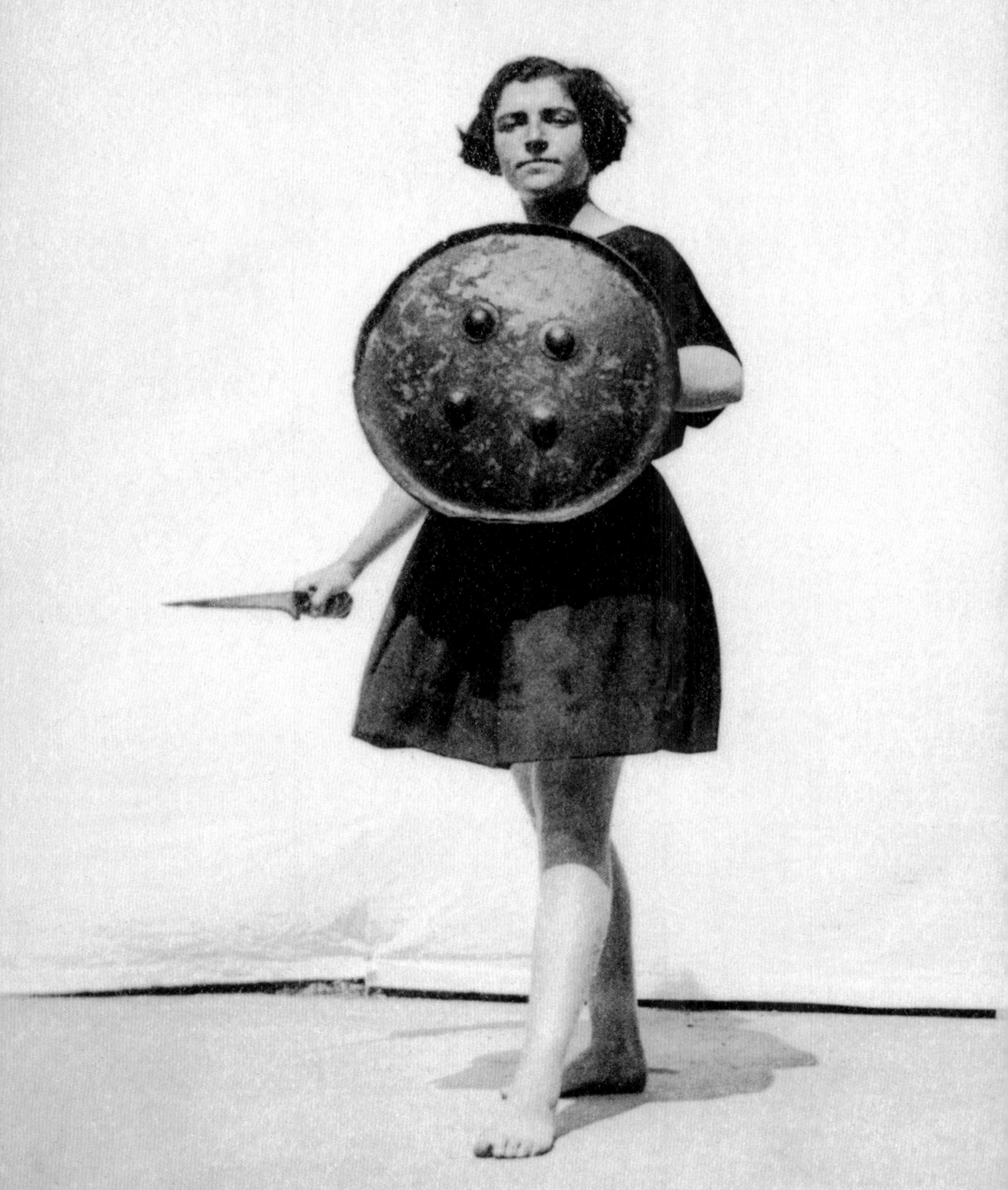

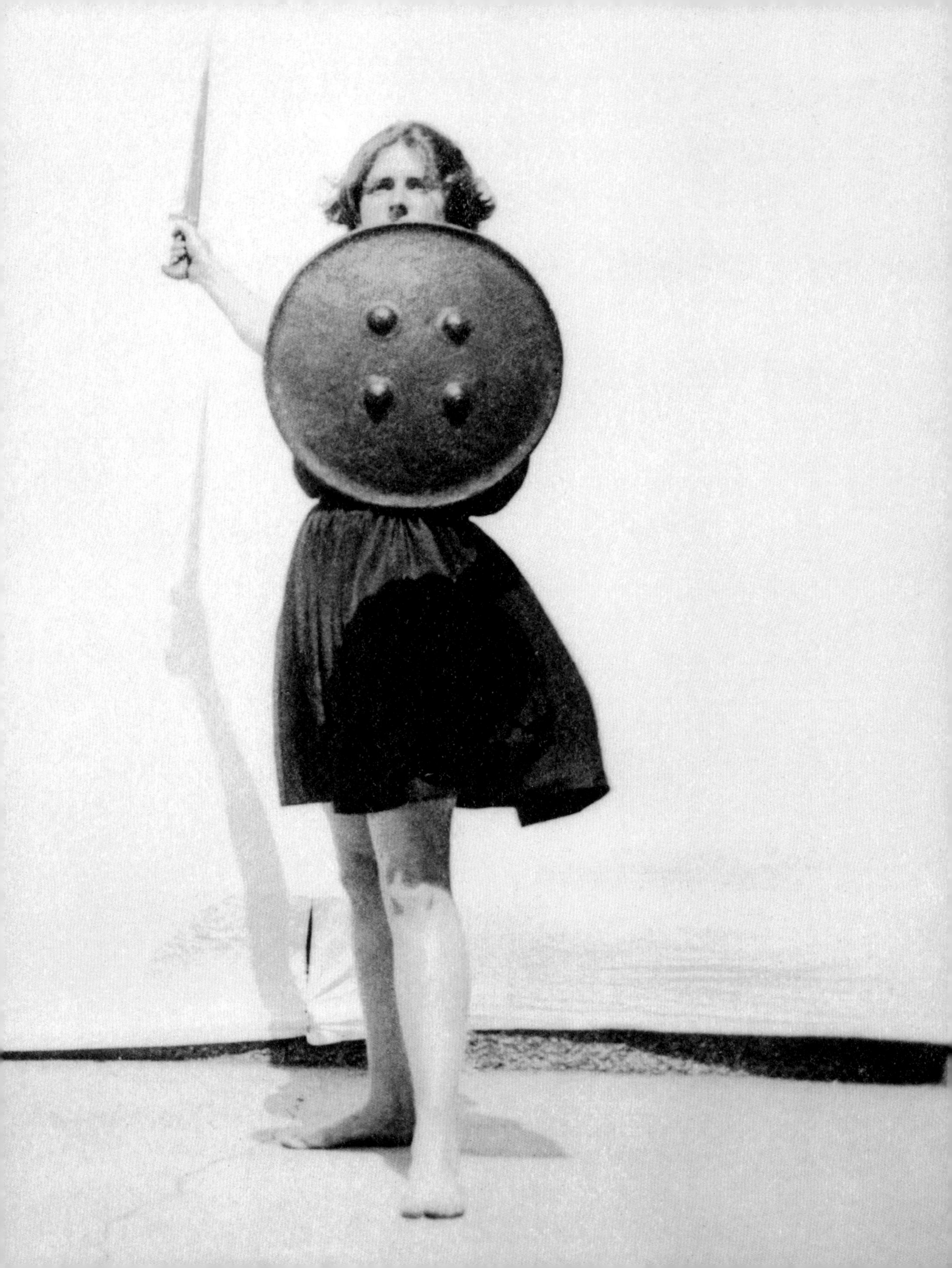

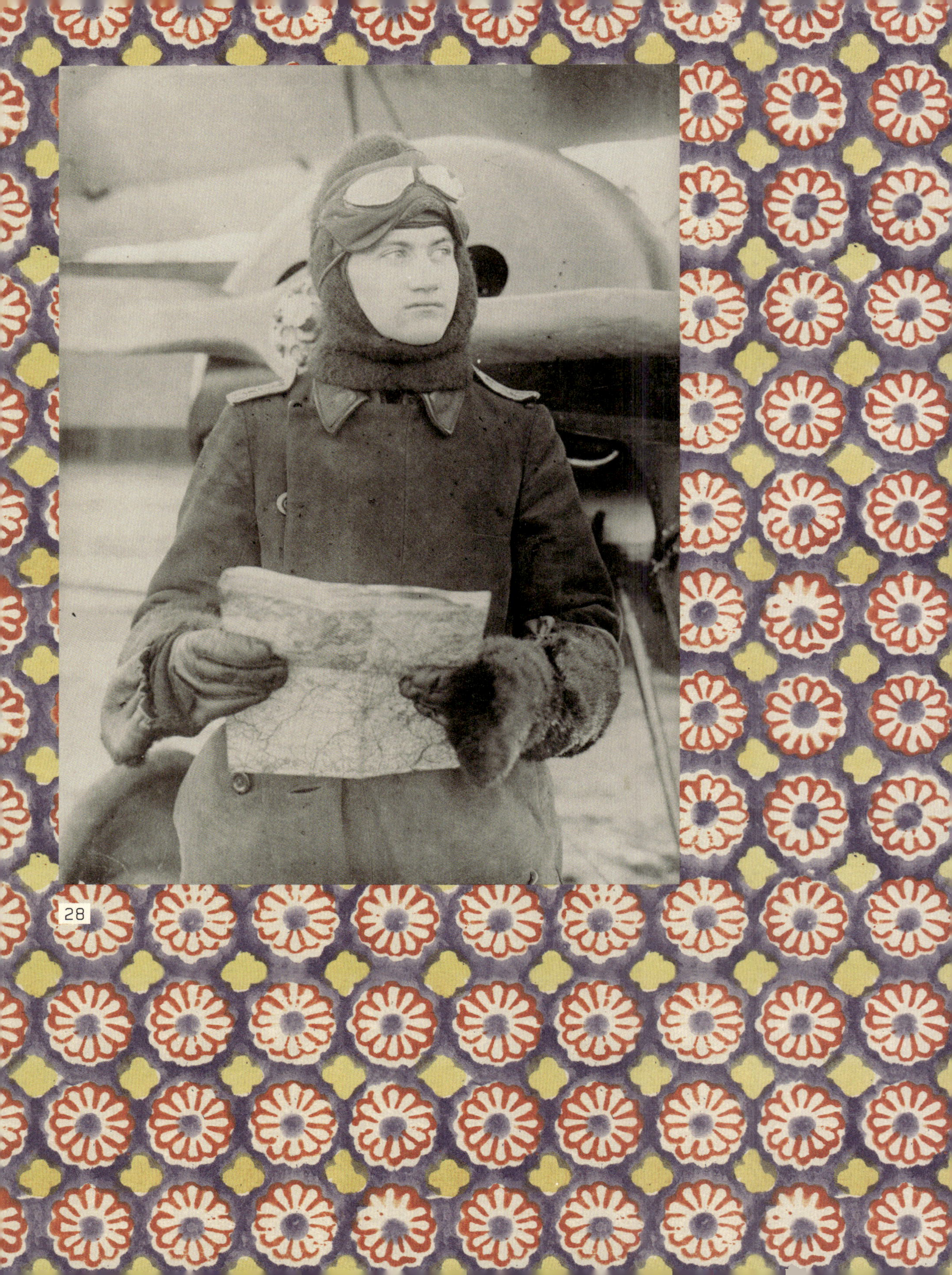

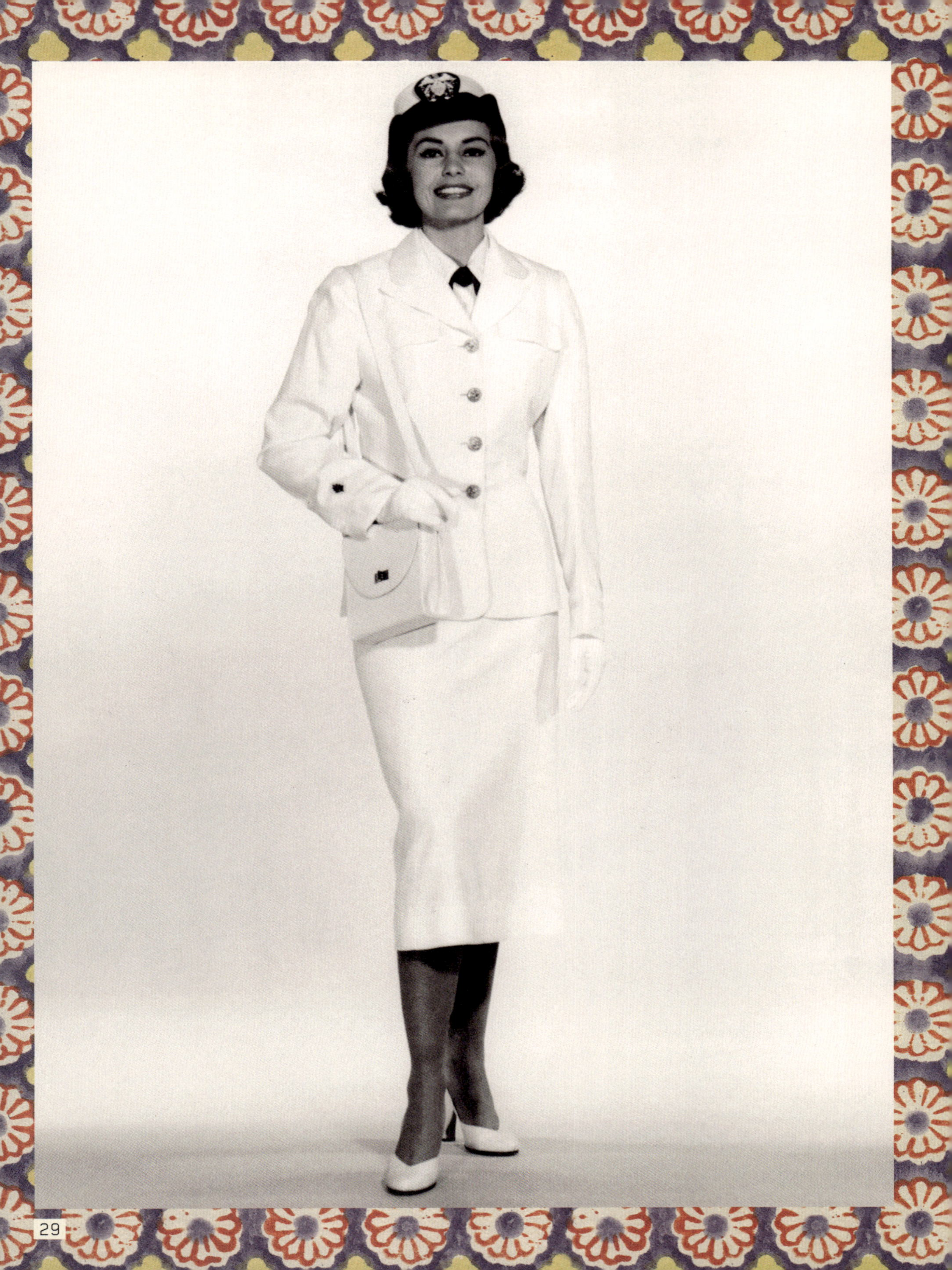

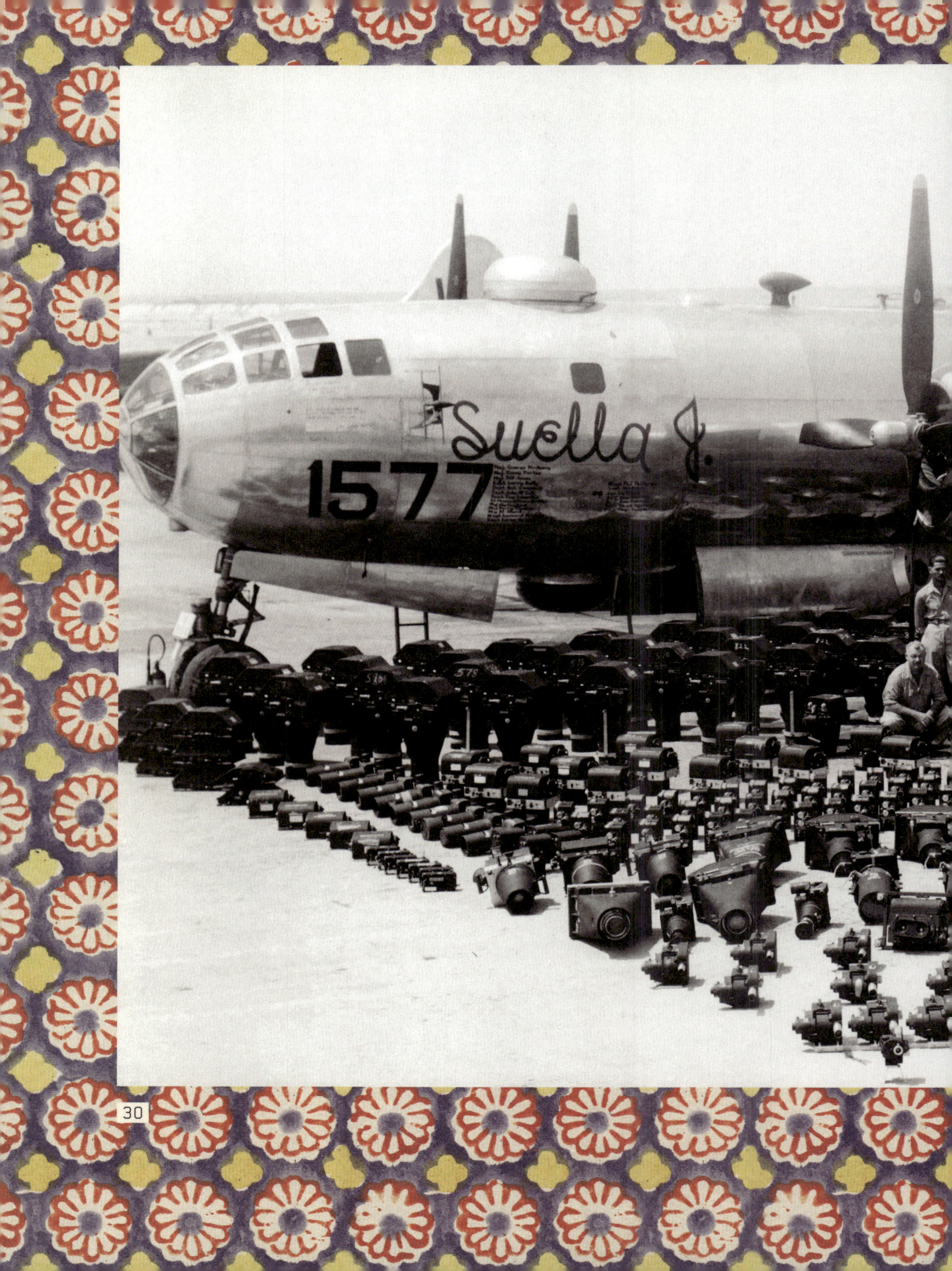

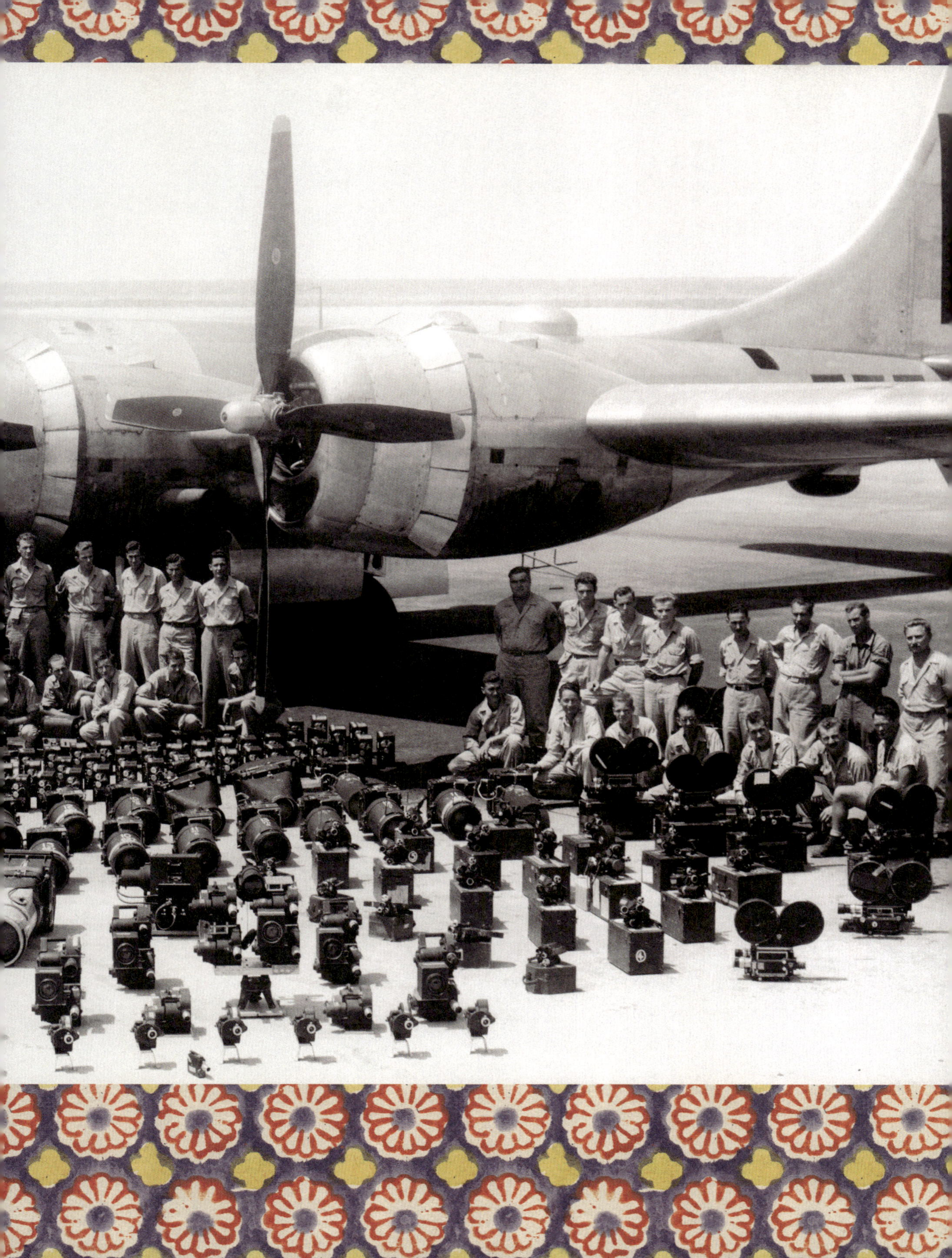

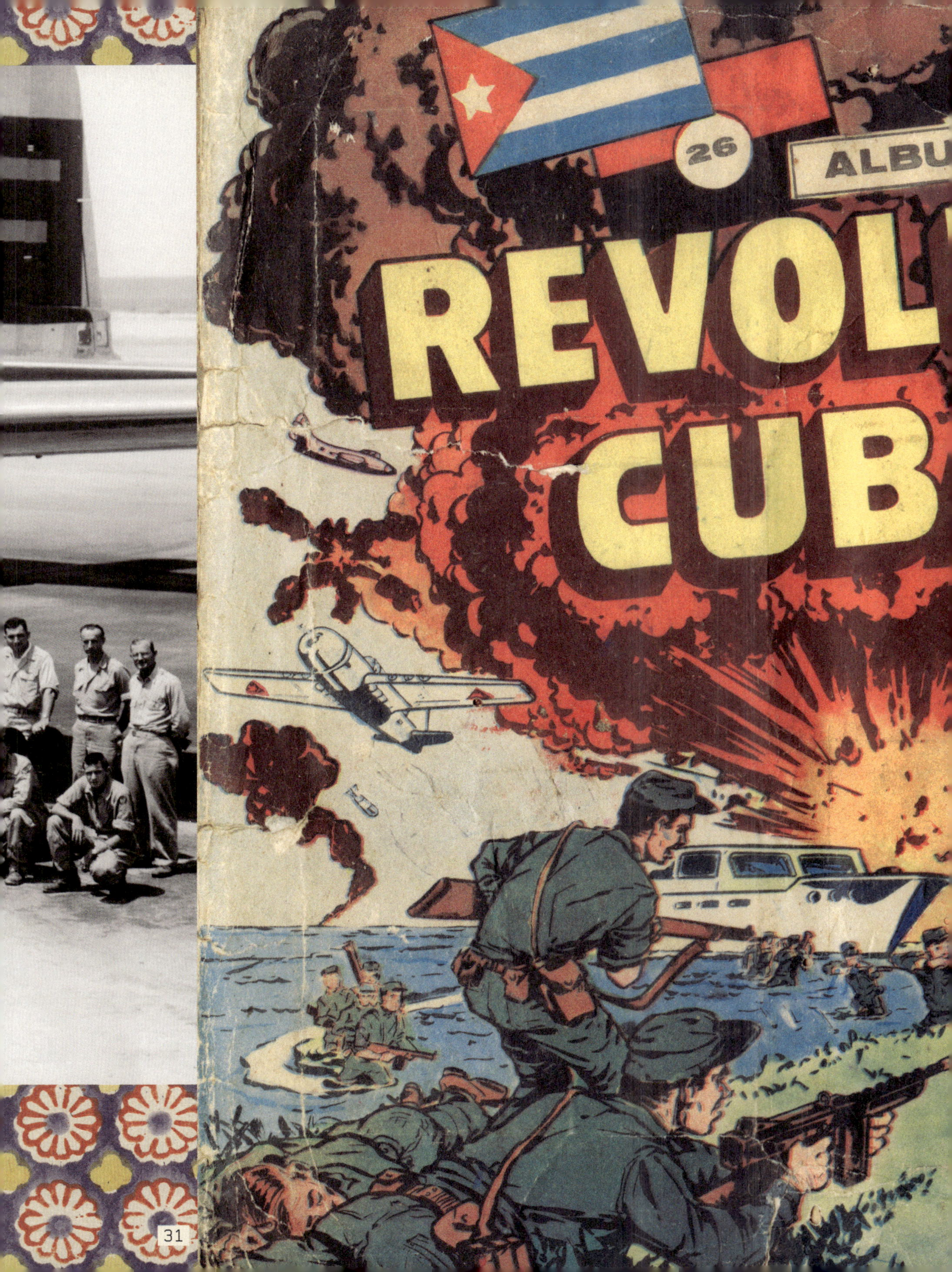
26
ALBU
REVOL
CUB
31

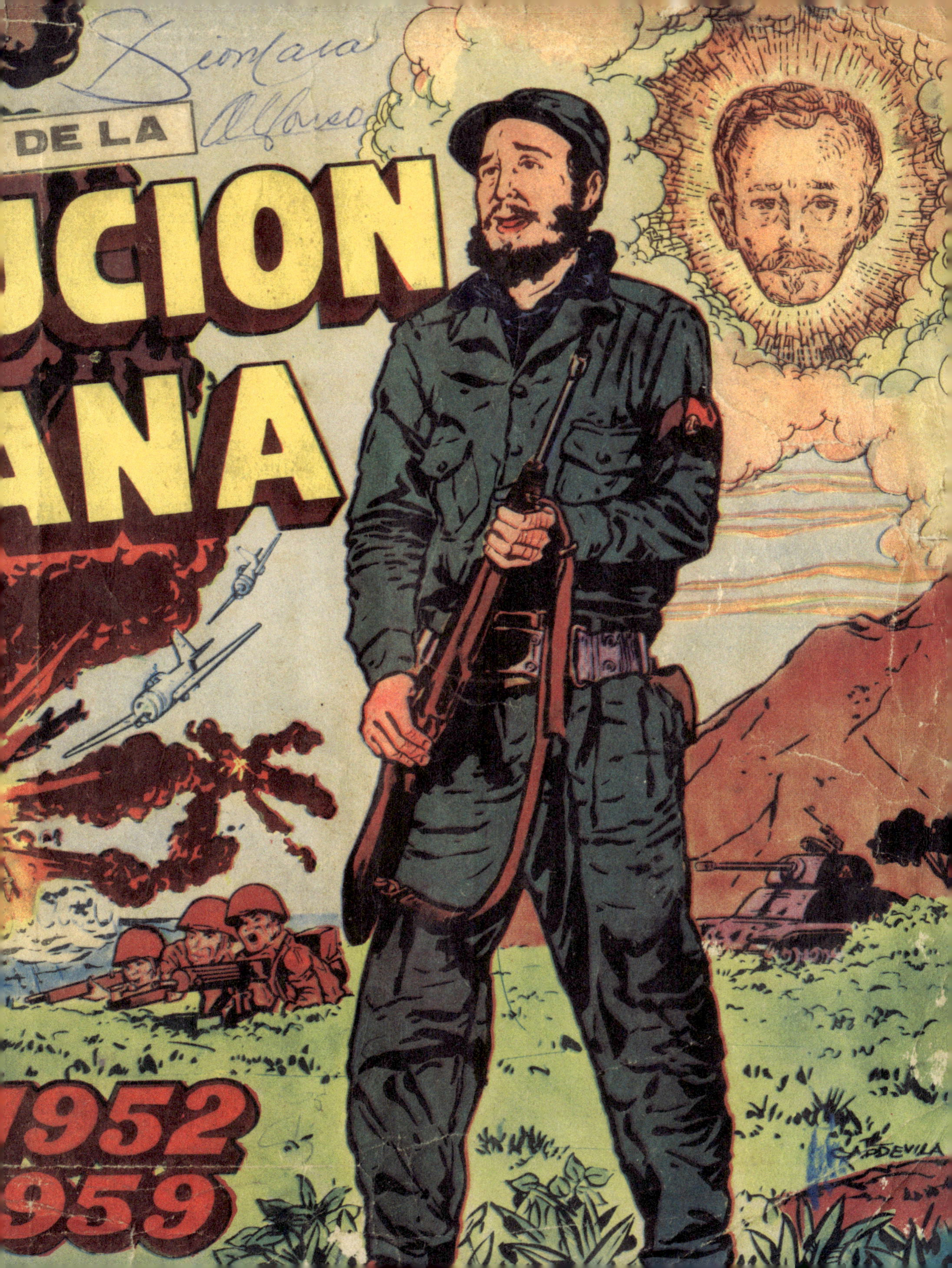
DE LA
UCION
ANA
1952
959

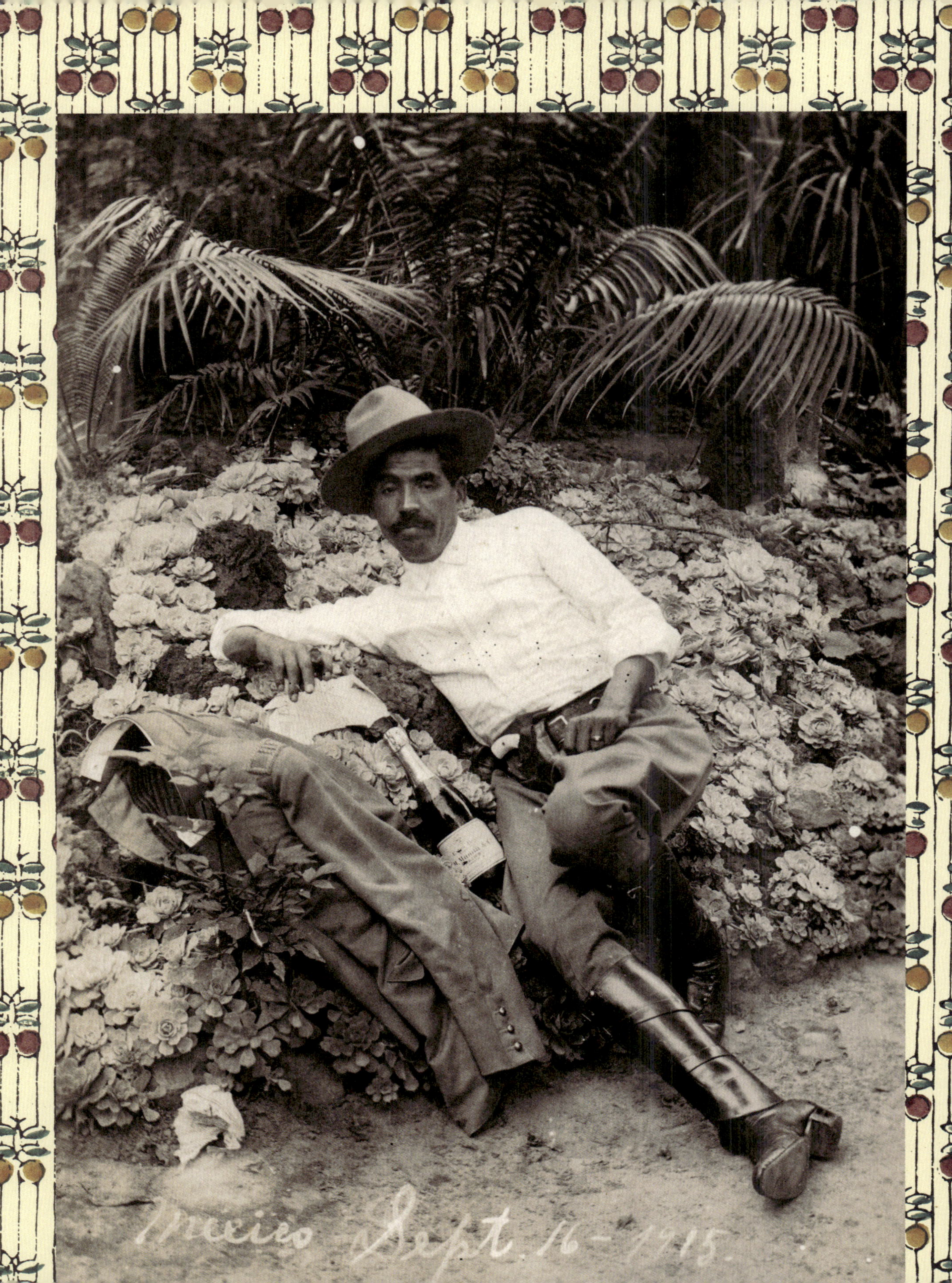
Mexico - Sept. 16 - 1915.

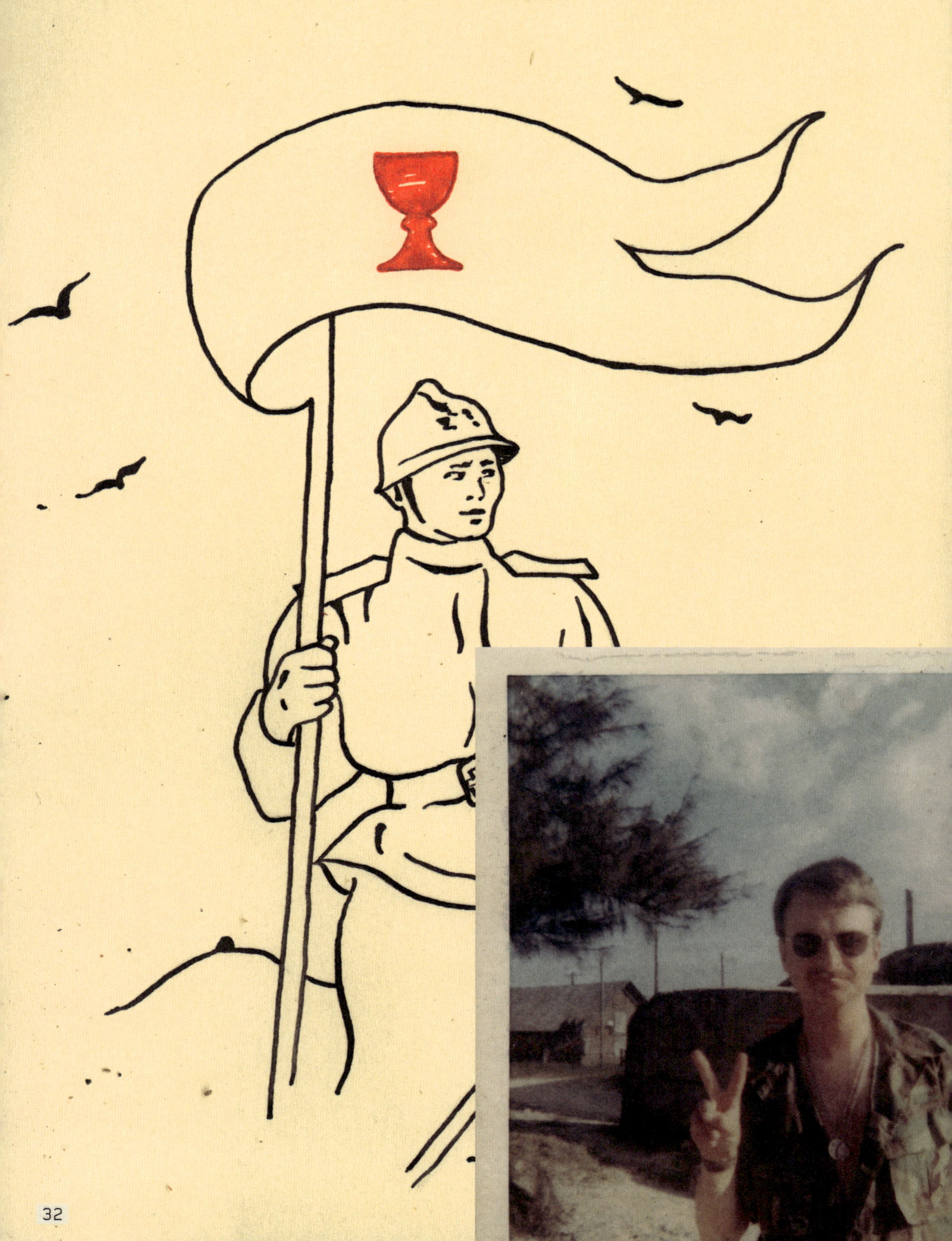

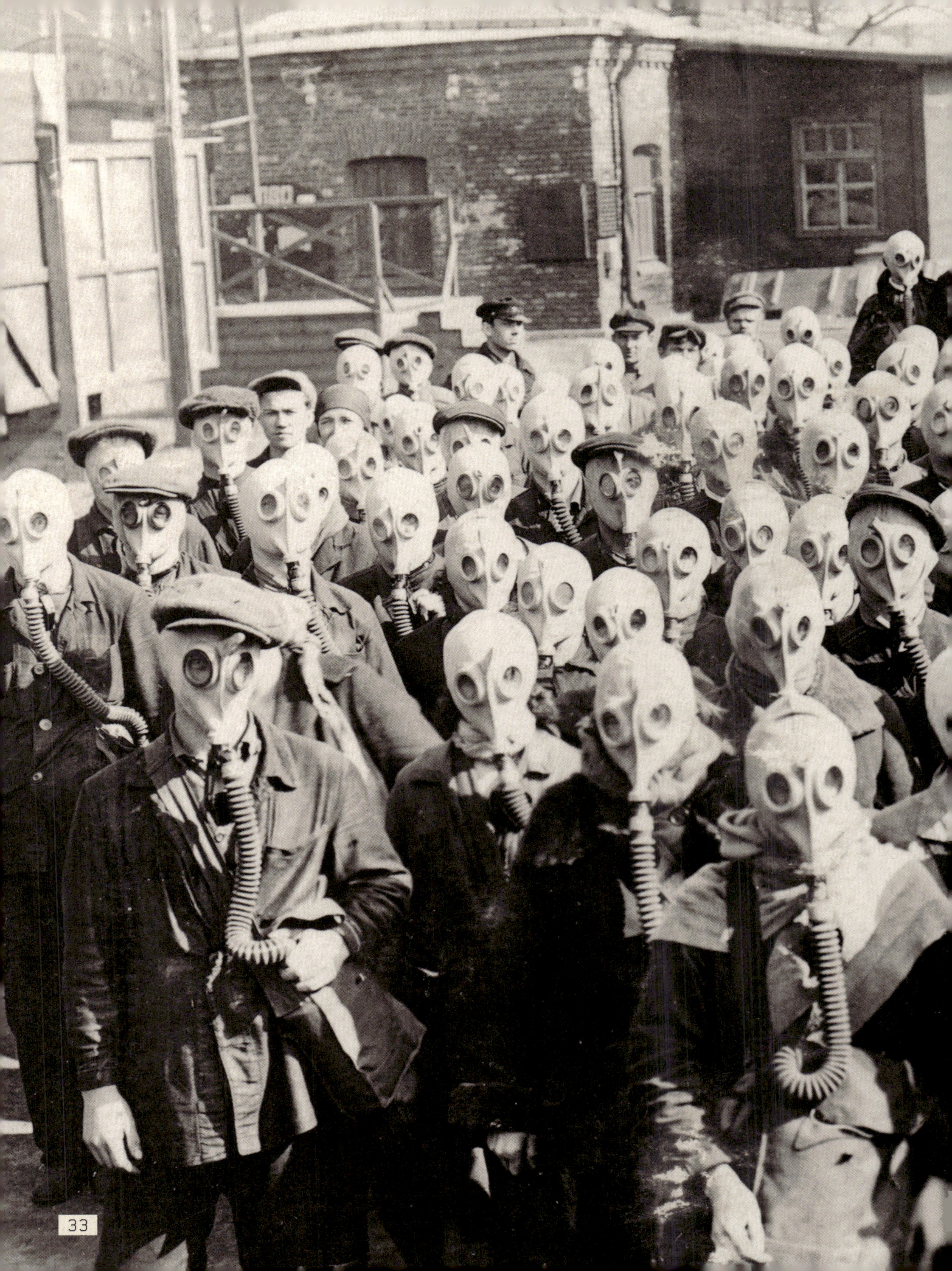
33

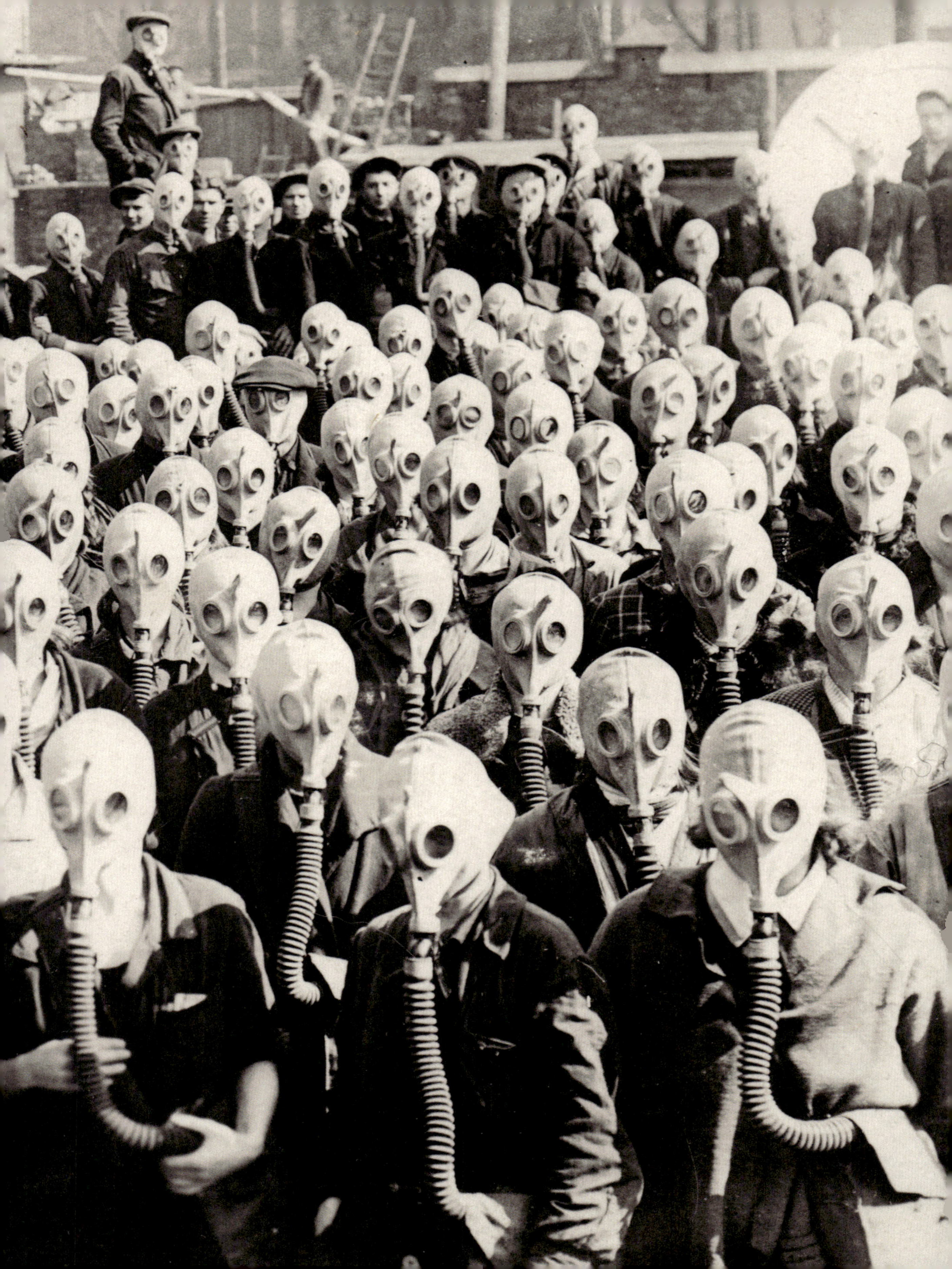

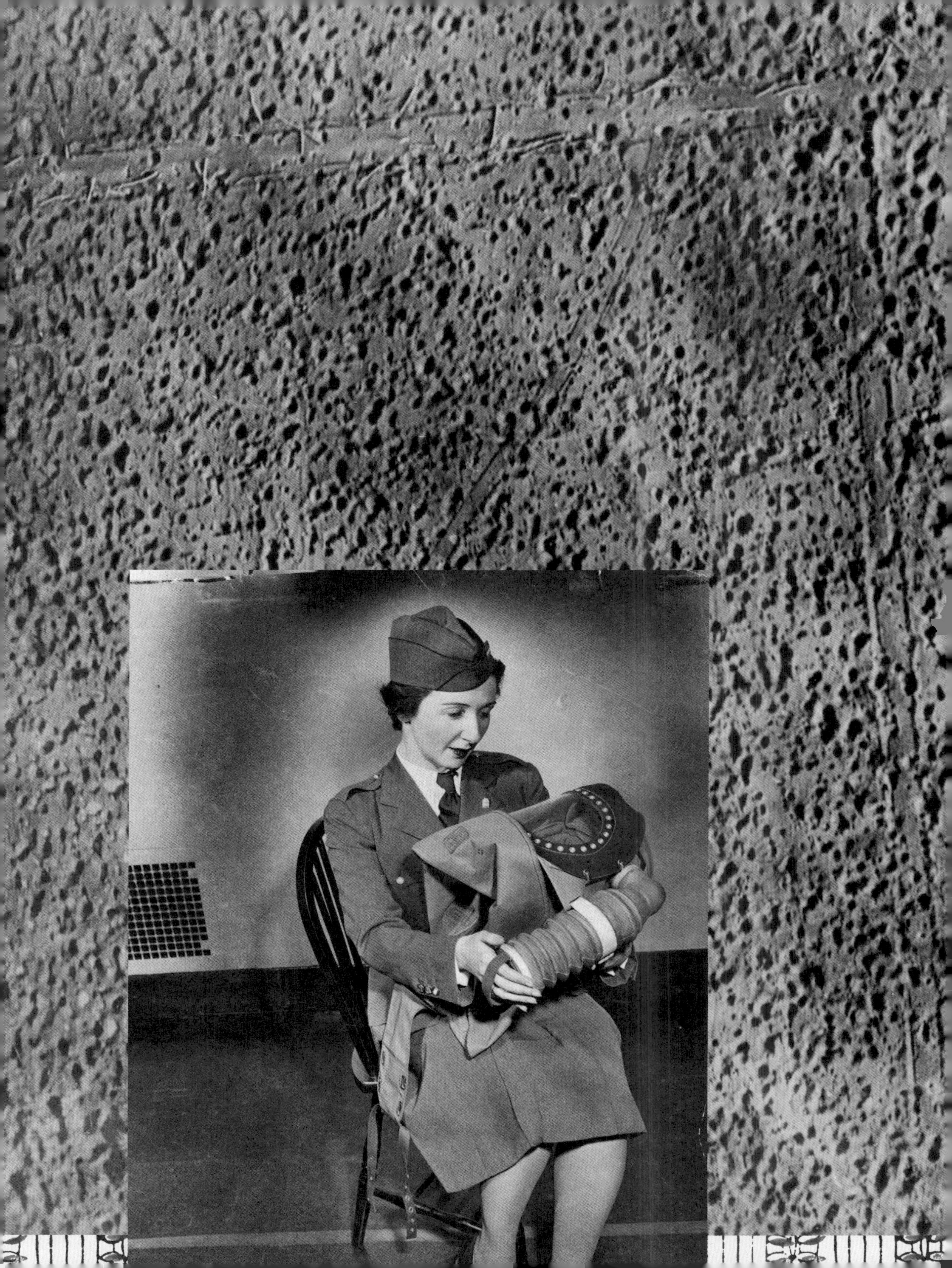

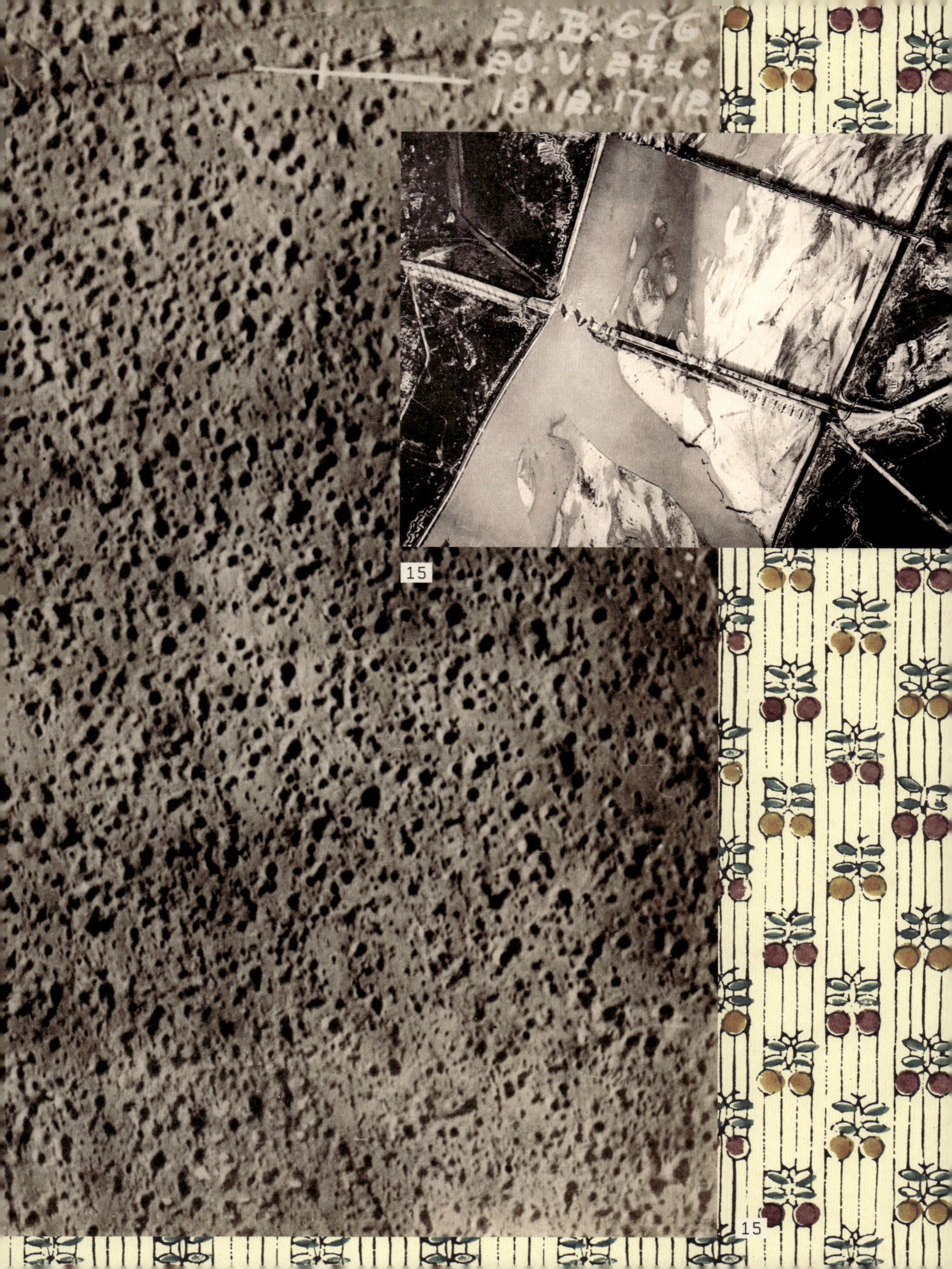

21.B.676
20.V.29 ac
18.12.17-12
15
15

The amnesia caused
memory of previous
transpiring while und
deferred death, the
enormous *longing for*
and effort it took to e

After arriving at
entirely dependent u
difference of languag
or any other reason
resorted to sensibilit
tests and the *military*
light bent under th
threatened and yelled at
in *a sea of liquid manur*
duped to the entrails
become incapable of
guts without knowing w

y *scopolamine and morphine* is not a loss of
ents but is an *inability to remember what is*
the *influence of the drug.* Condemned to a
ily thing that really mattered was an
, all the rest was torture, even the time

is conclusion he made his dosage almost
i the *depth of the amnesia.* In cases where a
r *extreme ignorance or dementia* of the patient
ecluded the use of the memory test, he
f the pupil and muscular coordination as
ture continued in its nocturnal aspect without
sacks that weighed more than a man,
iggard with no better prospect than to end
ckened at the thought we'd been tortured,
a *gang of vicious lunatics,* who had suddenly
ig anything else than *killing and spilling their*

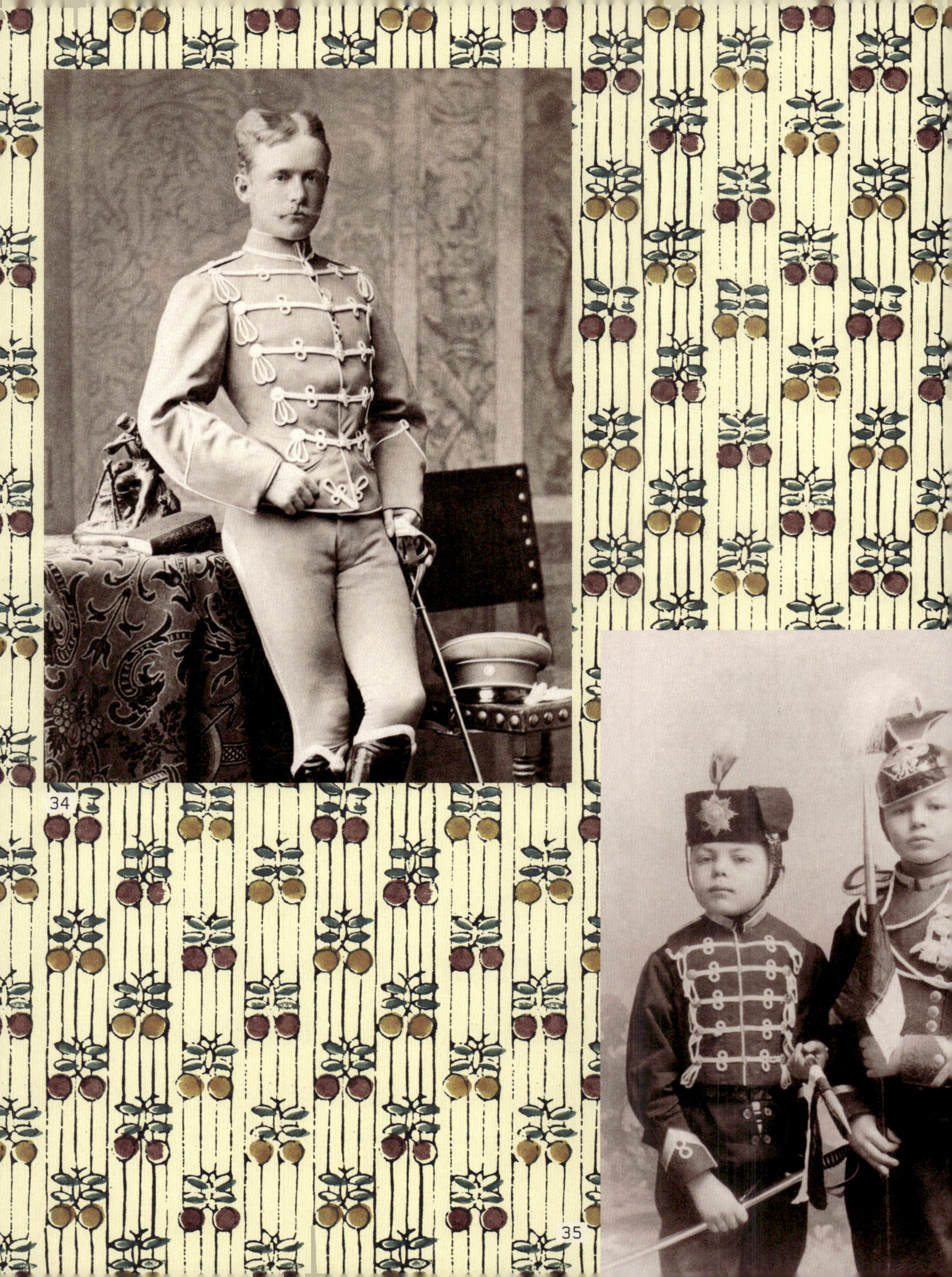

34

35

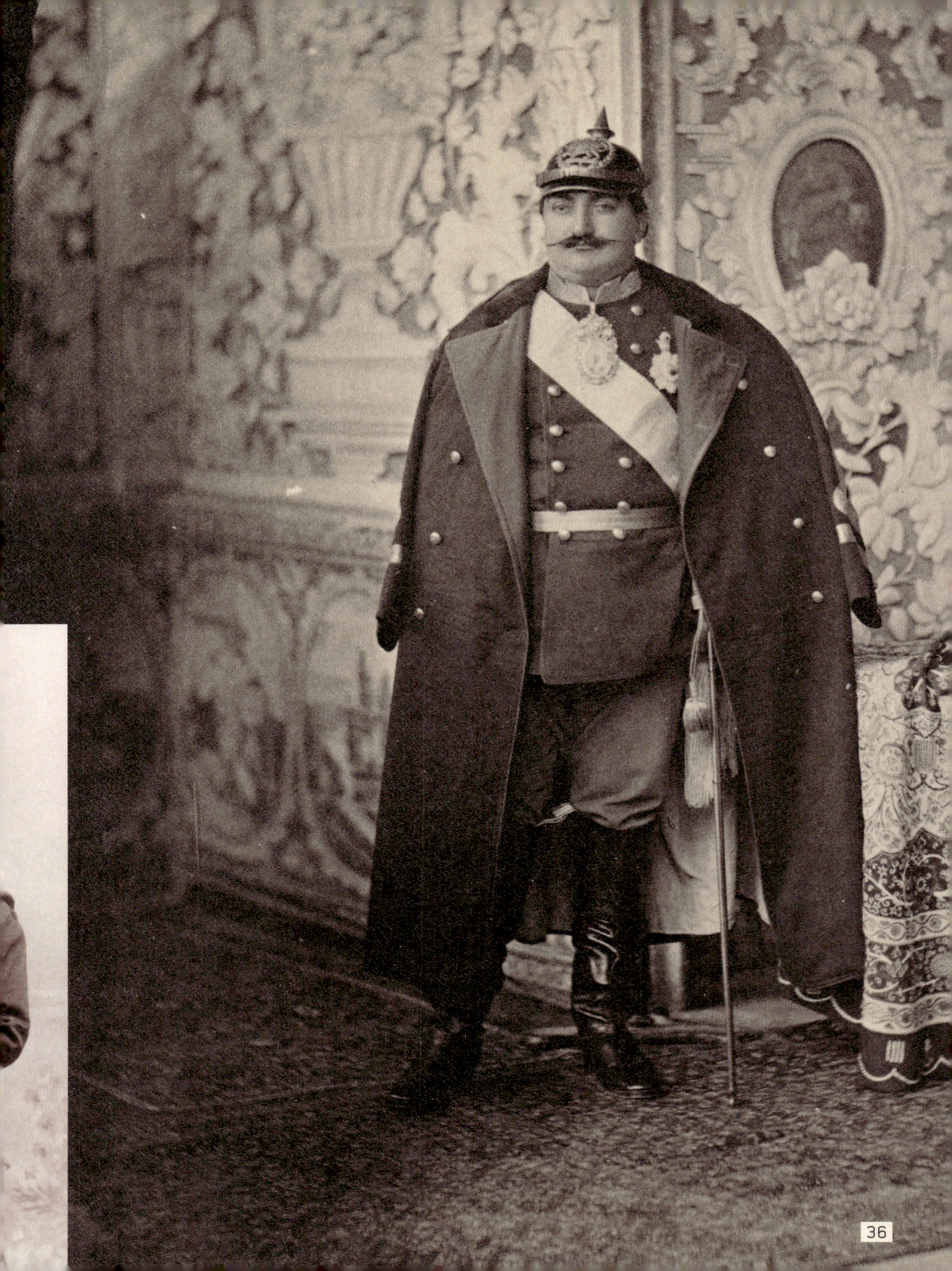

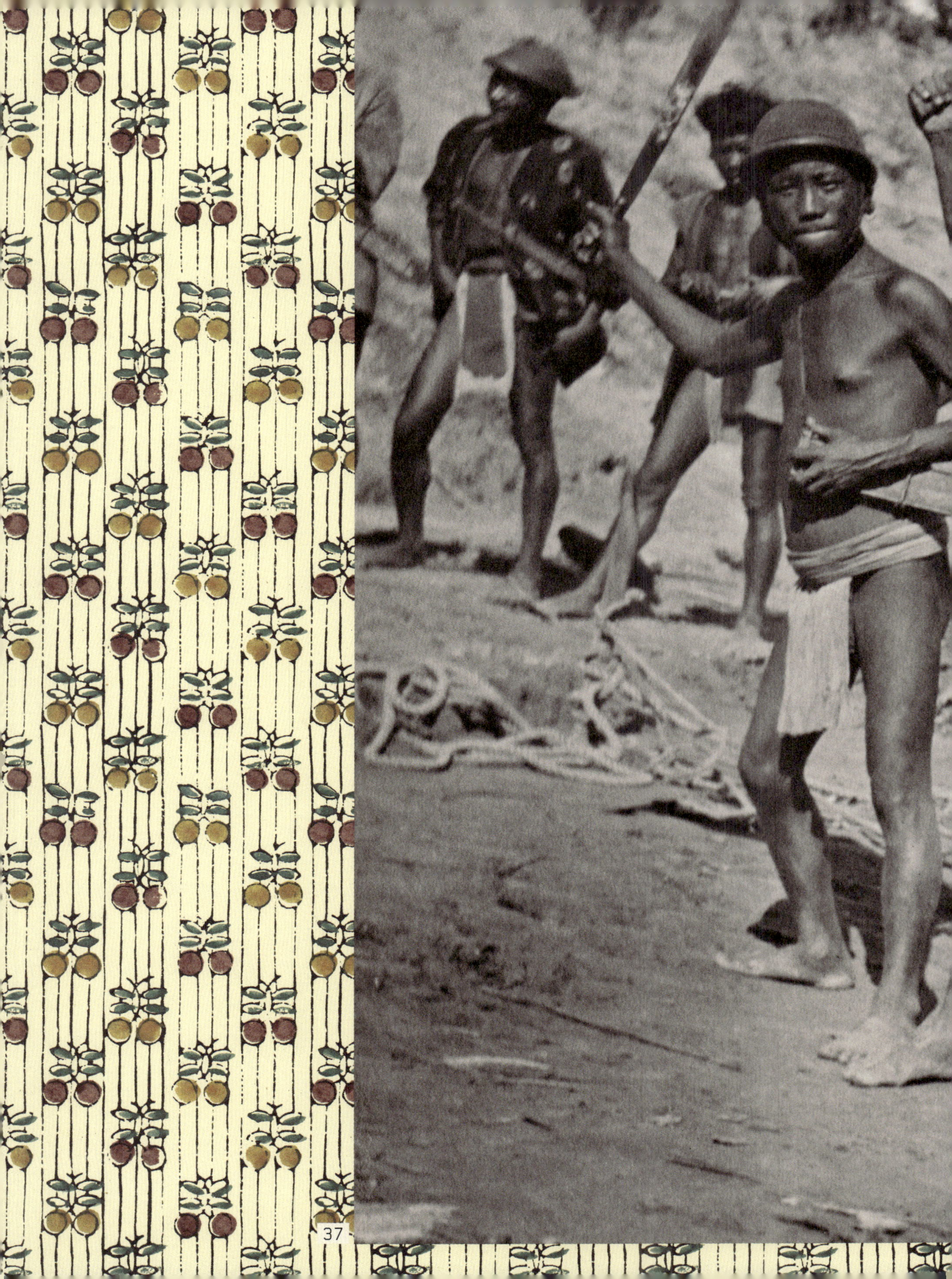

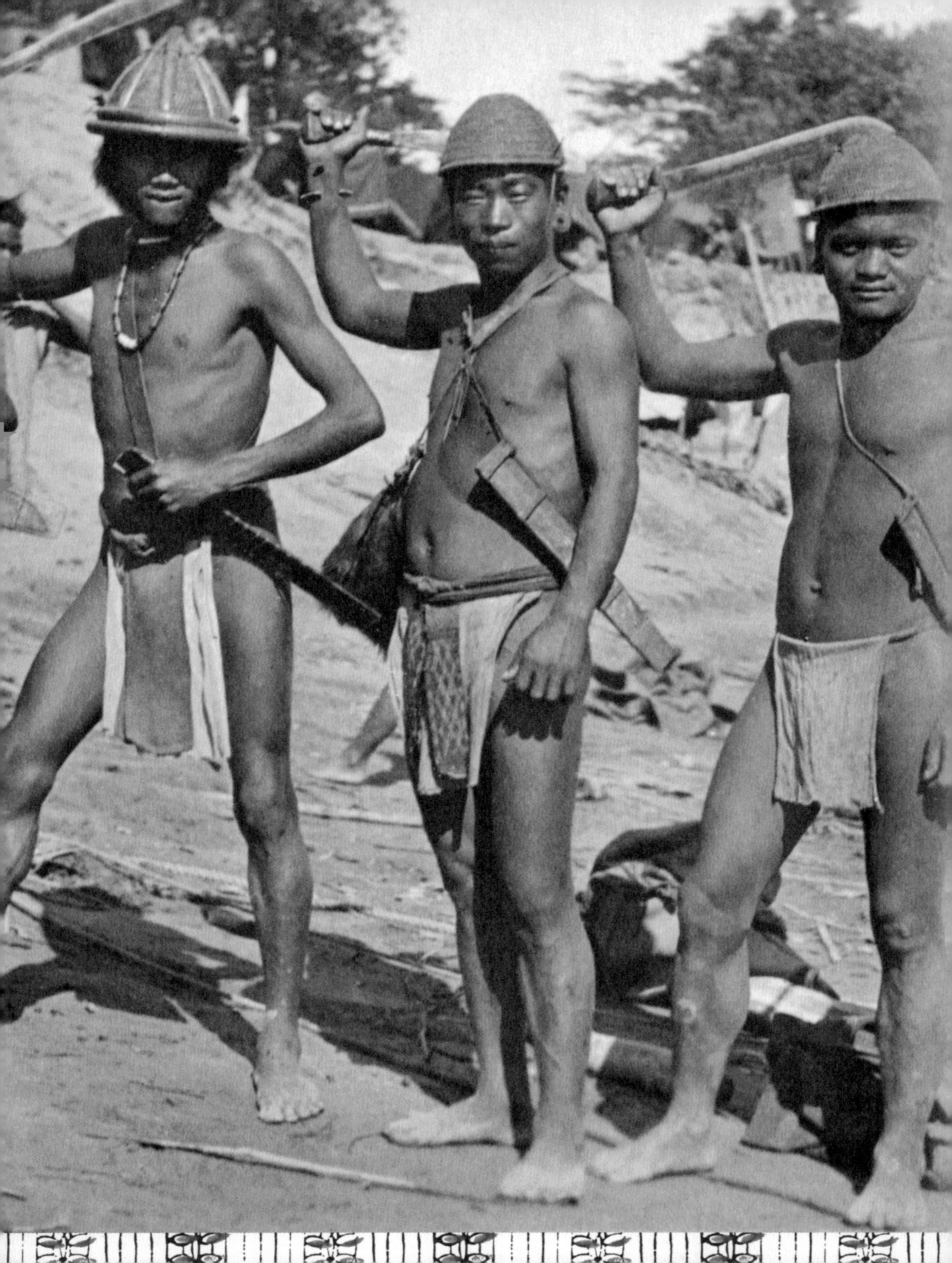

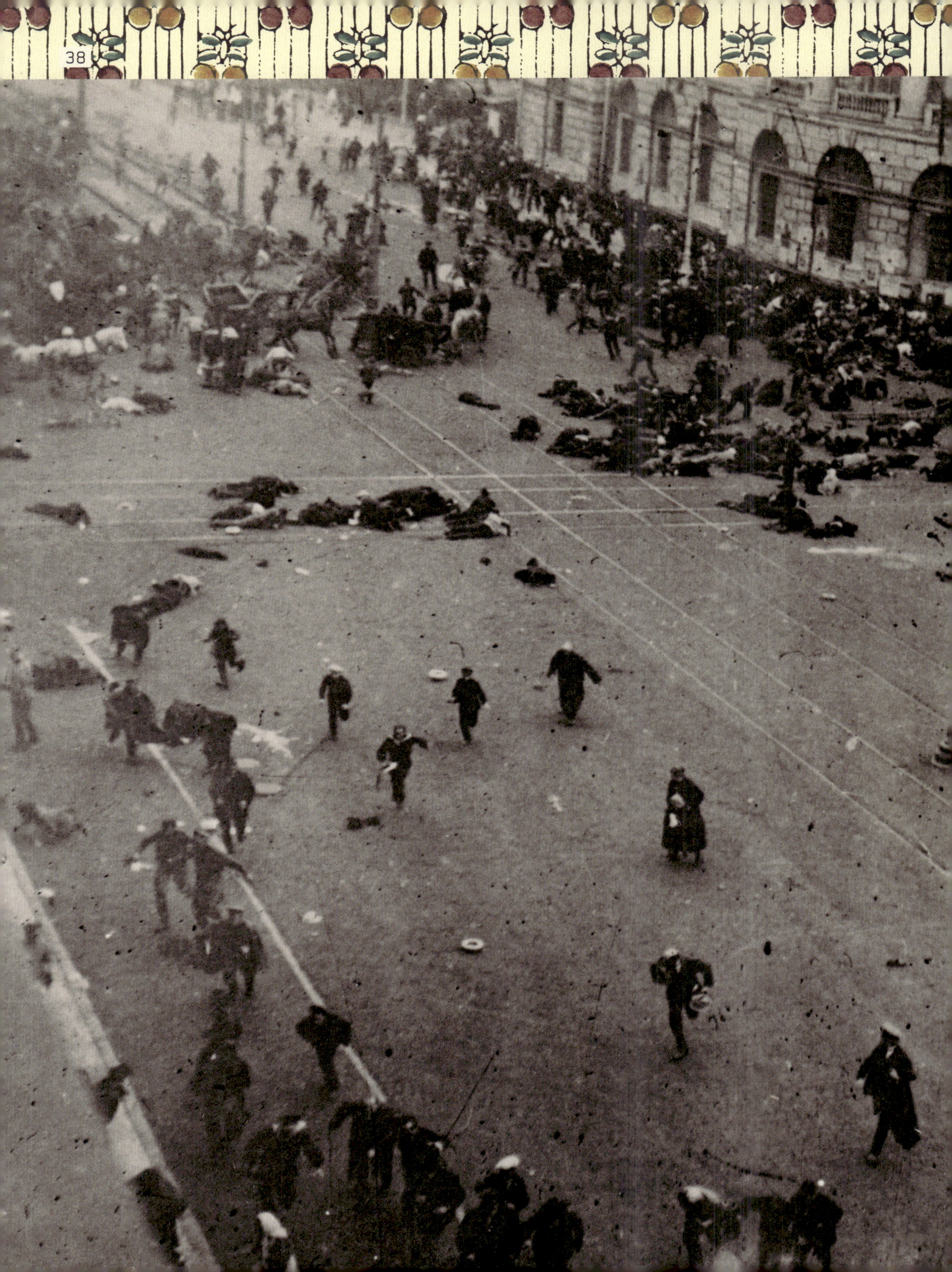

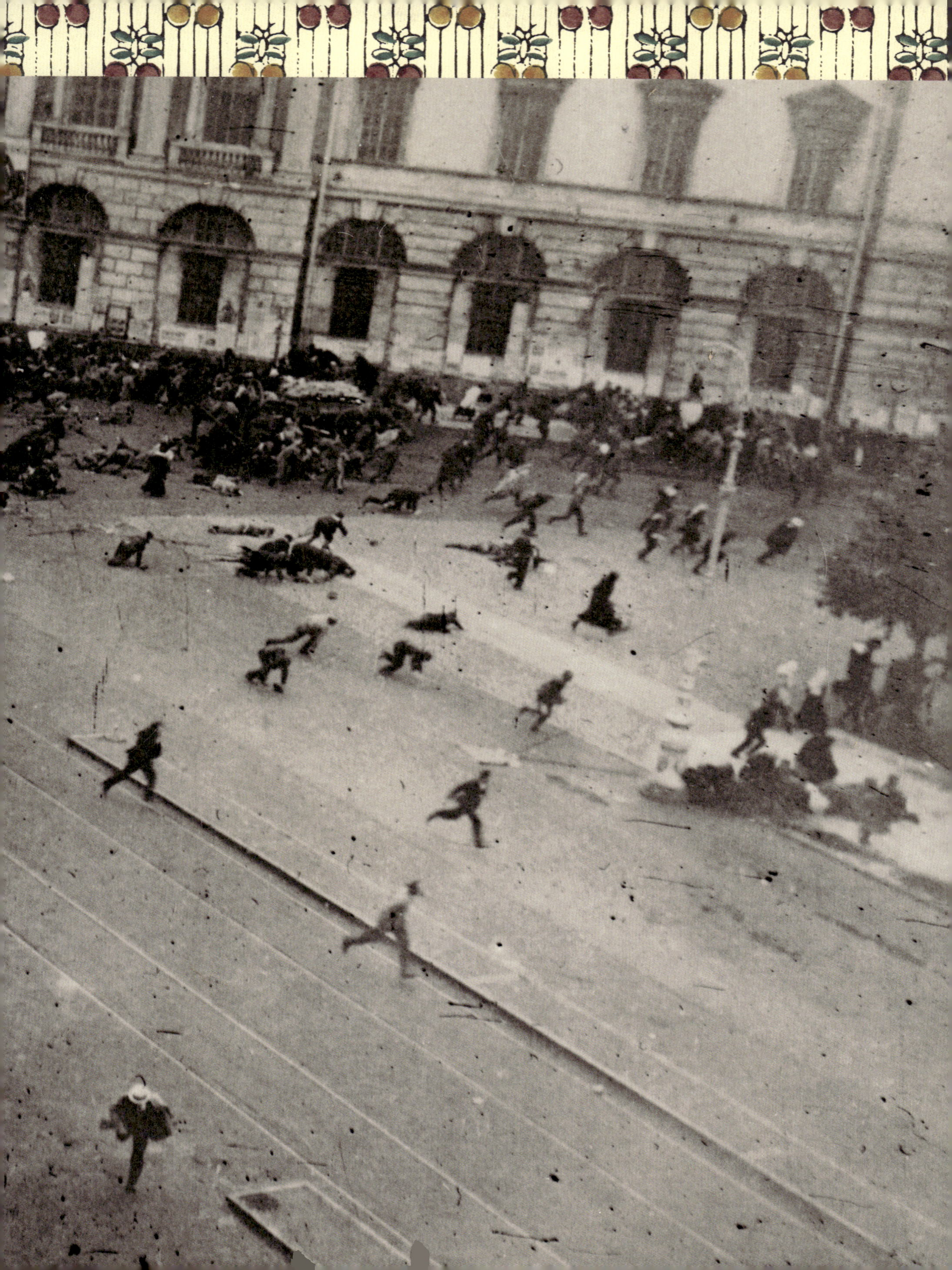

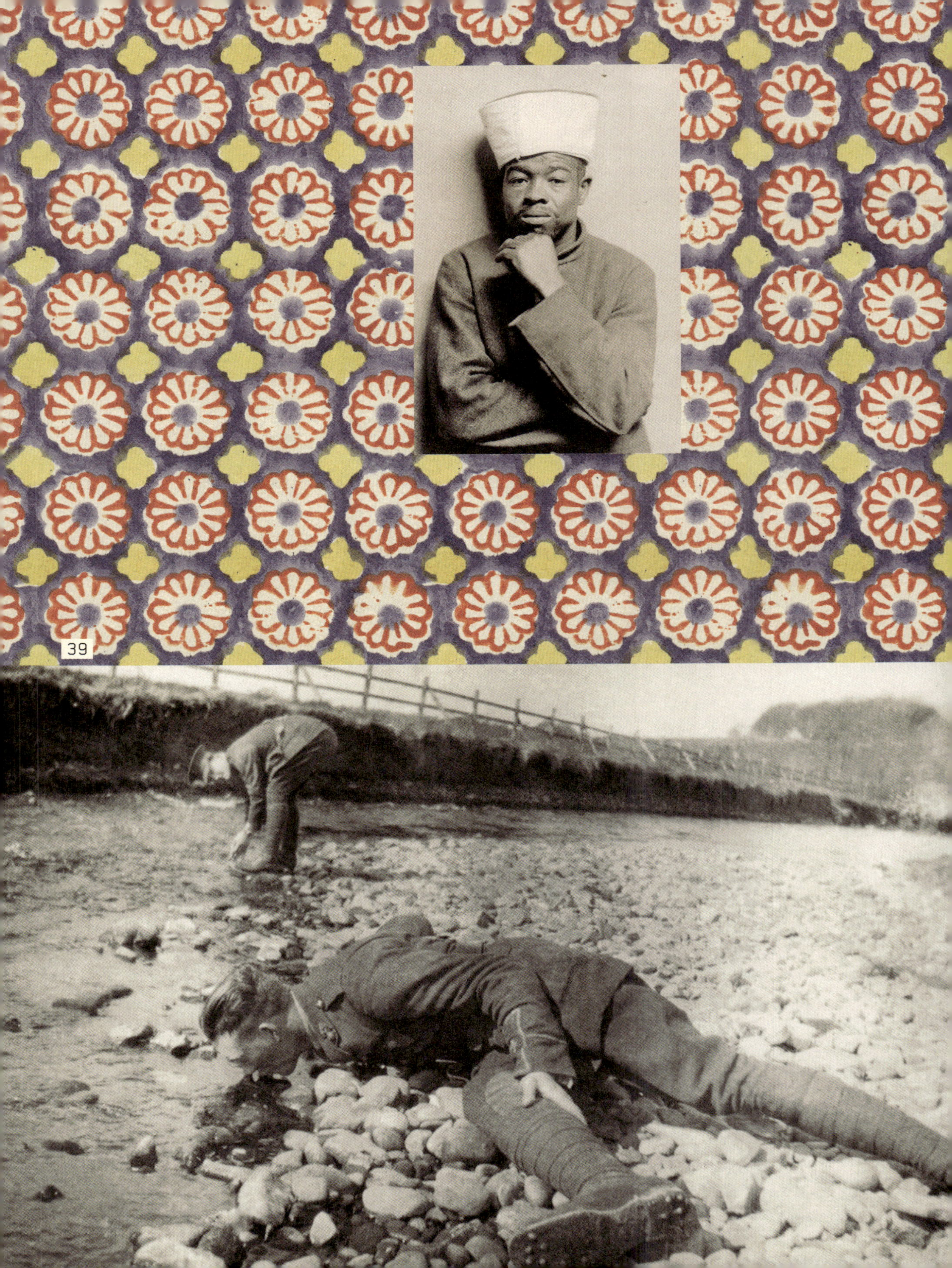

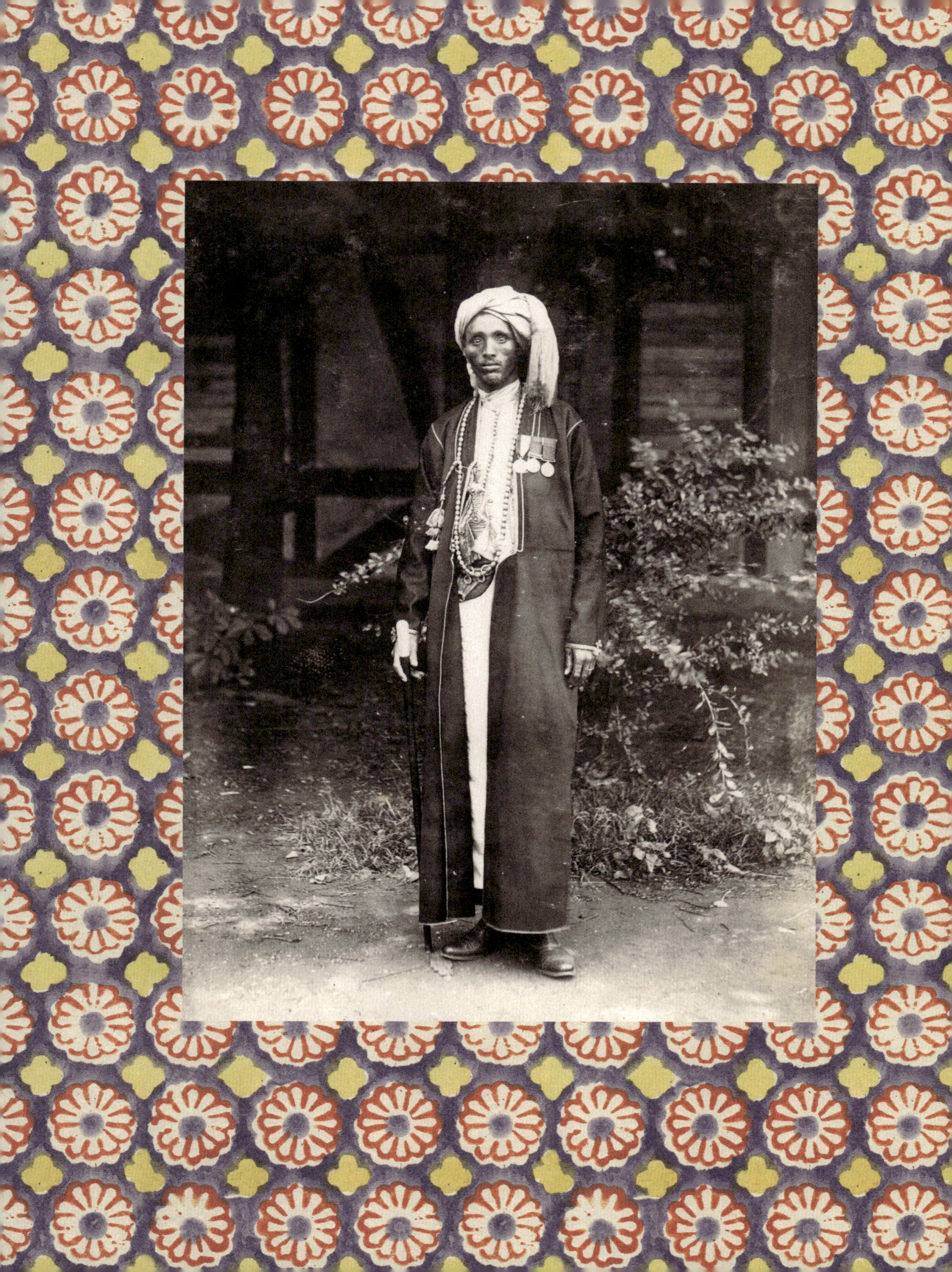

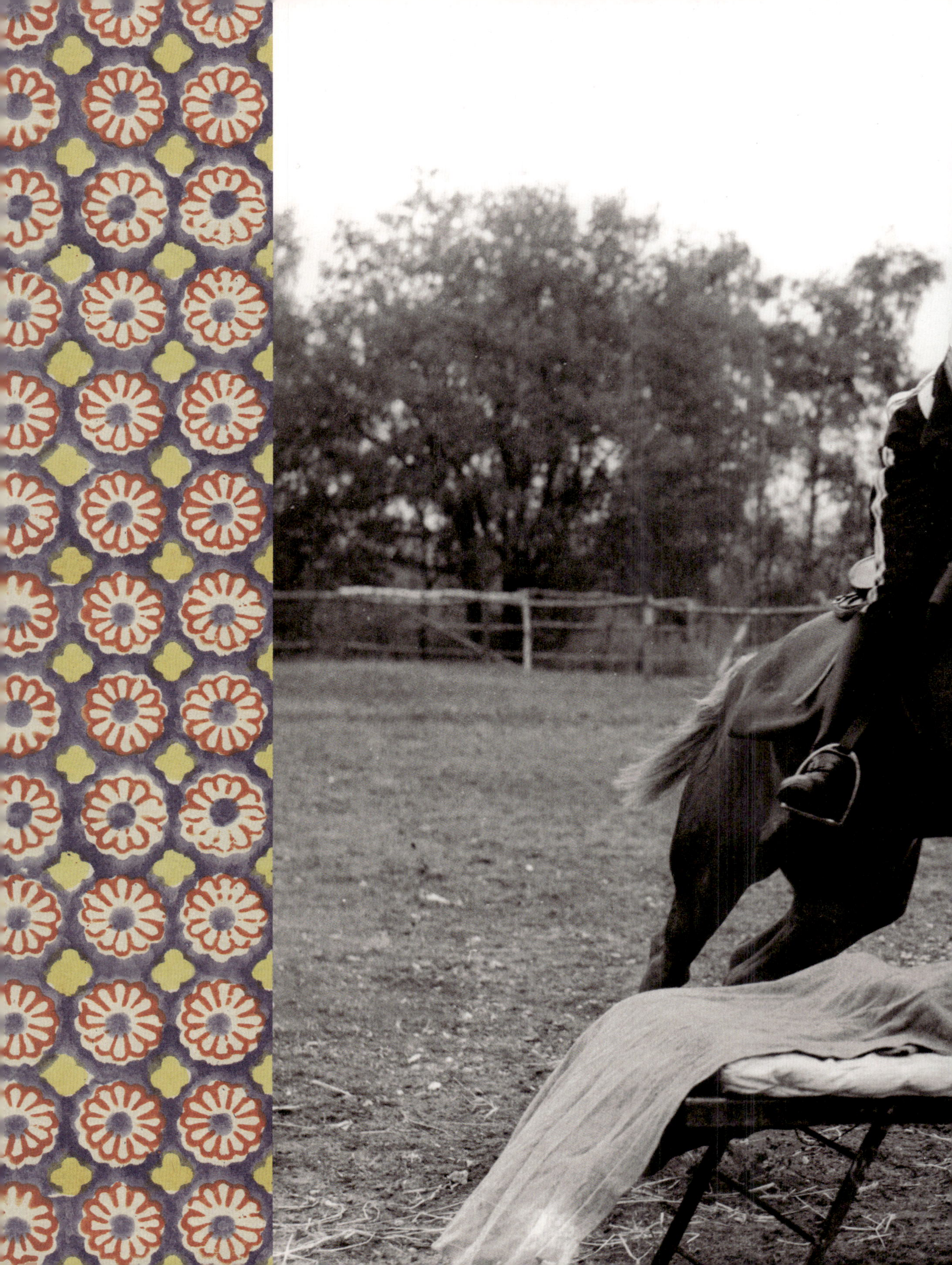

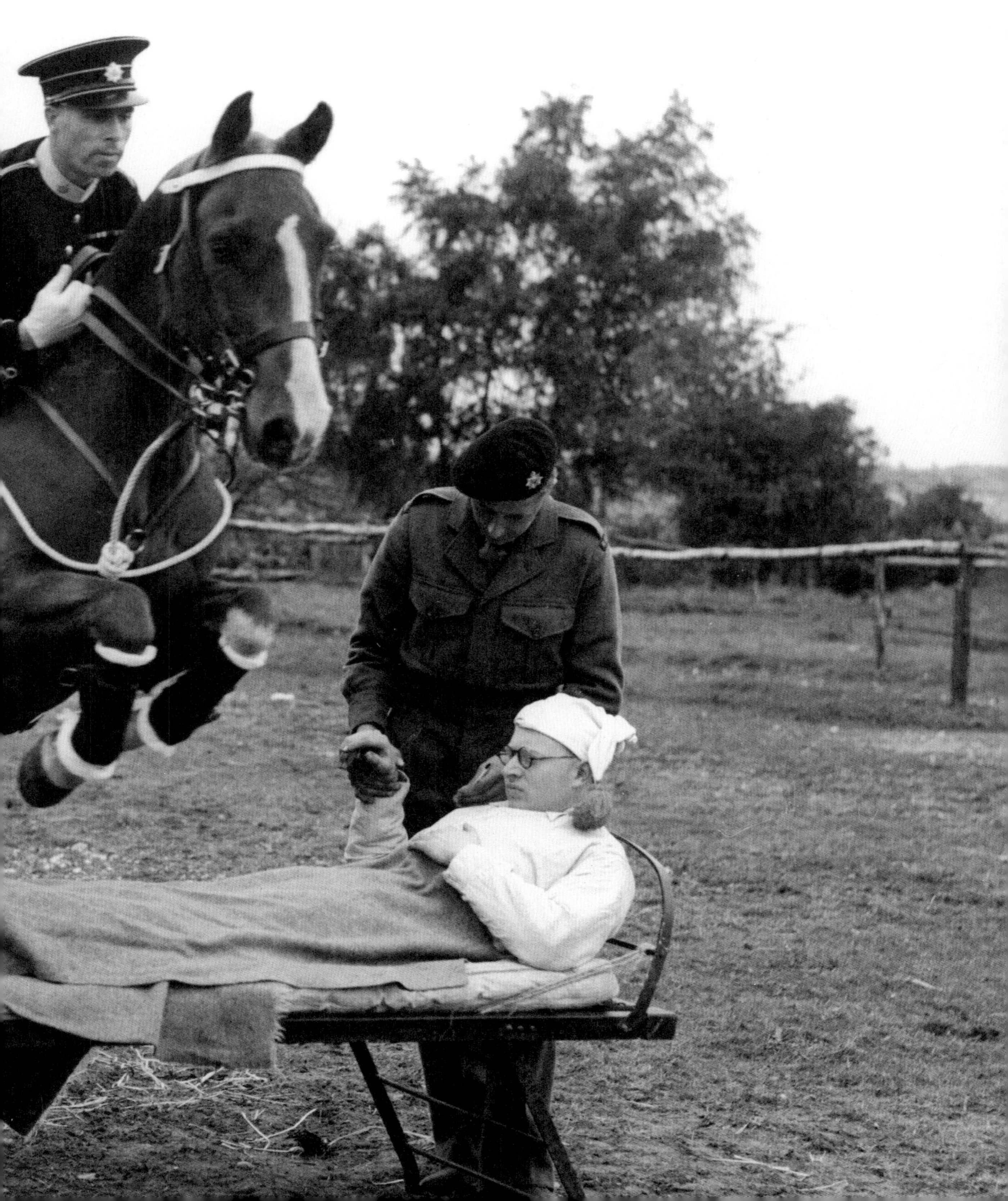

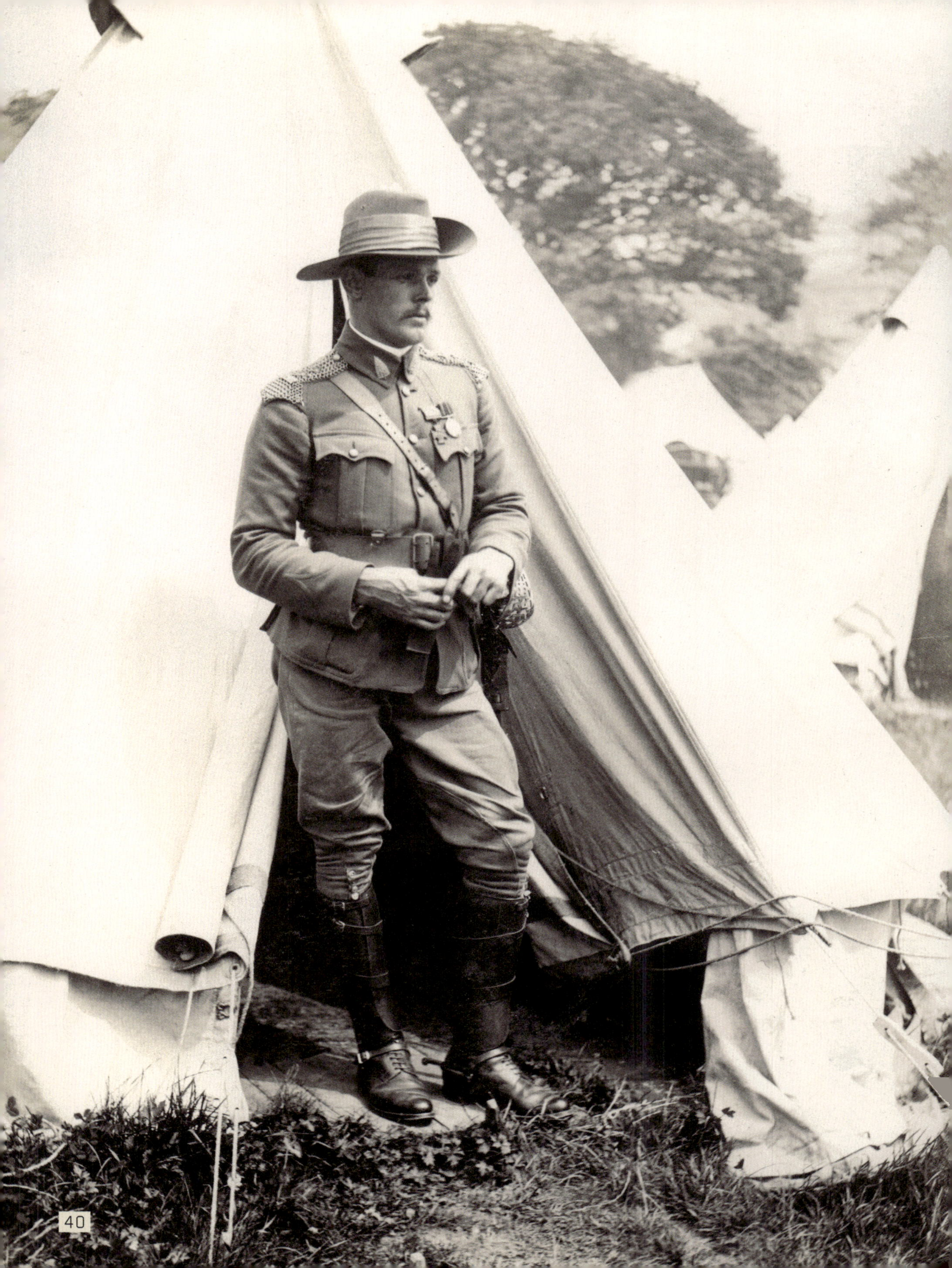

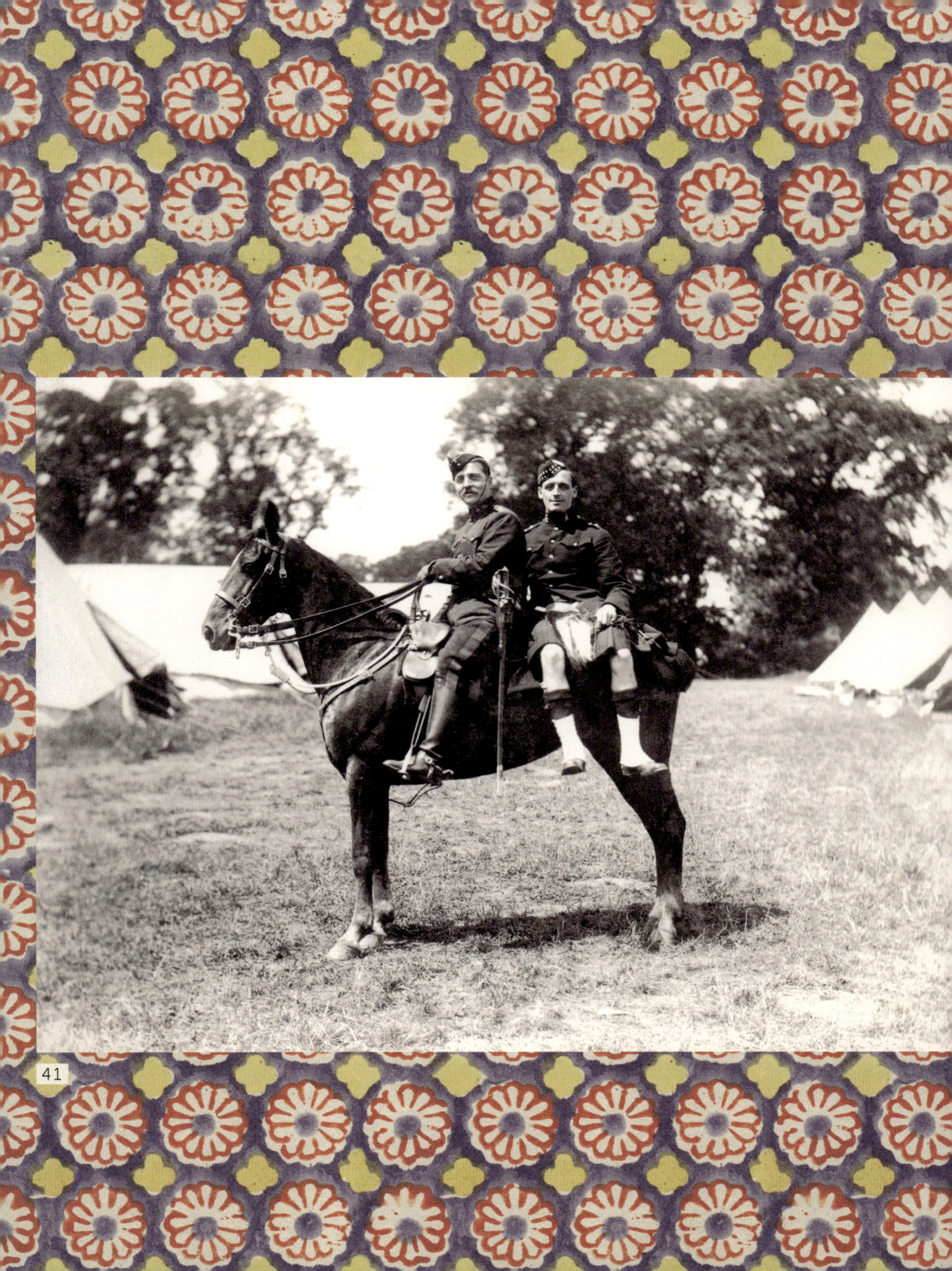

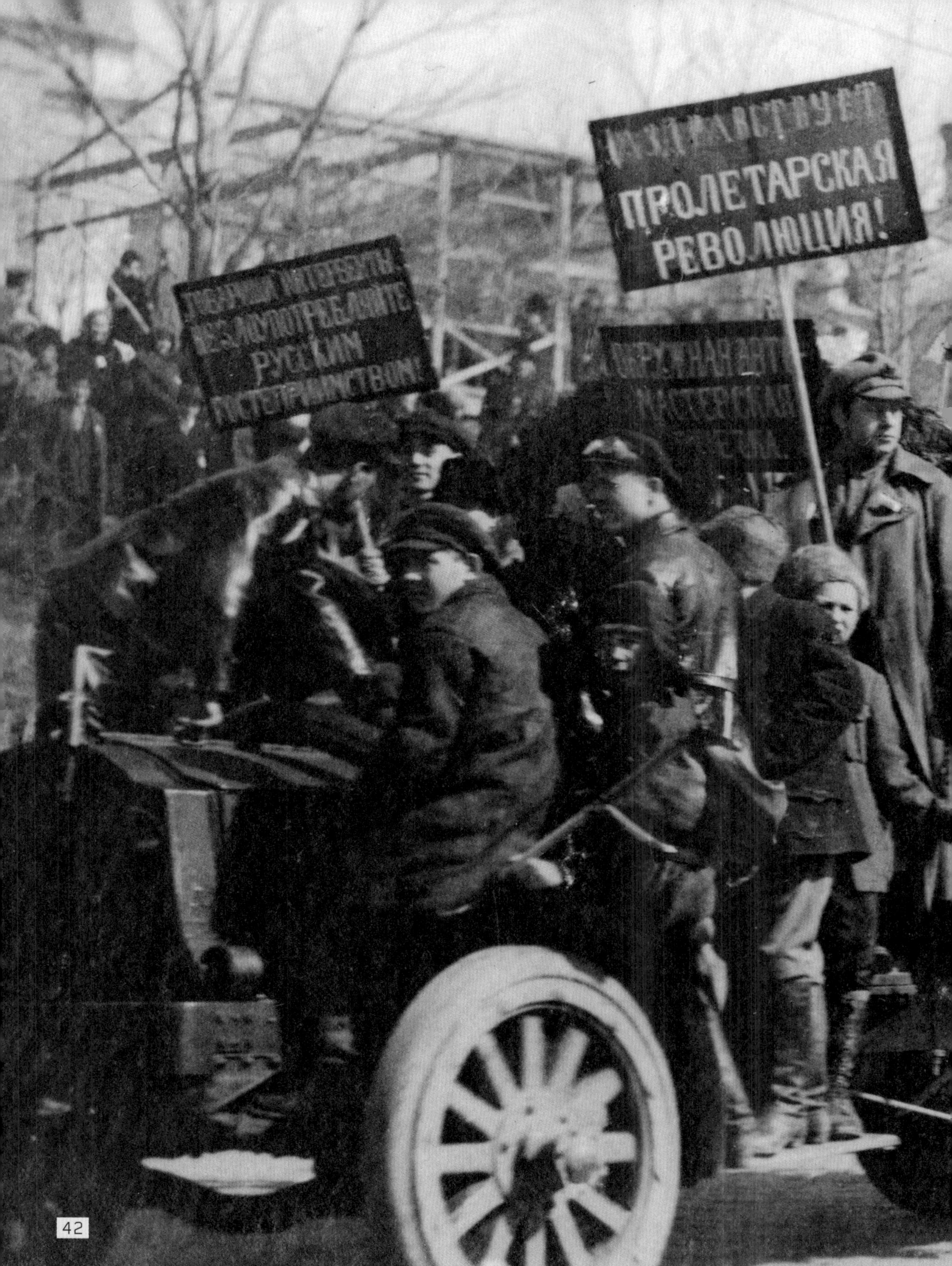
ДА ЗДРАВСТВУЕТ
ПРОЛЕТАРСКАЯ
РЕВОЛЮЦИЯ!
РУССКИМ
ПОТРЕБИТЕЛЯМ

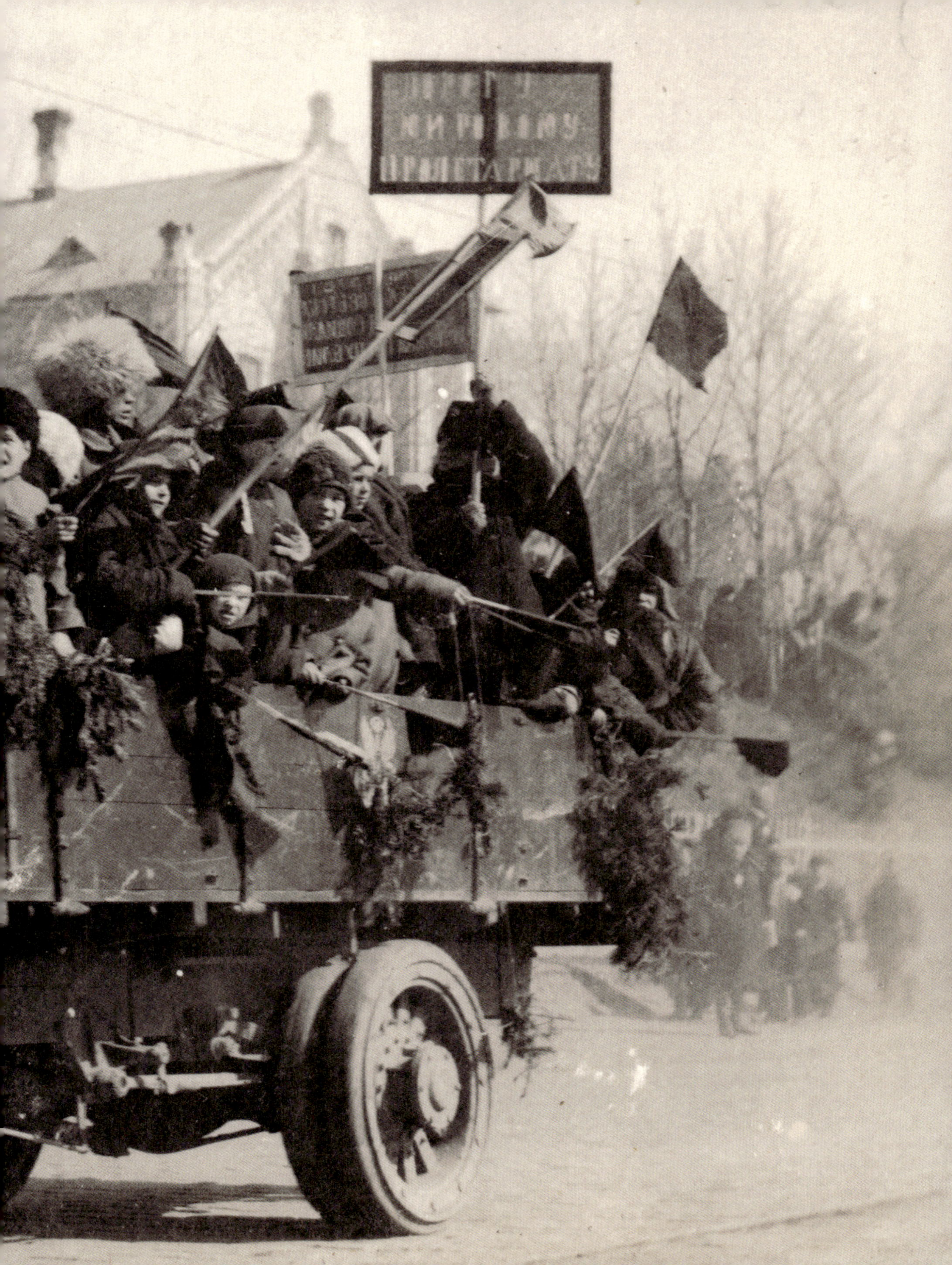
МИРОВОМУ
ПРОЛЕТАРИАТУ

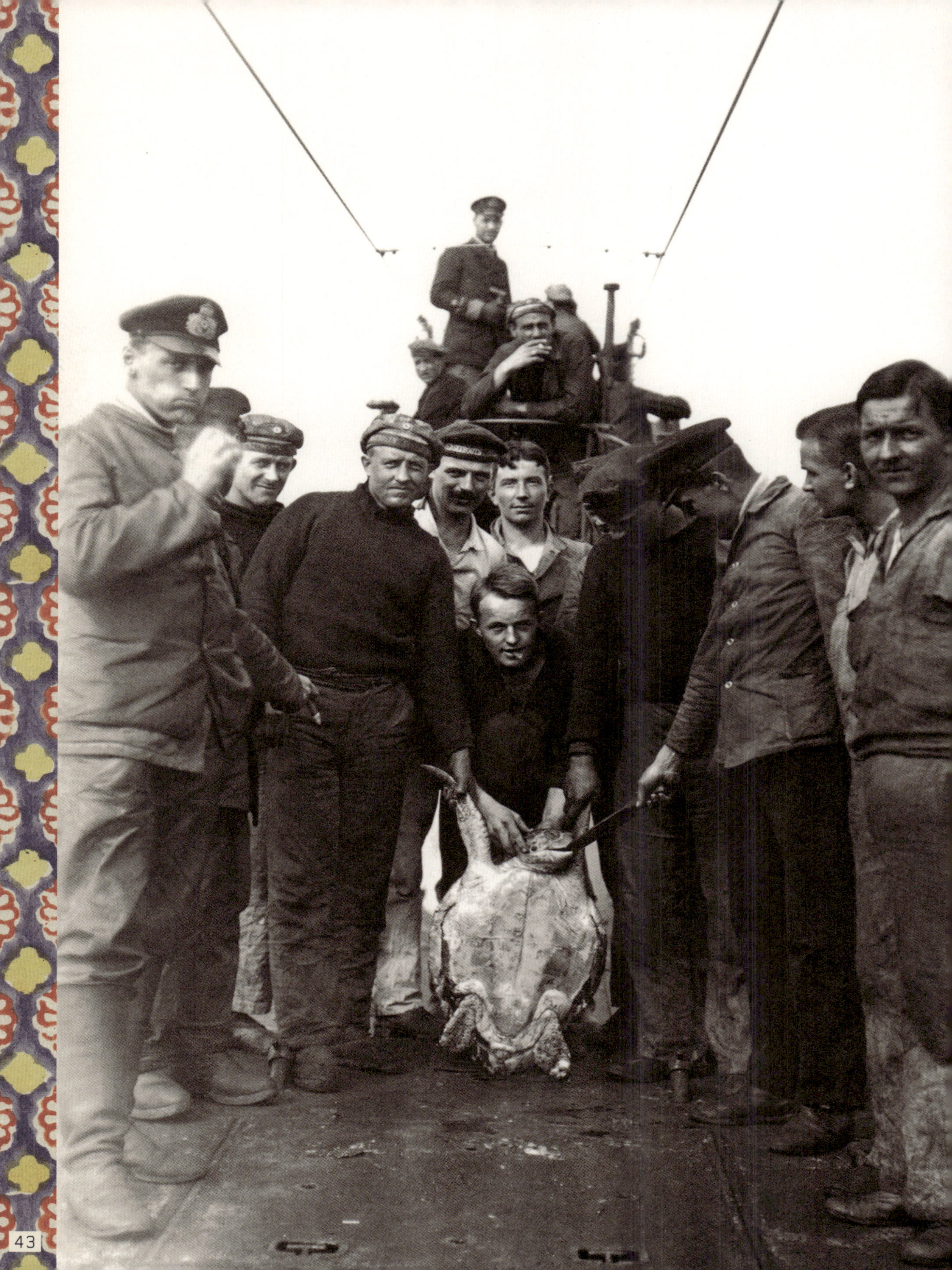

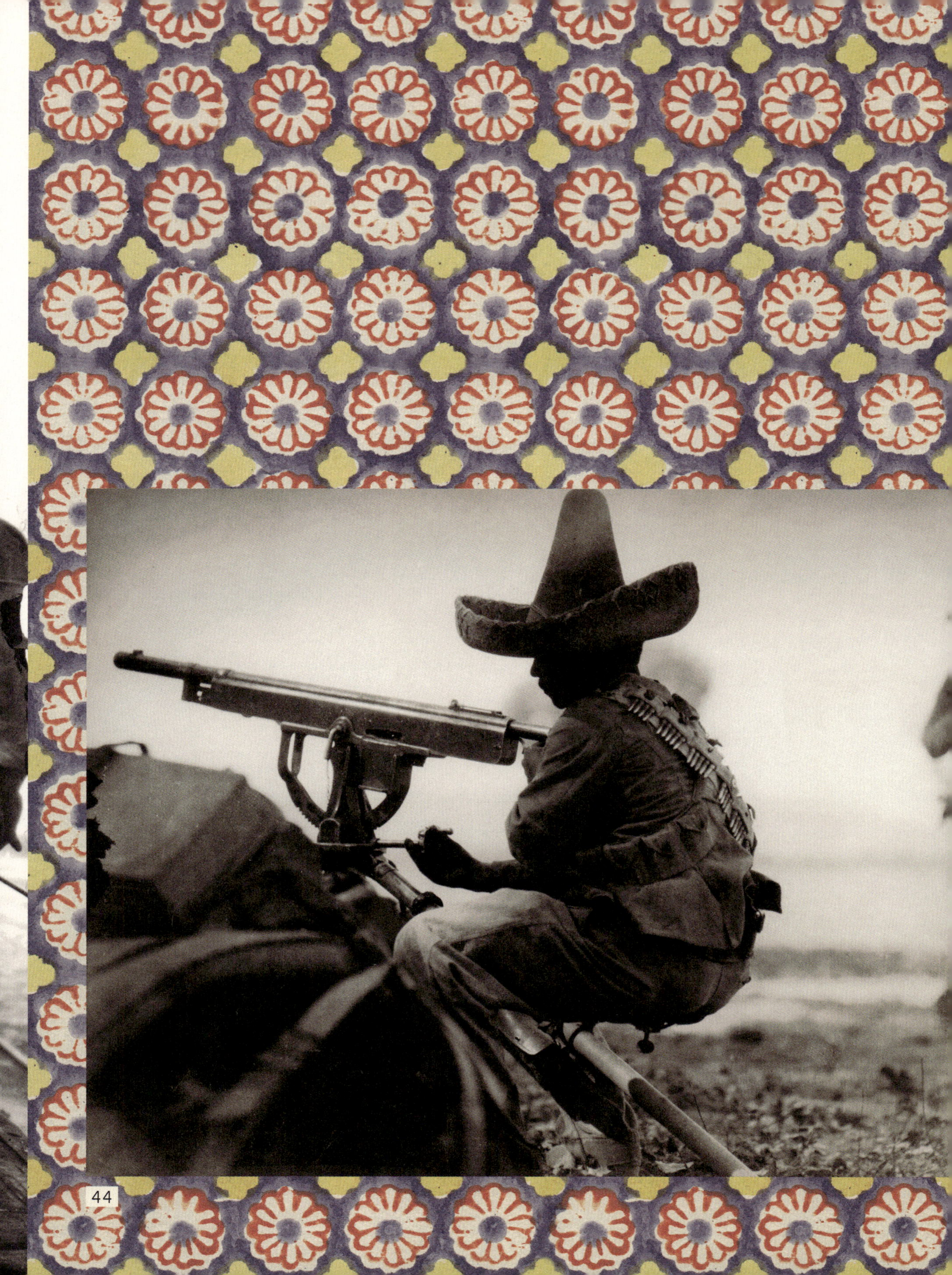

KÖNNIGGRÄTZ

Chlum Heights

taken from the Gitschin – Königgrätz road near Dub facing S.E.

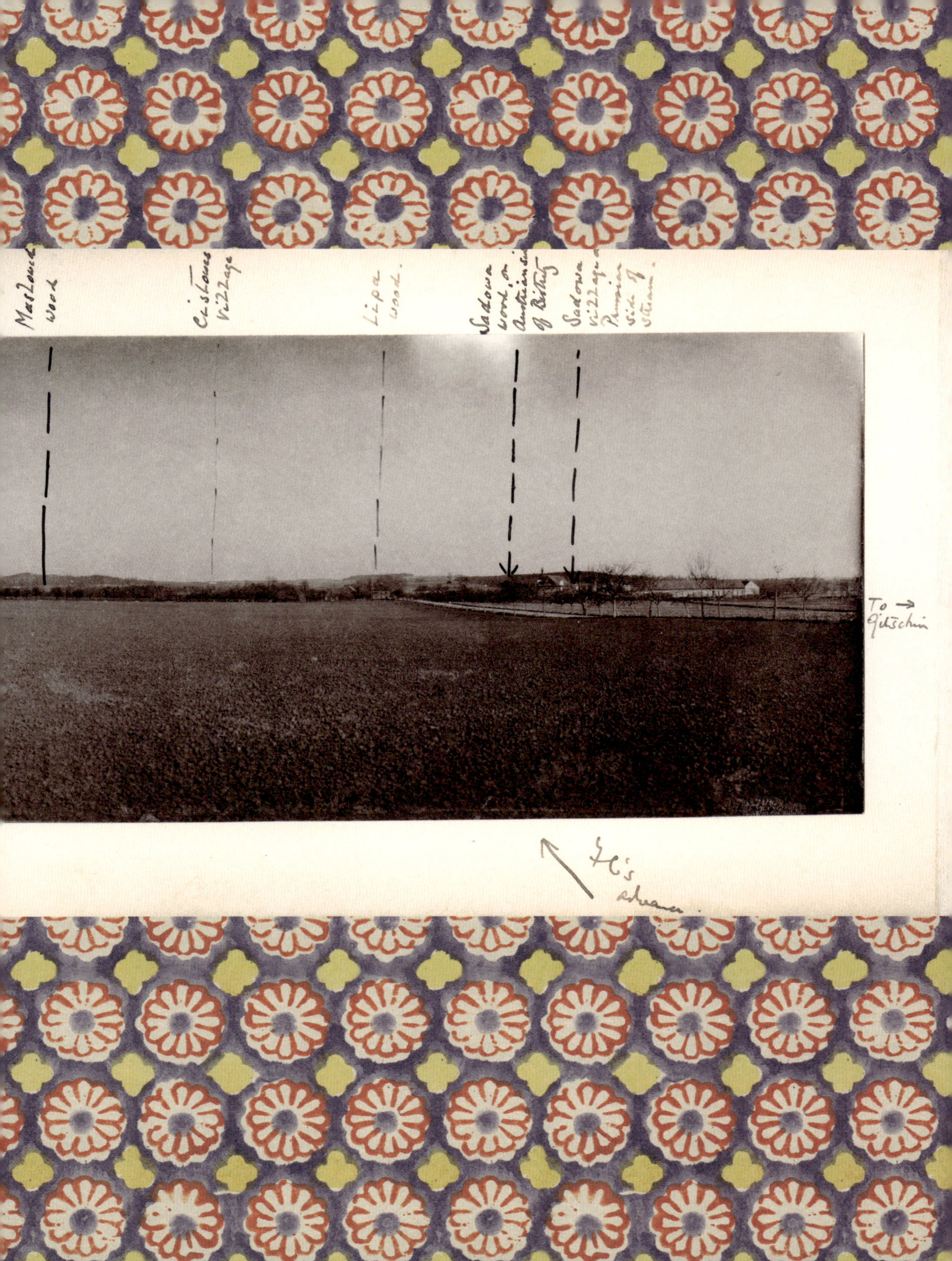

Maslowed wood
Cistowes village
Lipa wood.
Sadowa wood, in continuation of Birch
Sadowa village & Prussian site of stream.
To → Gitschin
7 C's advance.

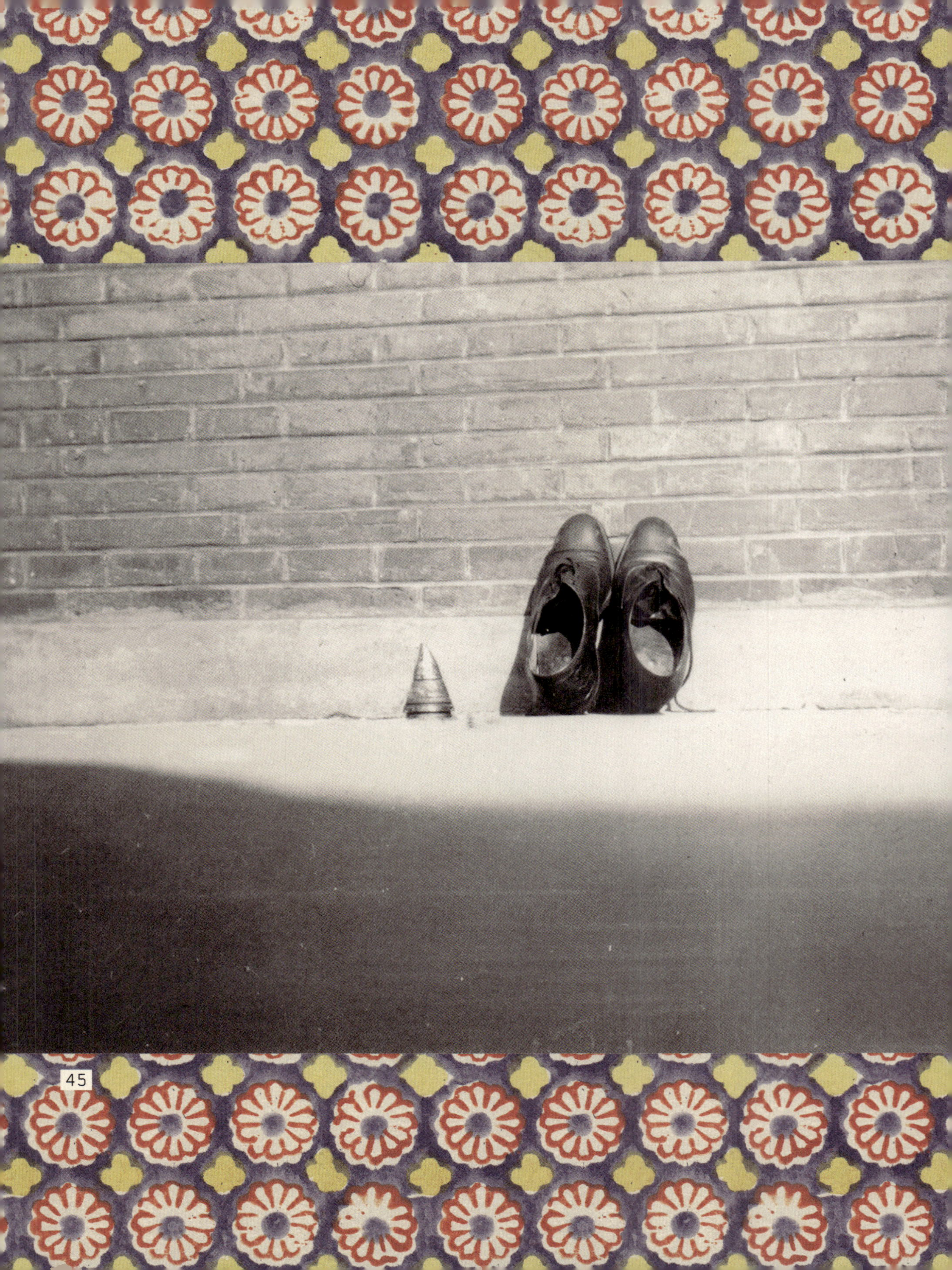

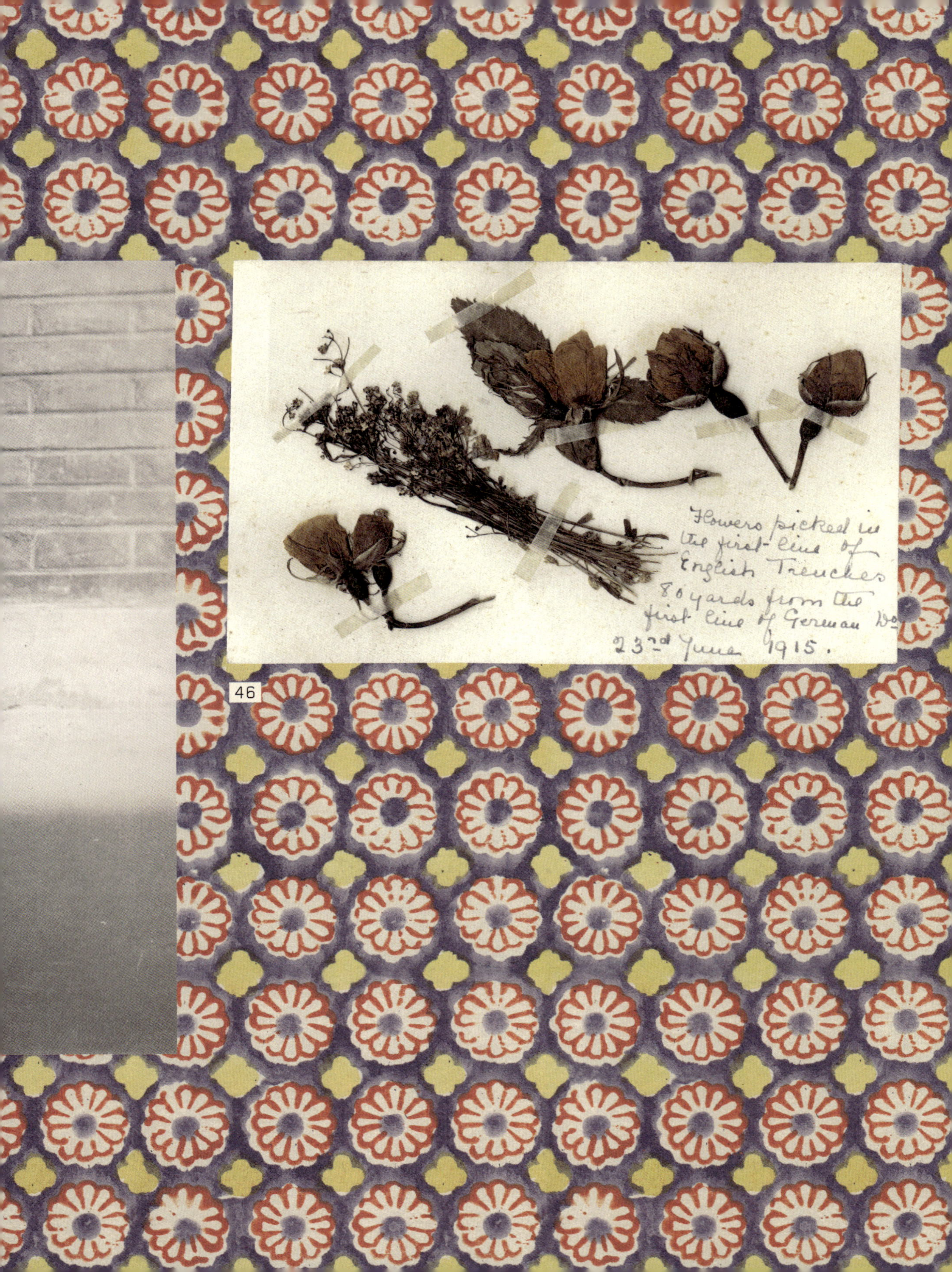

Flowers picked in
the first line of
English Trenches
80 yards from the
first line of German Do
23rd June 1915.

46

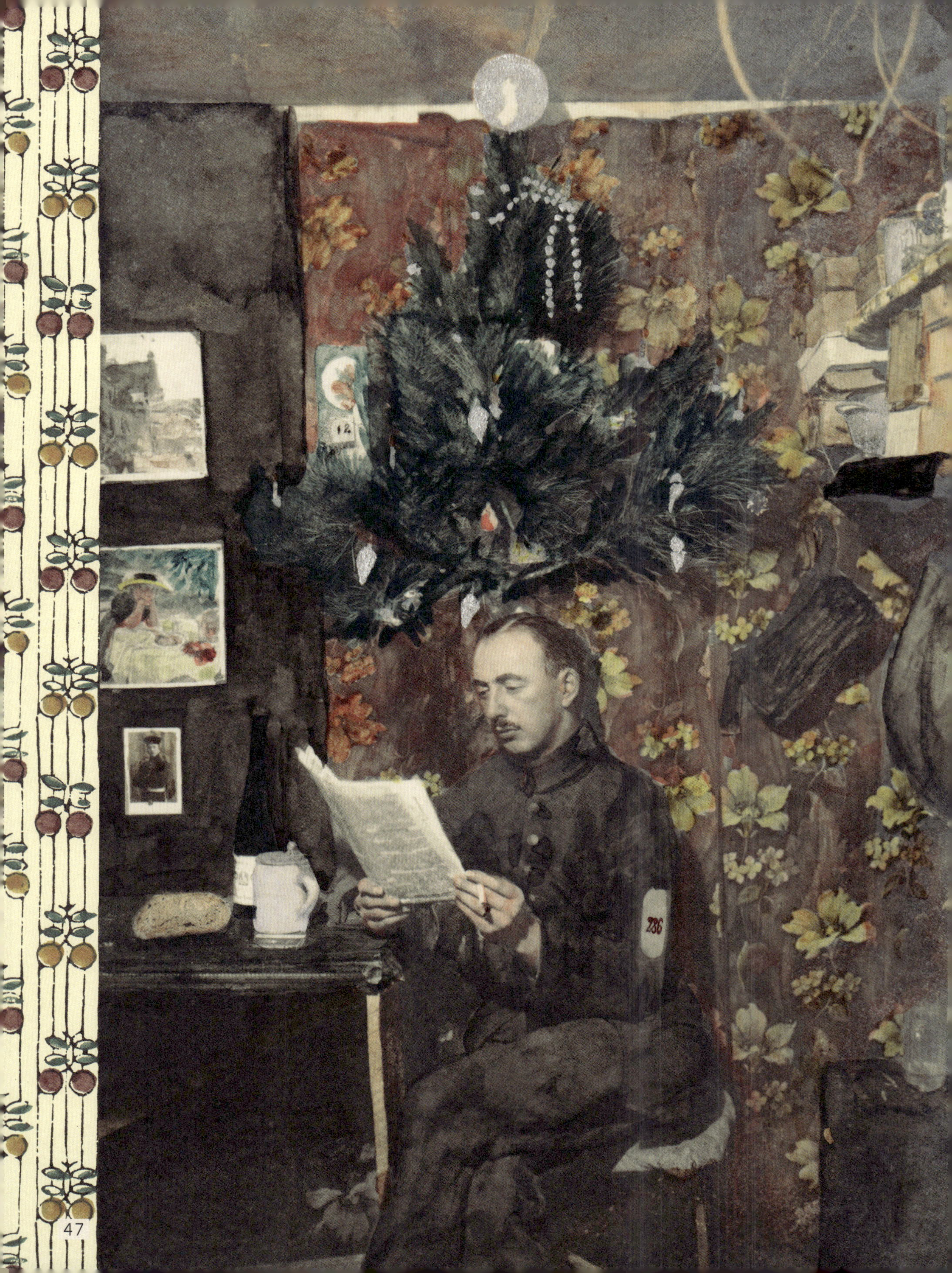

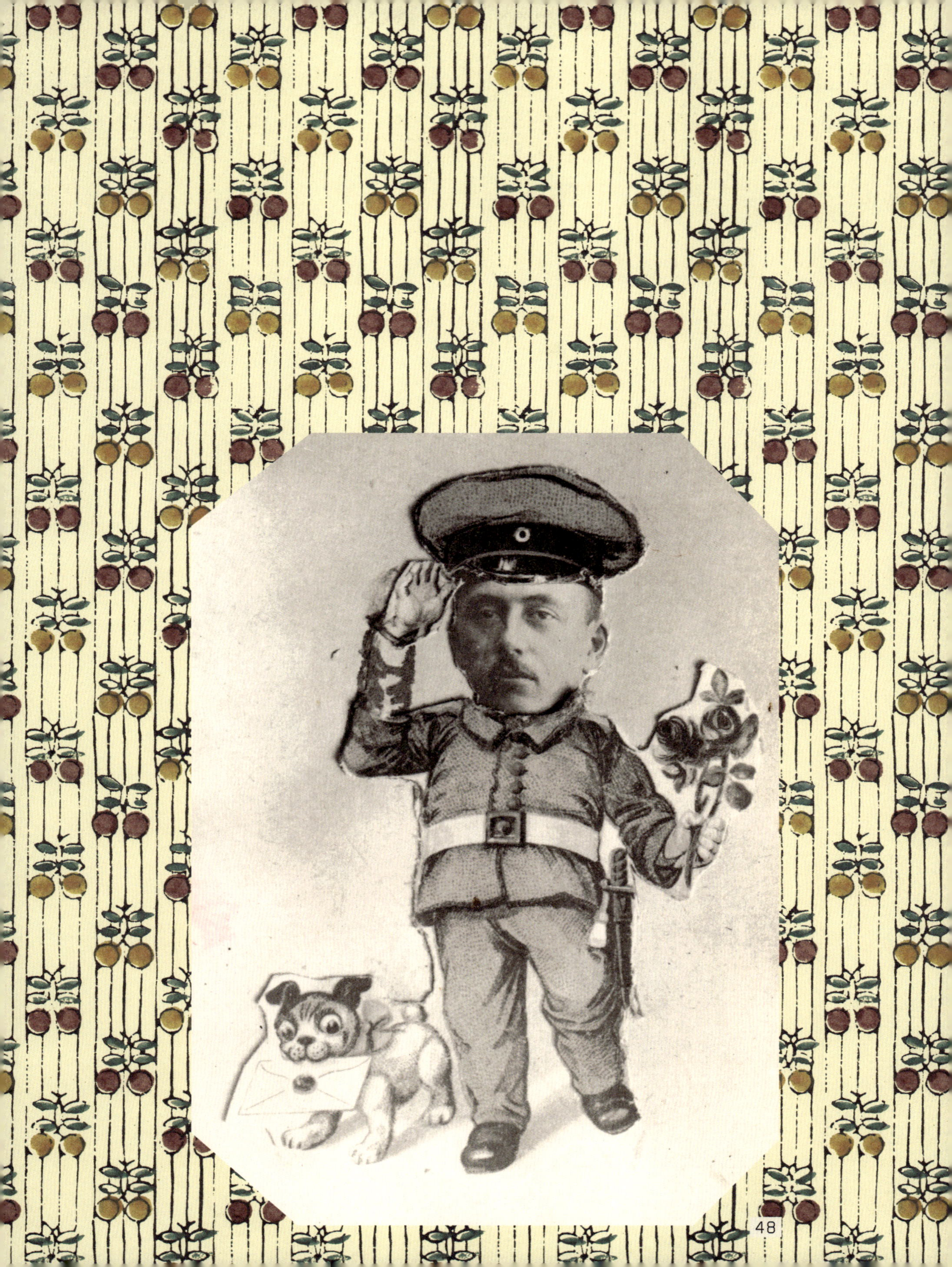

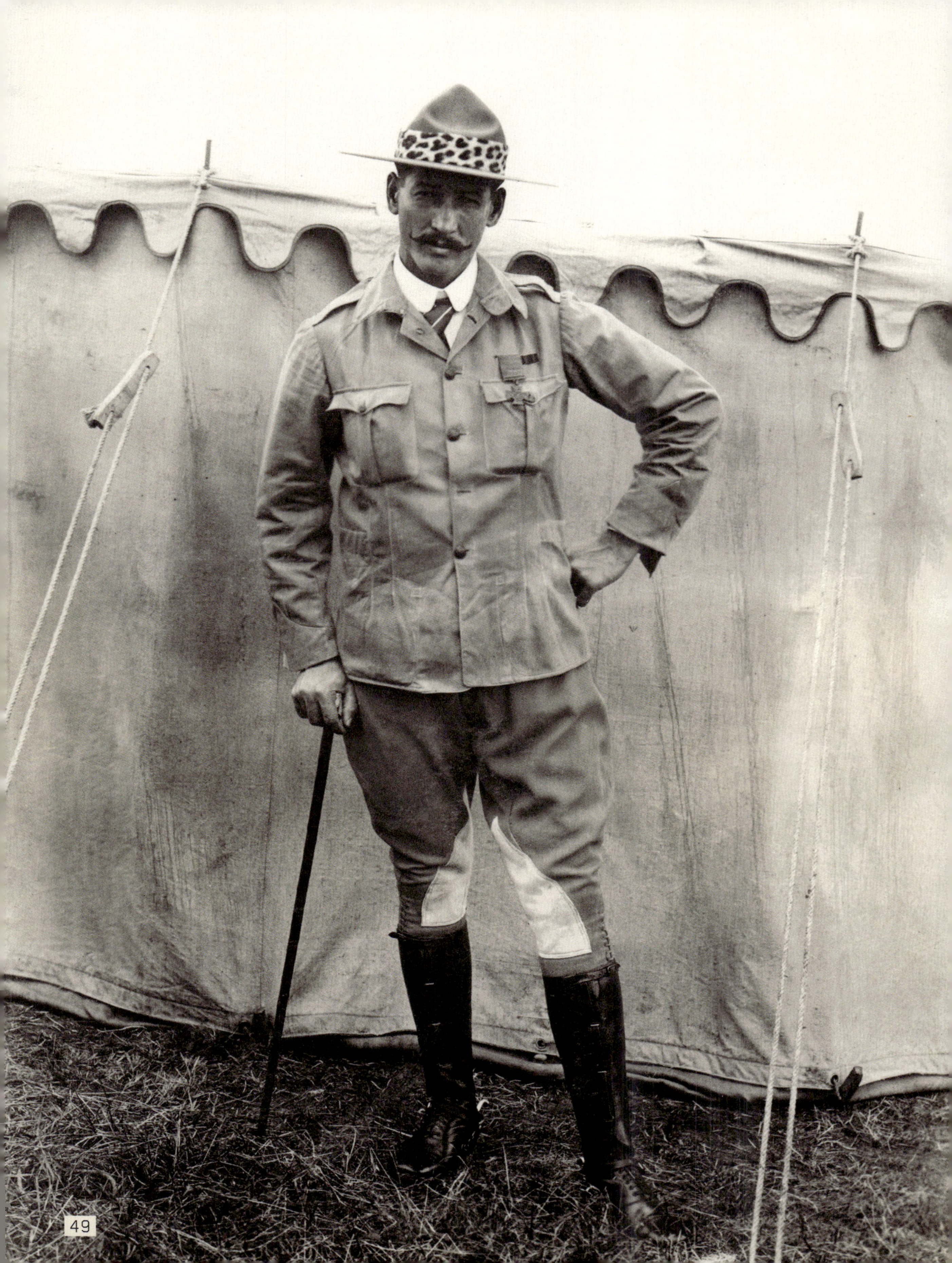

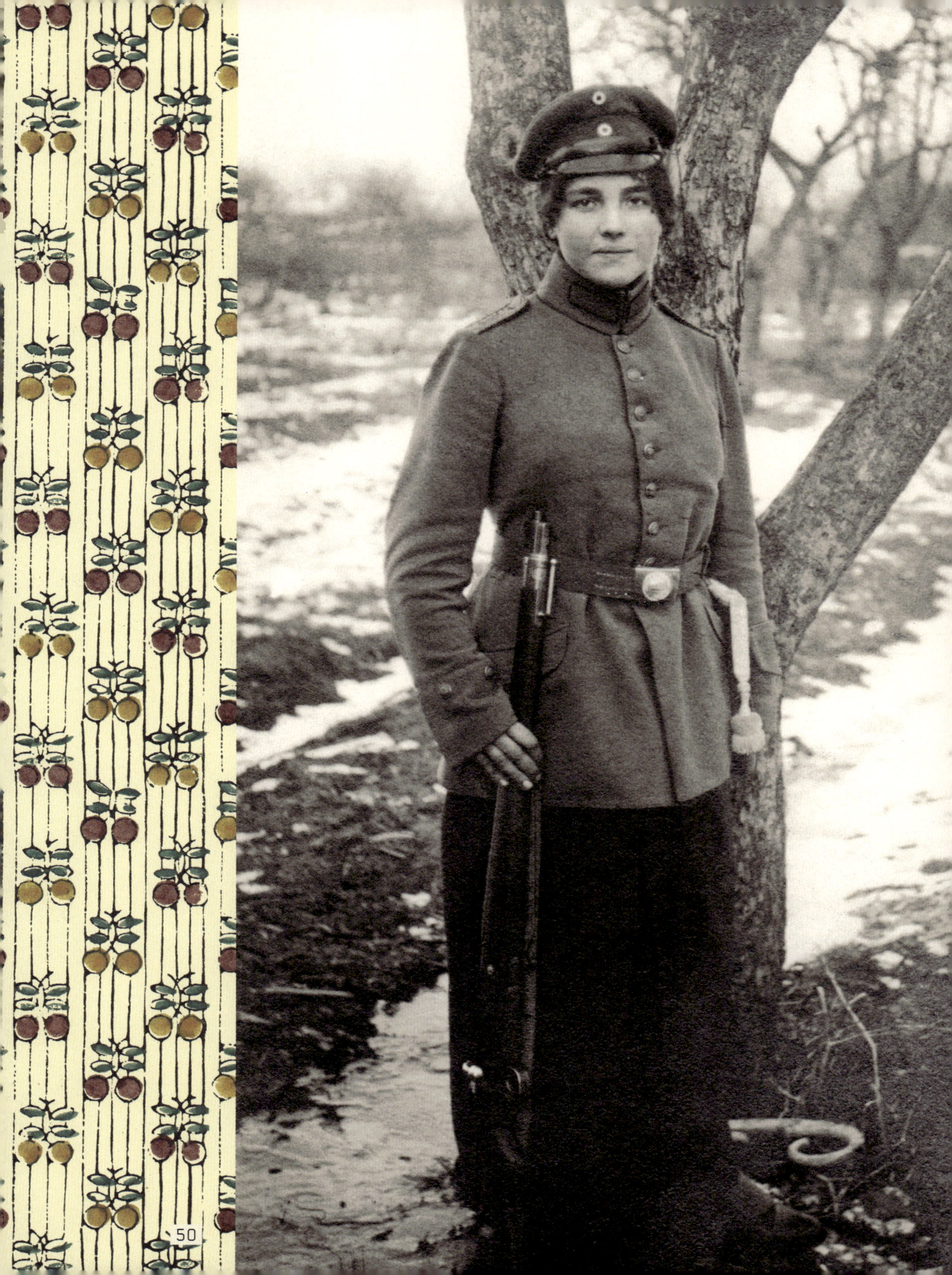

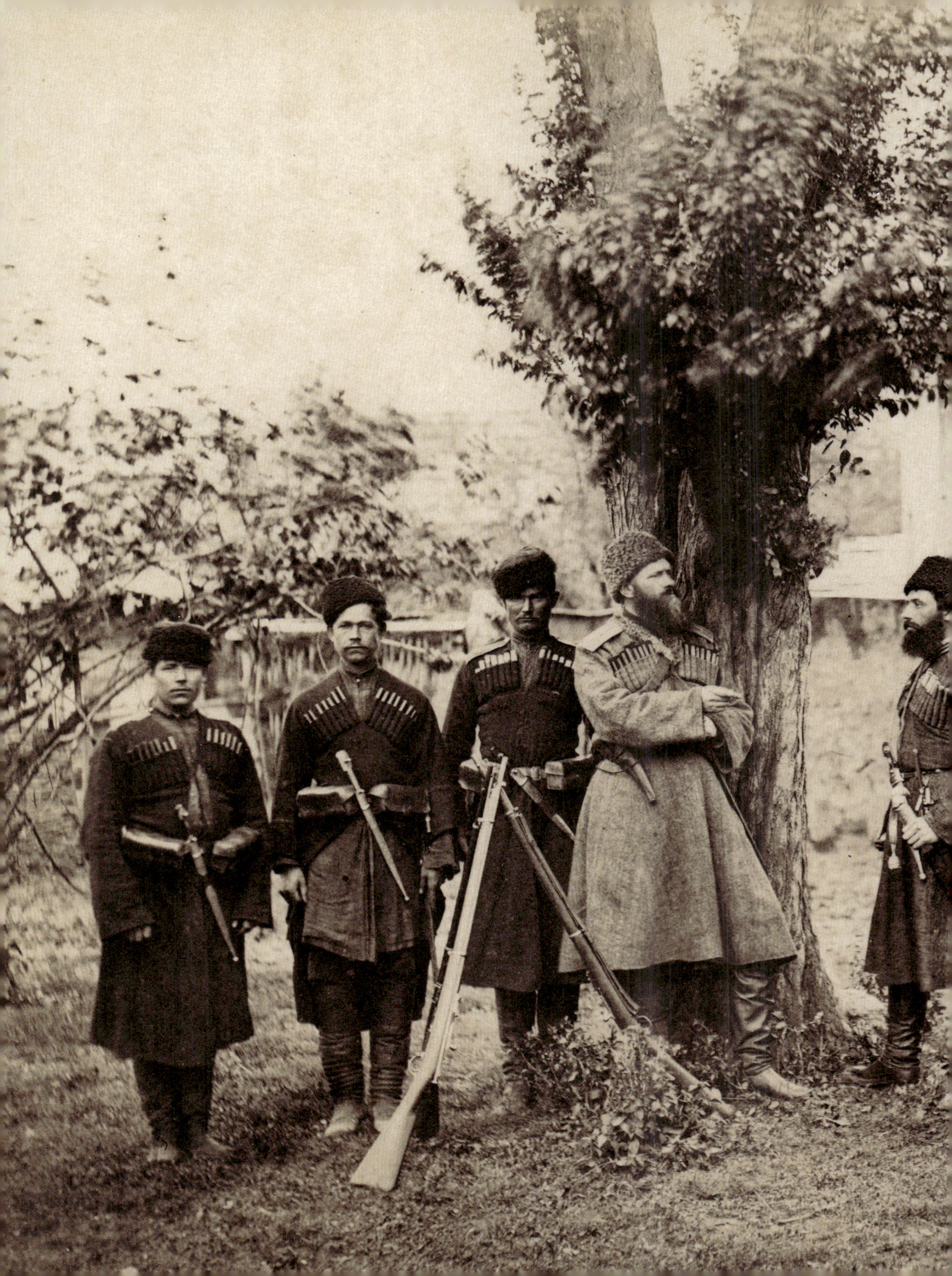

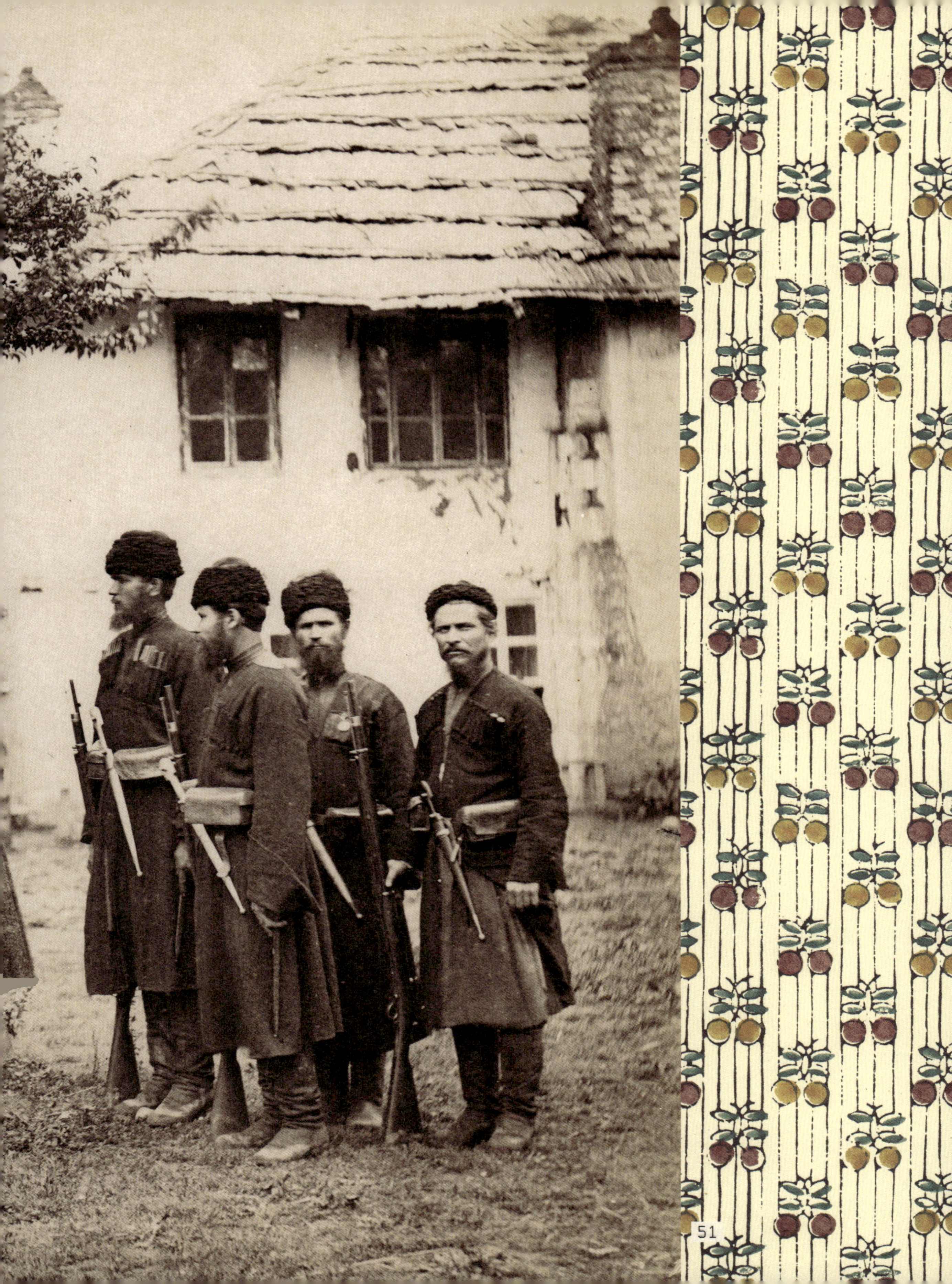

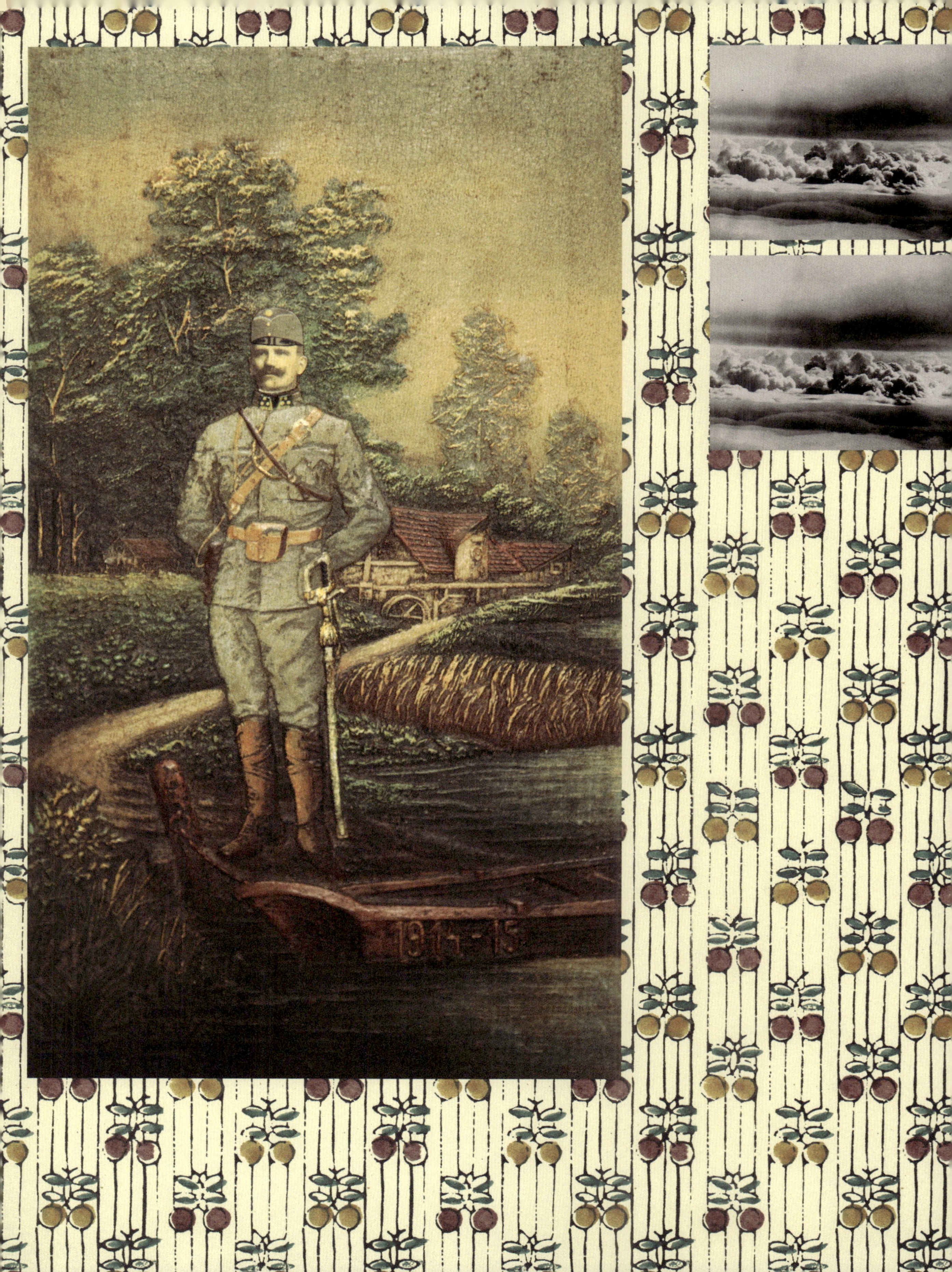

1914-15

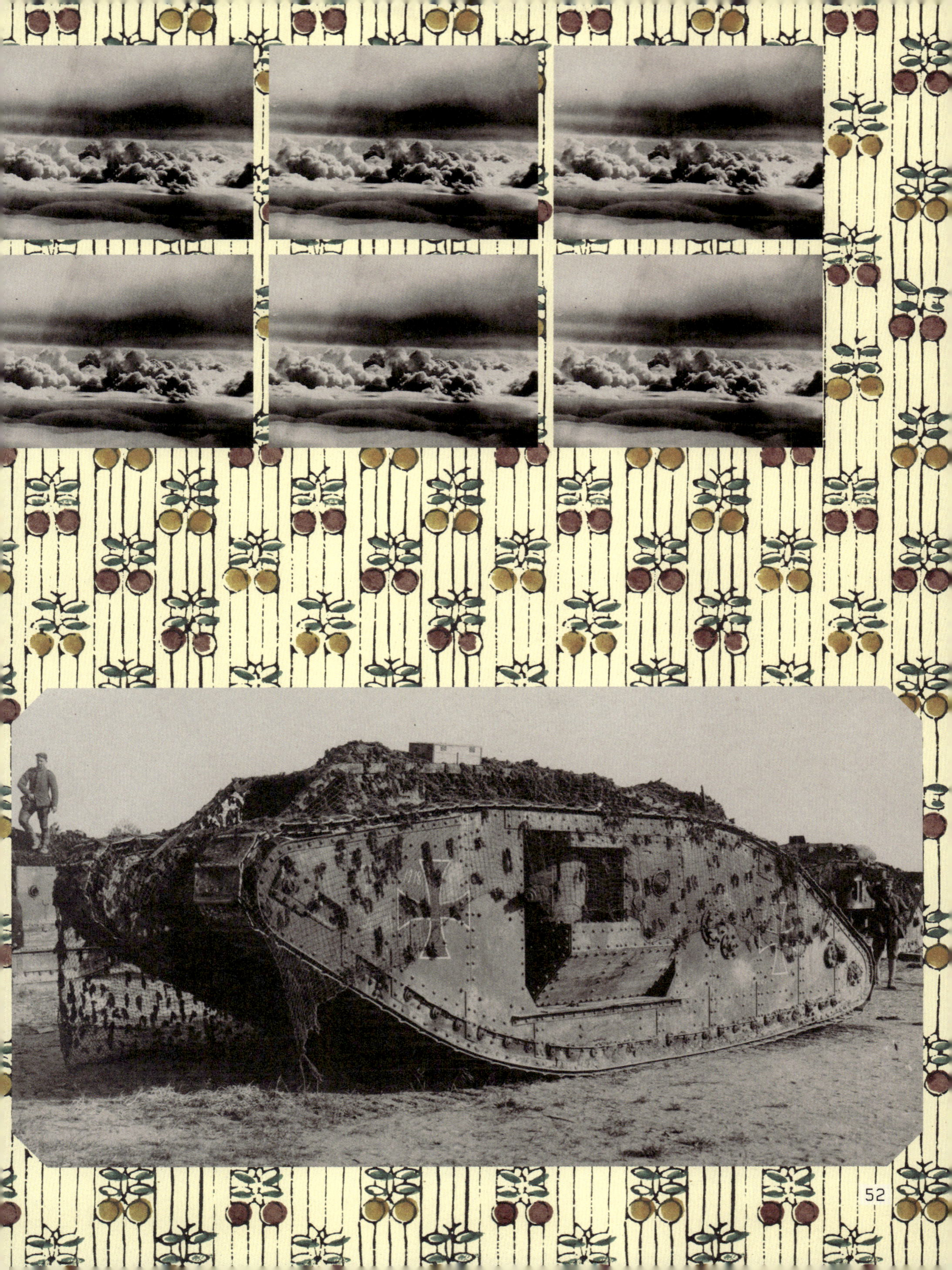

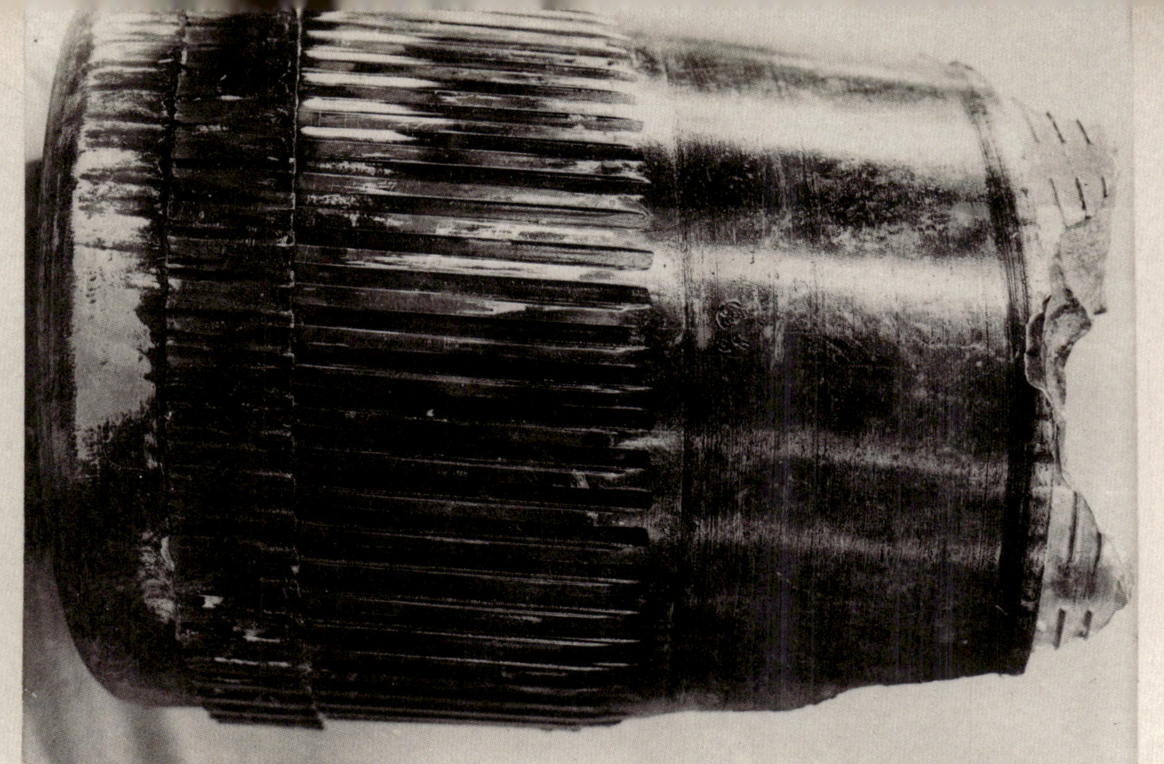

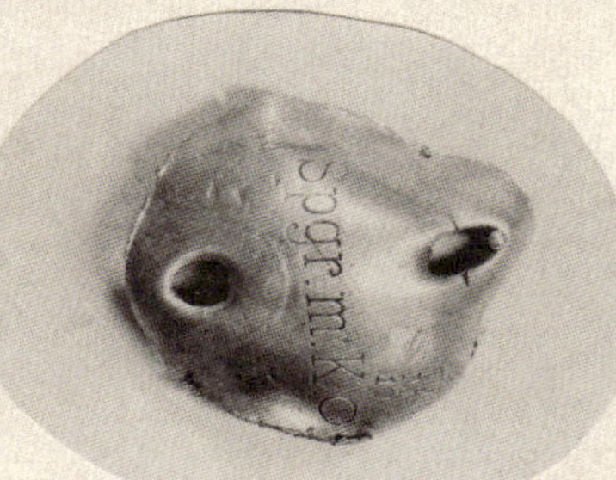

Obus de la Bertha.   1918.

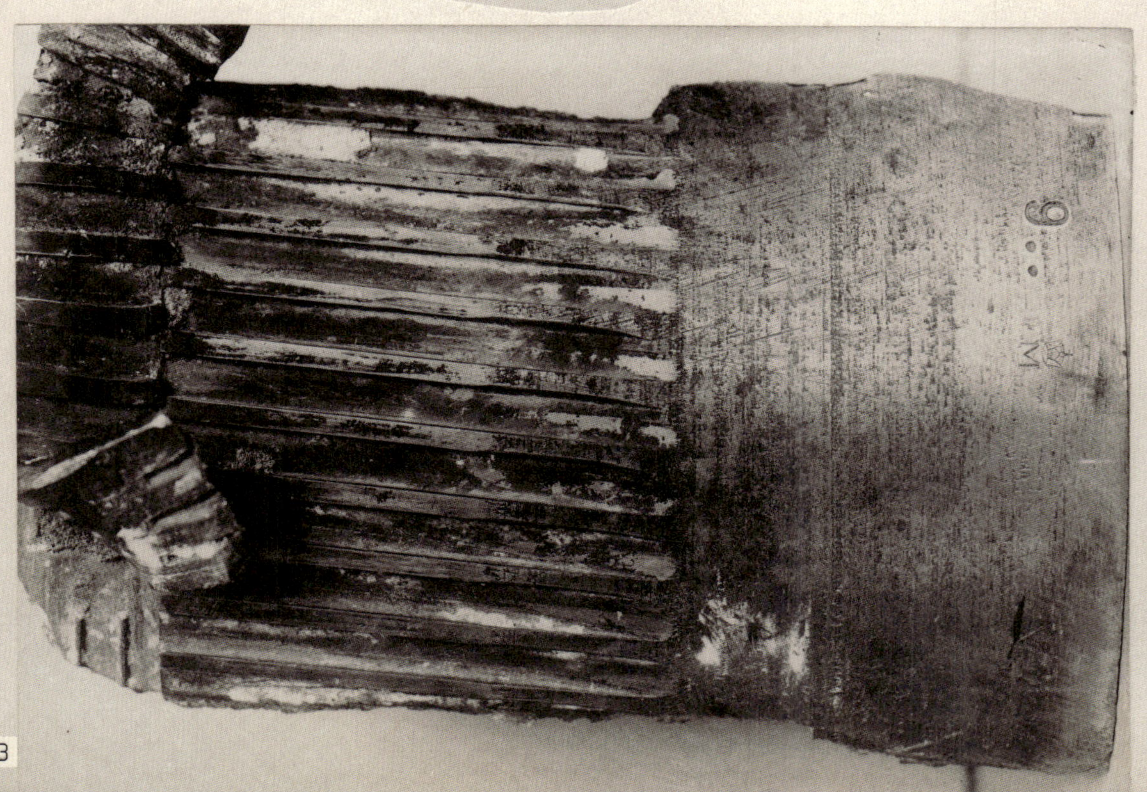

WD SOAP
WD
WD
WD
WD SOCKS FOR FEET FOR USE OF
TROUSERS FOR COVERINGS OF
WD

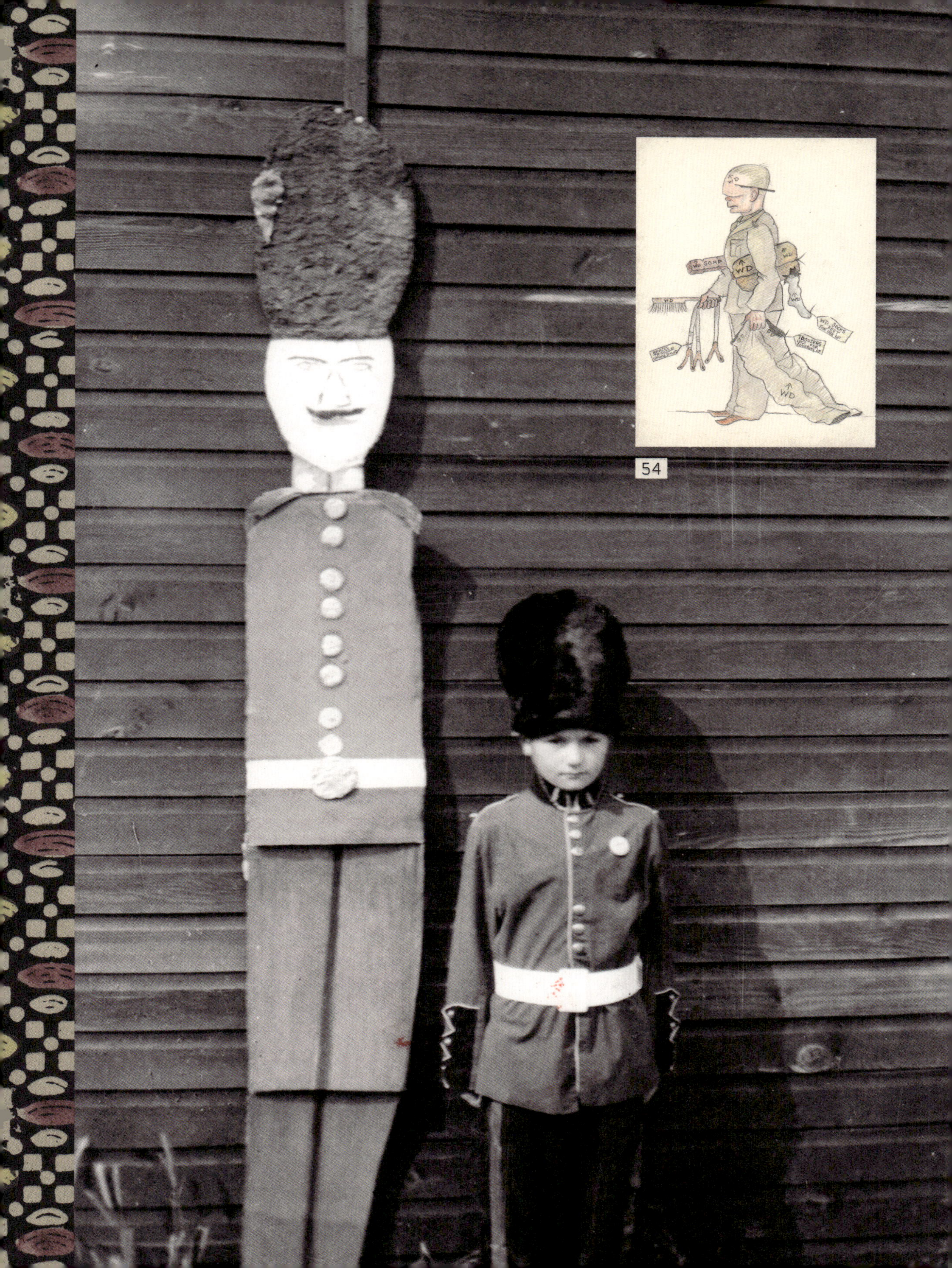

54

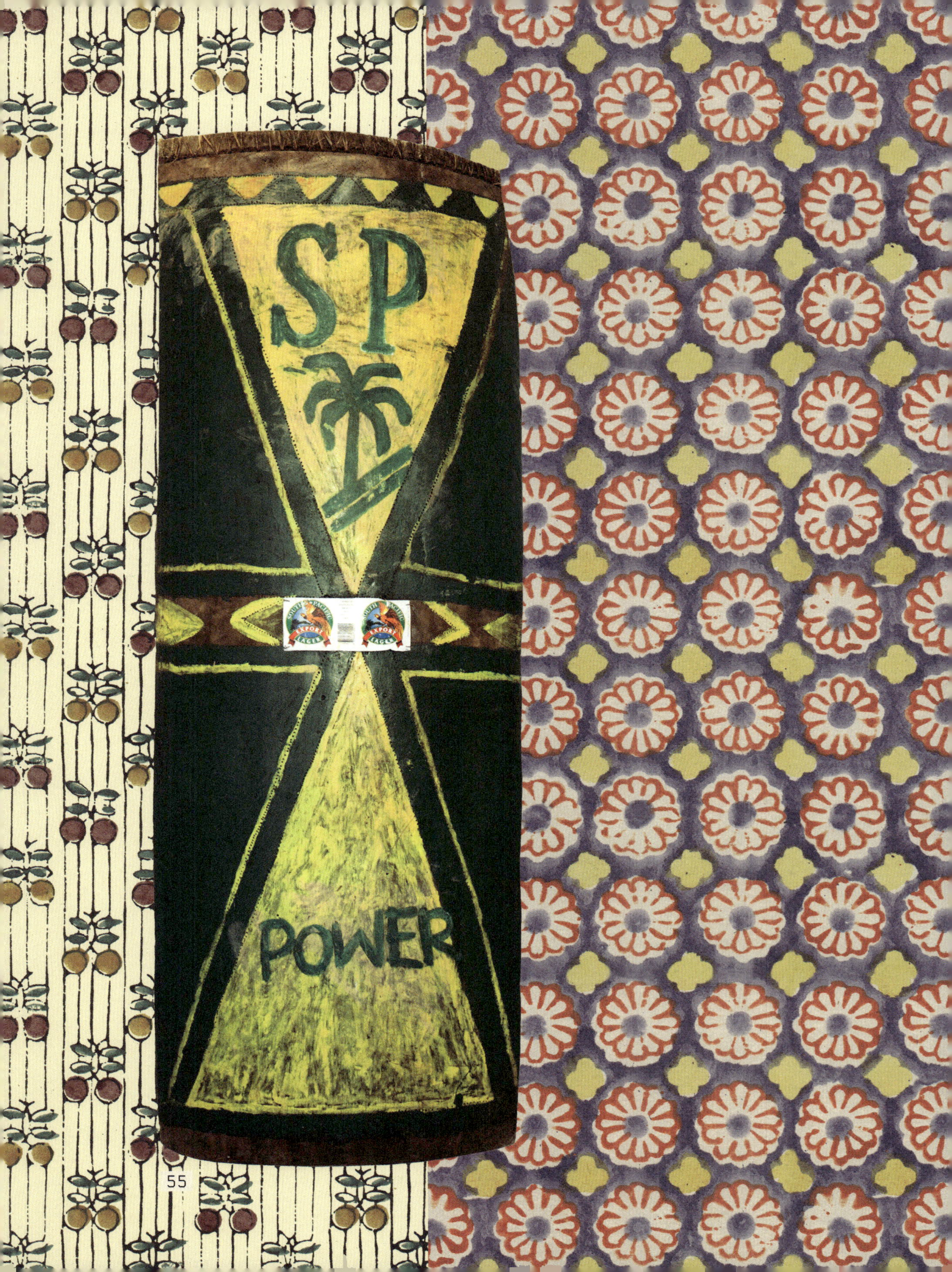

SP
POWER

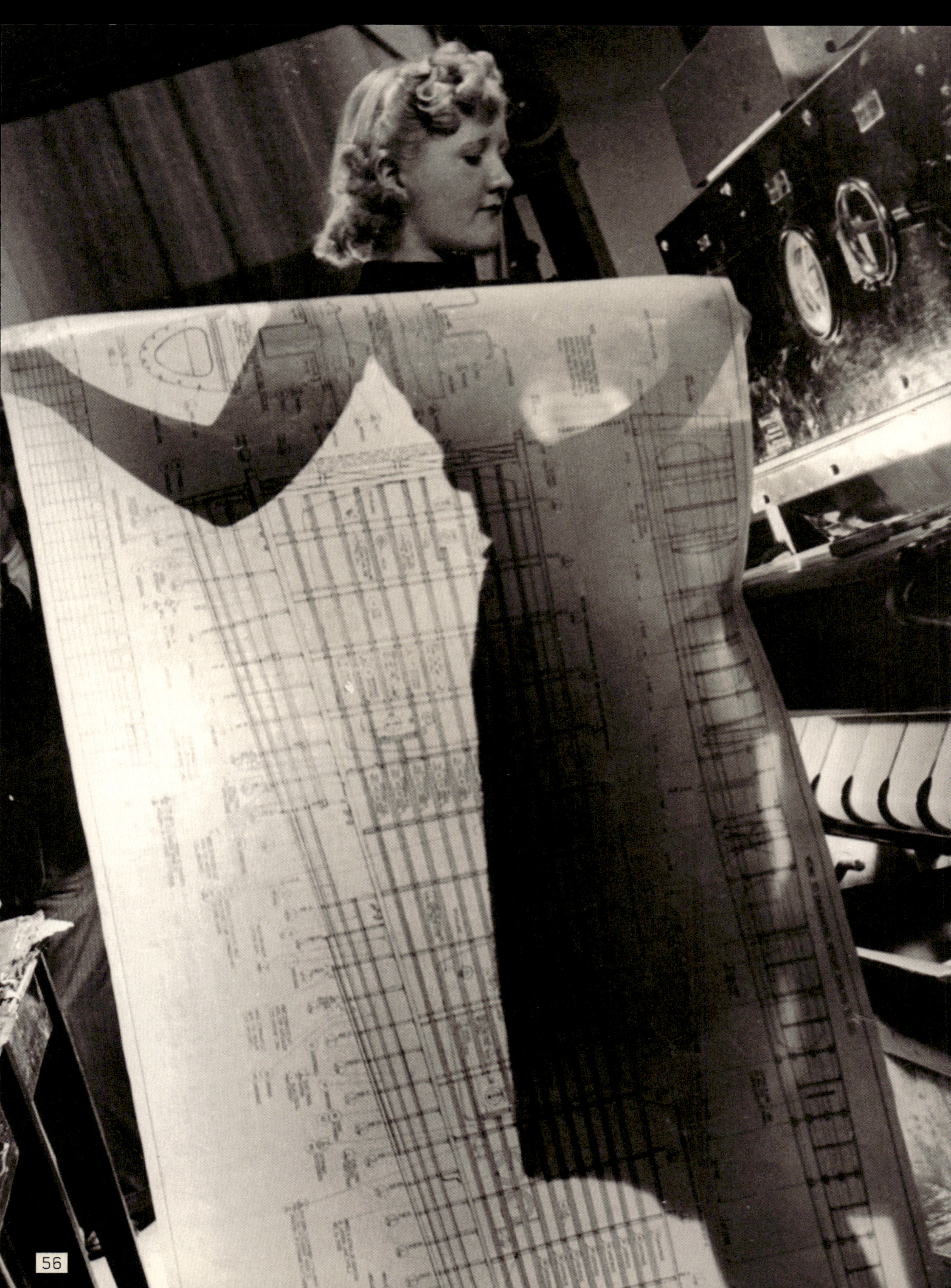

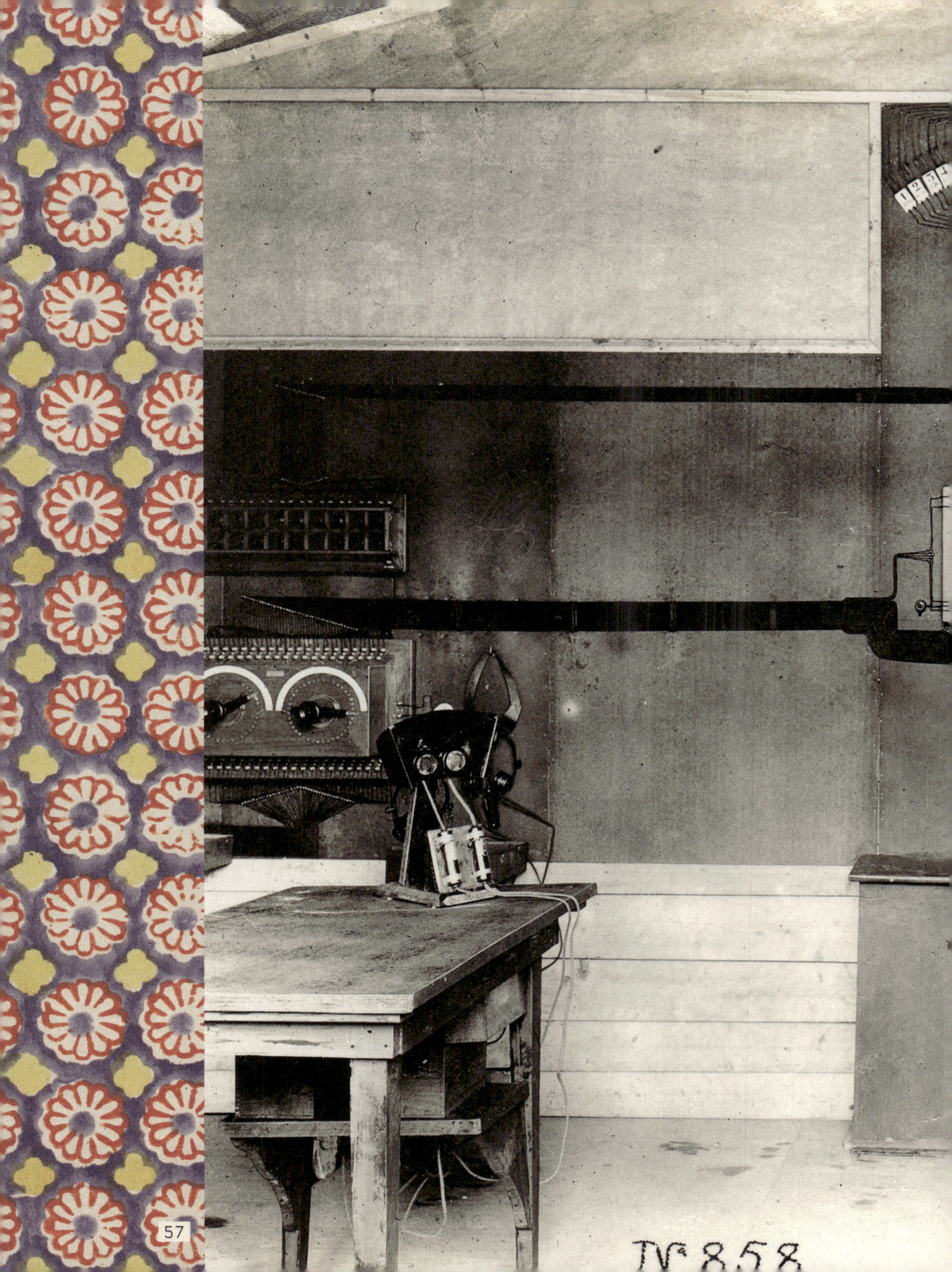
TV 858

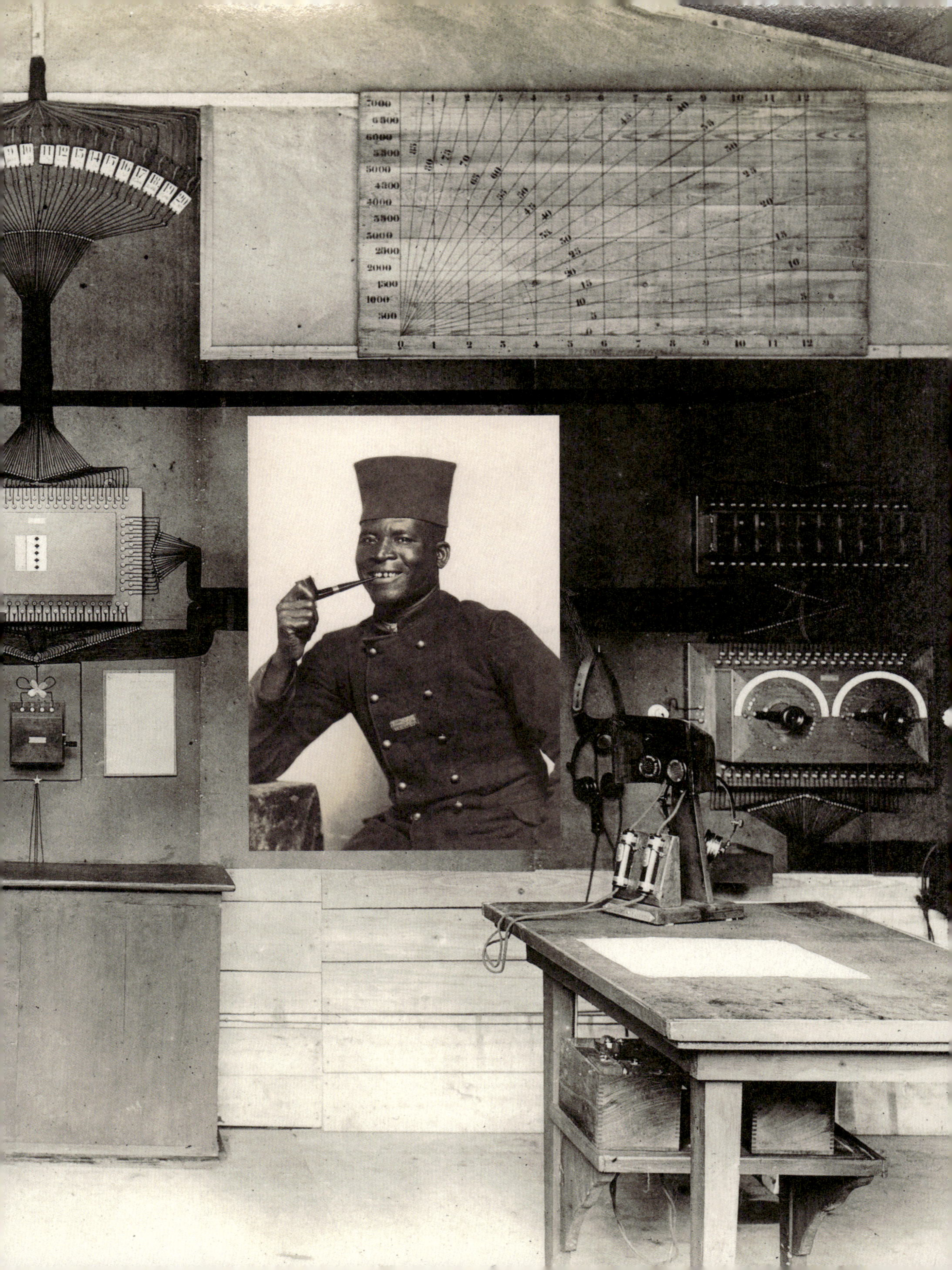

7000 6500 6000 5500 5000 4500 4000 3500 3000 2500 2000 1500 1000 500
1 2 3 4 5 6 7 8 9 10 11 12
0 1 2 3 4 5 6 7 8 9 10 11 12

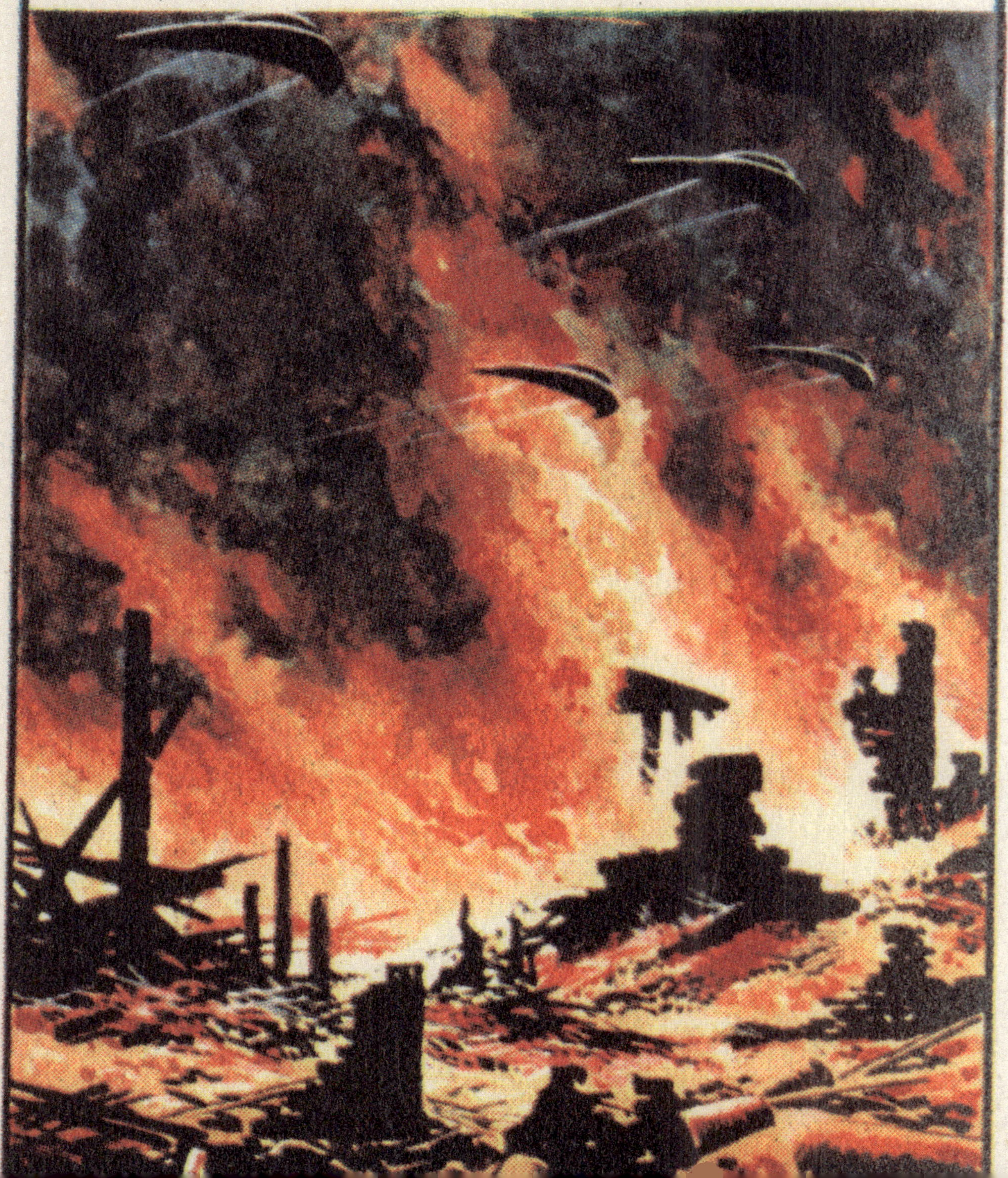
While this was happening, the air fleets of the vicious Lokans were pounding to rubble the last remains of the lovely city of the peace-loving Tharvs . . . the city that Peric had built and loved.

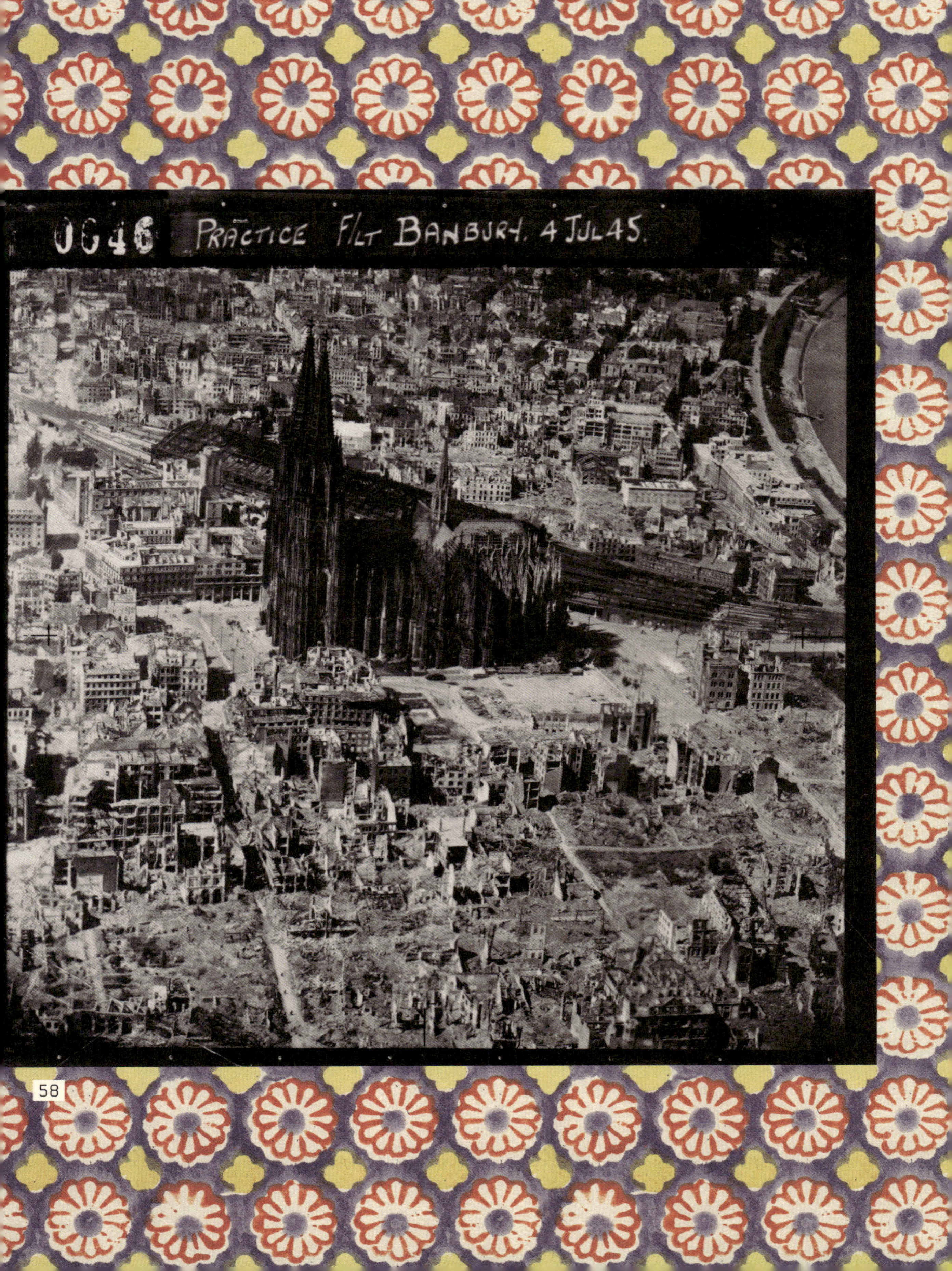
0646 PRACTICE F/LT BANBURY. 4 JUL 45.

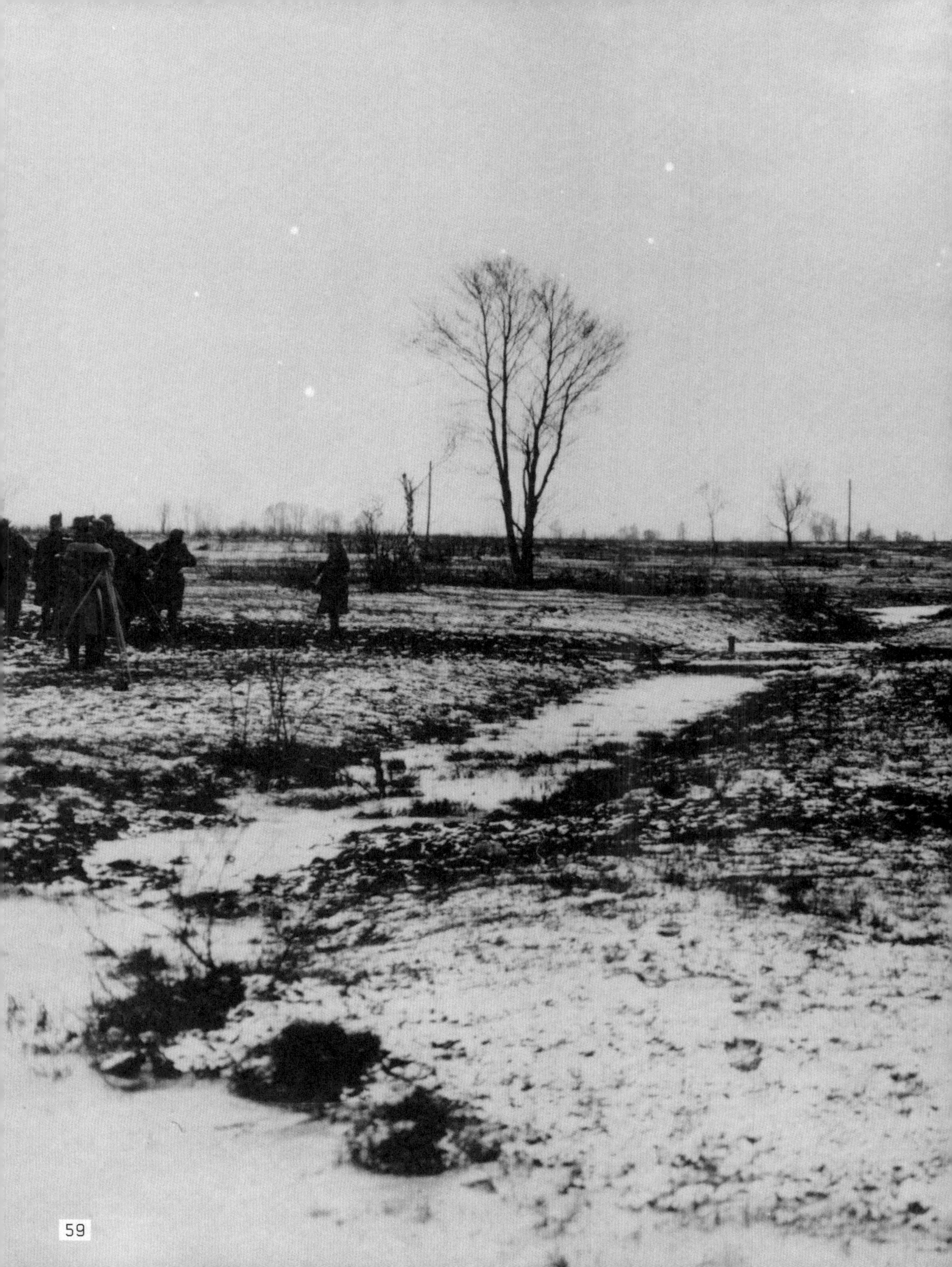

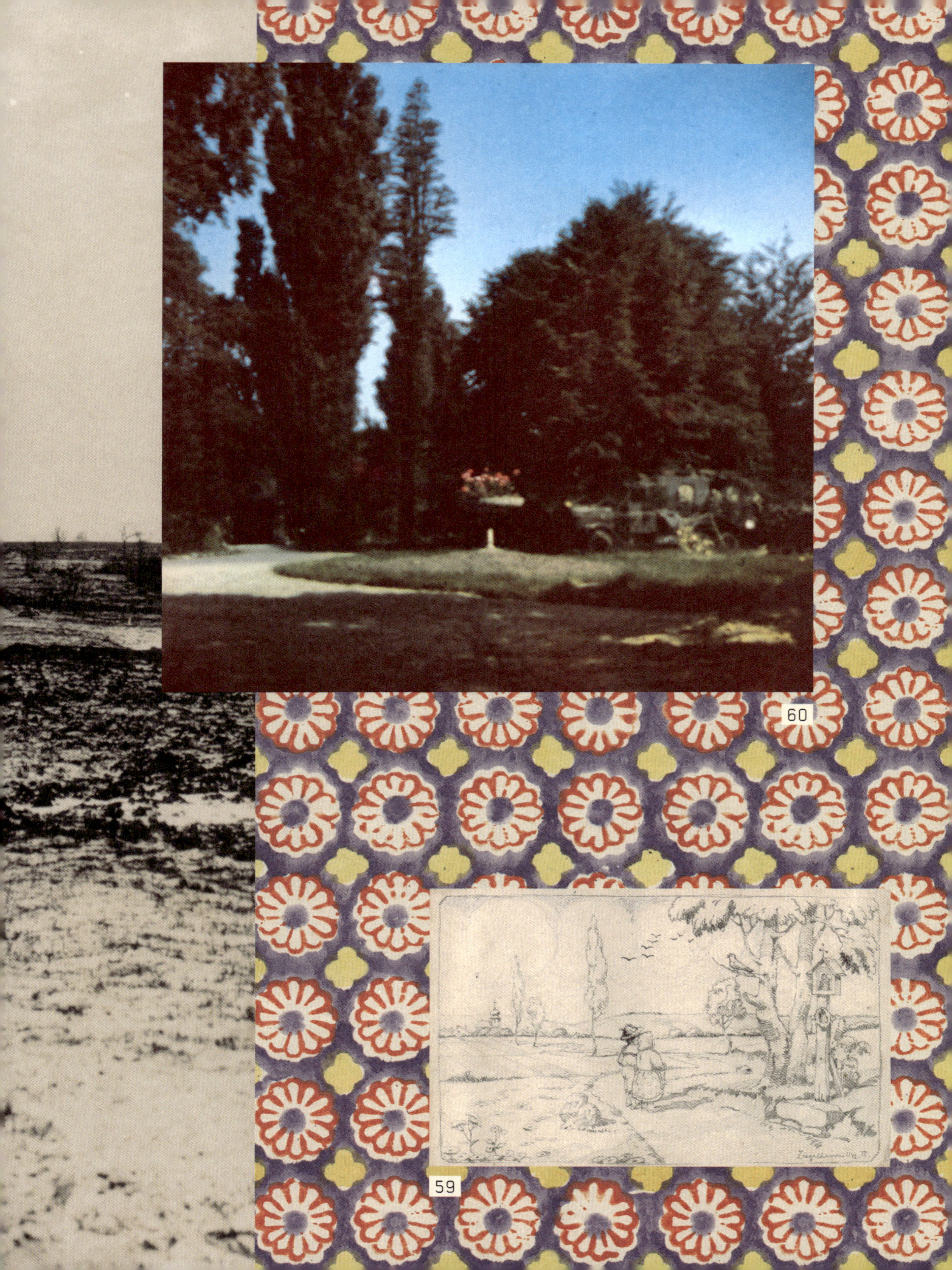

59

60

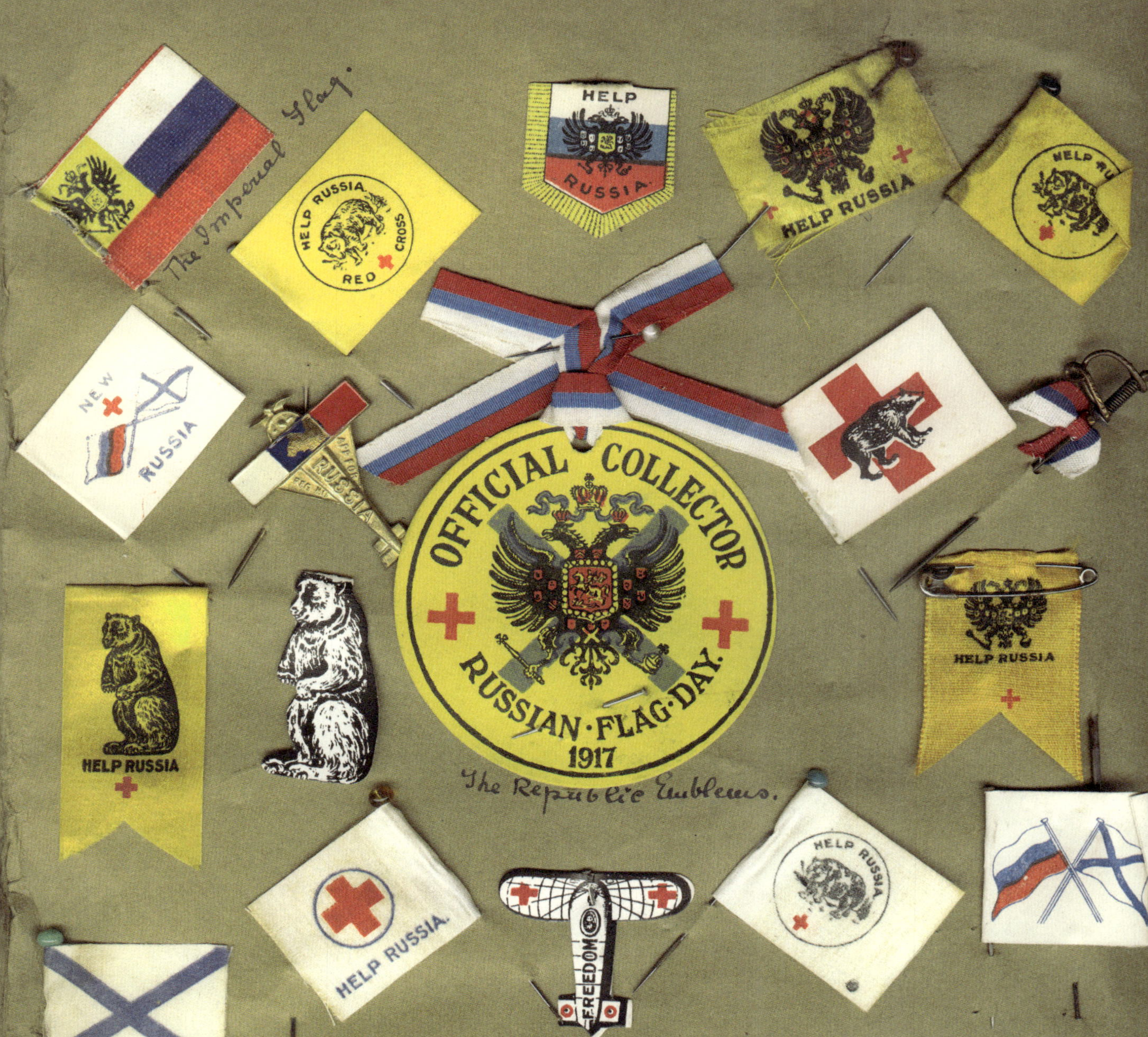

The Imperial Flag.
HELP RUSSIA
RED CROSS
HELP
RUSSIA.
HELP RUSSIA
HELP RU
NEW RUSSIA
OFFICIAL COLLECTOR
RUSSIAN · FLAG · DAY.
1917
The Republic Emblems.
HELP RUSSIA
HELP RUSSIA
HELP RUSSIA
FREEDOM
HELP RUSSIA
Sold by A. F. Onock at the Law Courts
15th May. 1917.
RUSSIA

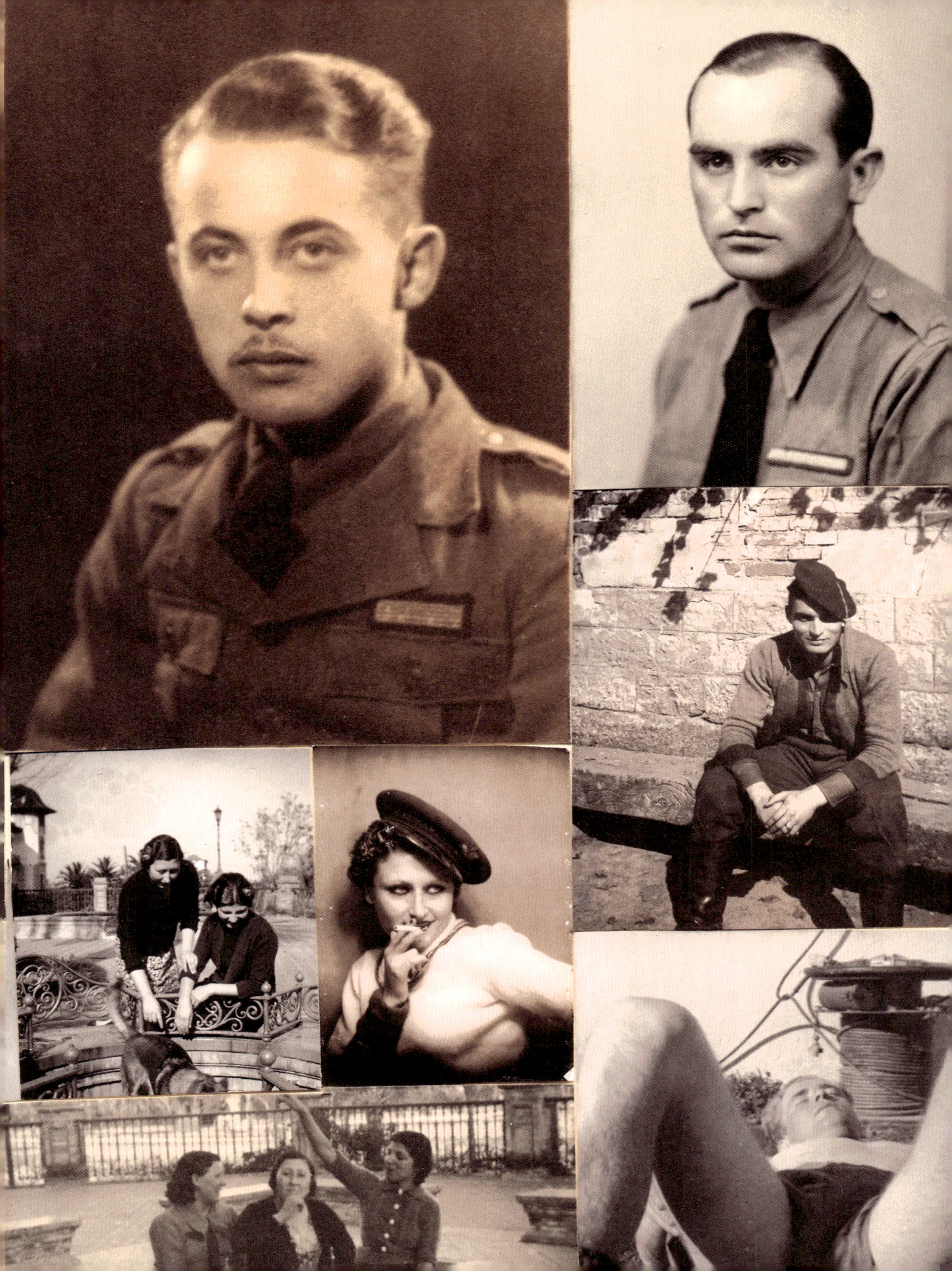

Although it is always easy to be
that a number of features are dif
of organic amnesia. In the first pla
appear to have attracted the noti
charge of the case. In the second
to an hour only which must be
the third place, *disorientation for*
fixed. The plain truth, I may as
have never been really right in the hea

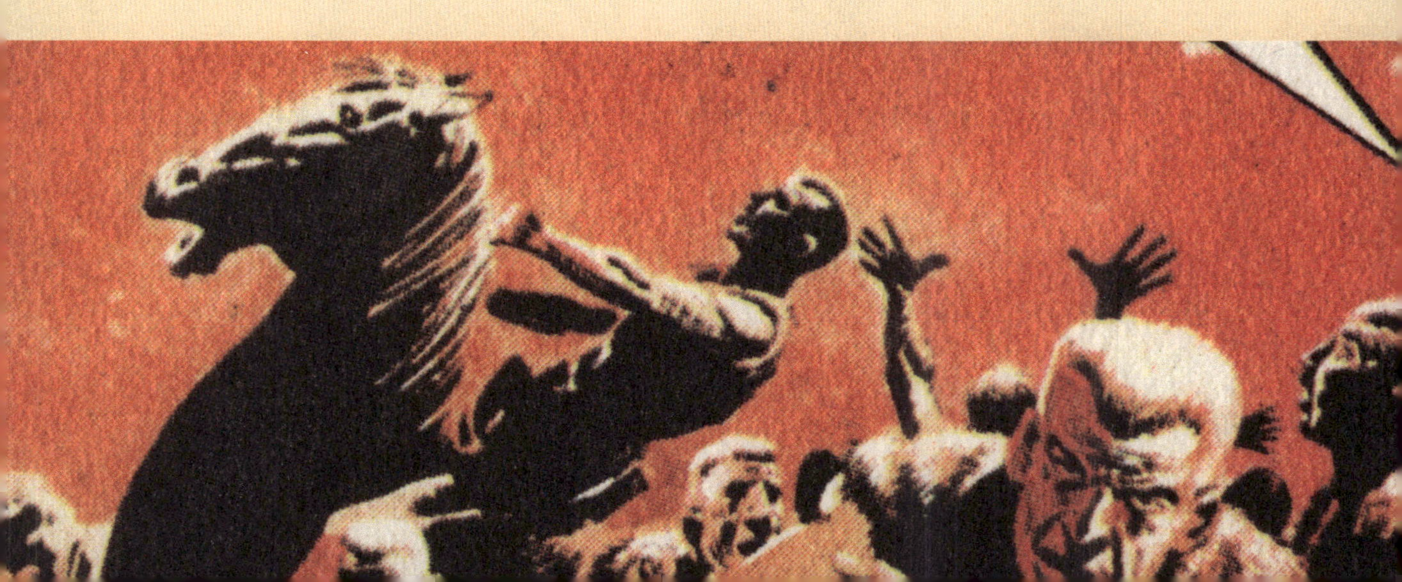

ise after the event, one may agree
ult to reconcile with the *diagnosis*
, the *gross memory defect* does not
of the physicians at that time in
ace, *retrograde amnesia* was limited
garded as exceptionally brief. In
h time and place was suspiciously
ll admit it, is that as animals *we*

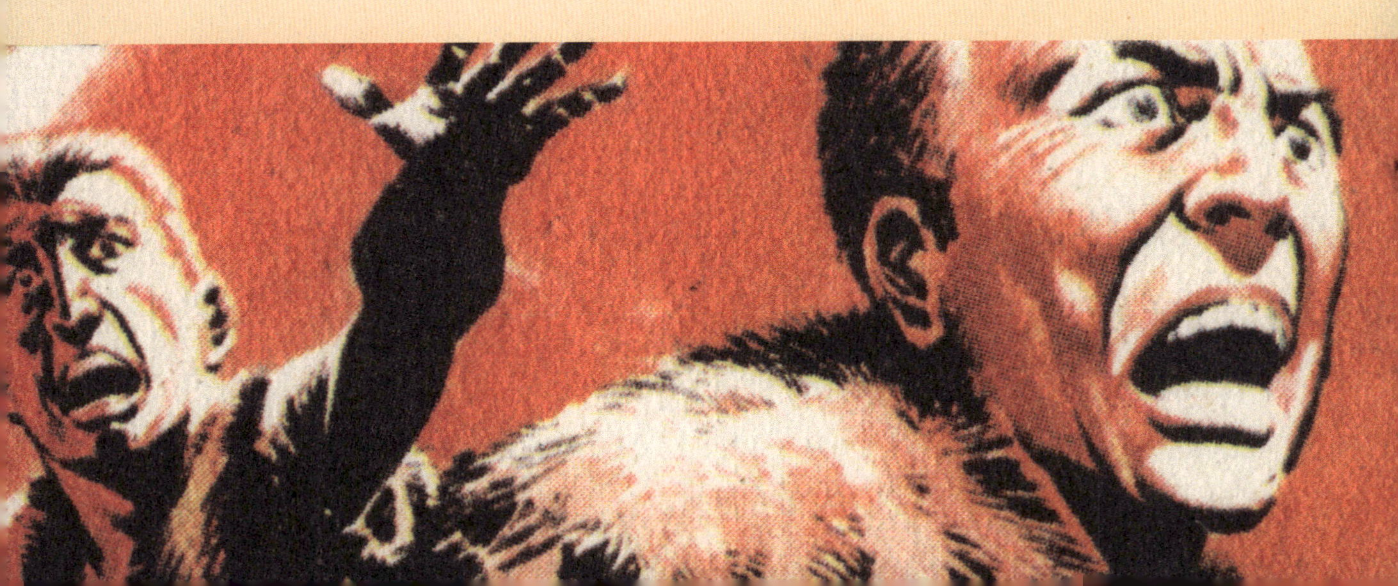

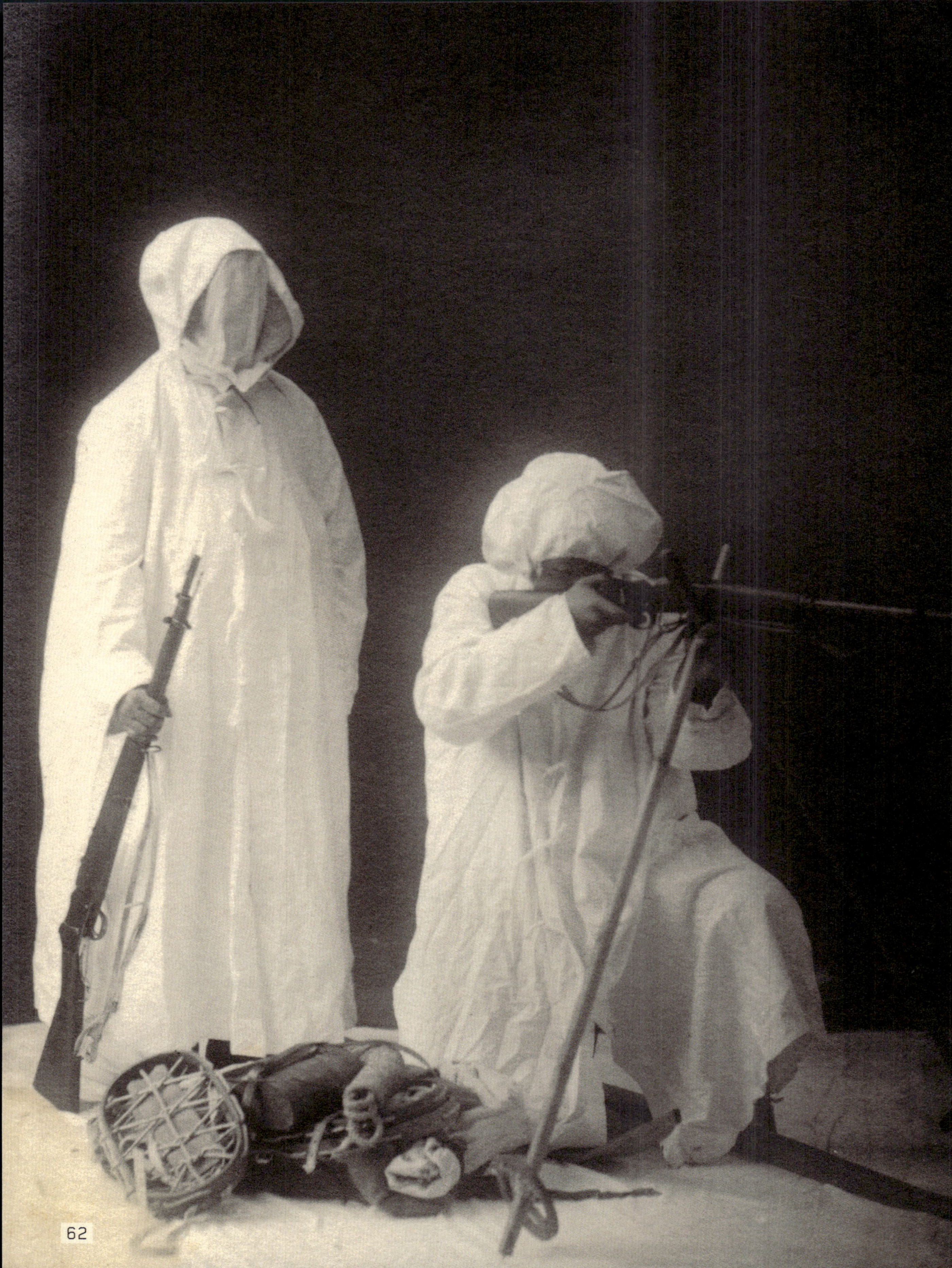

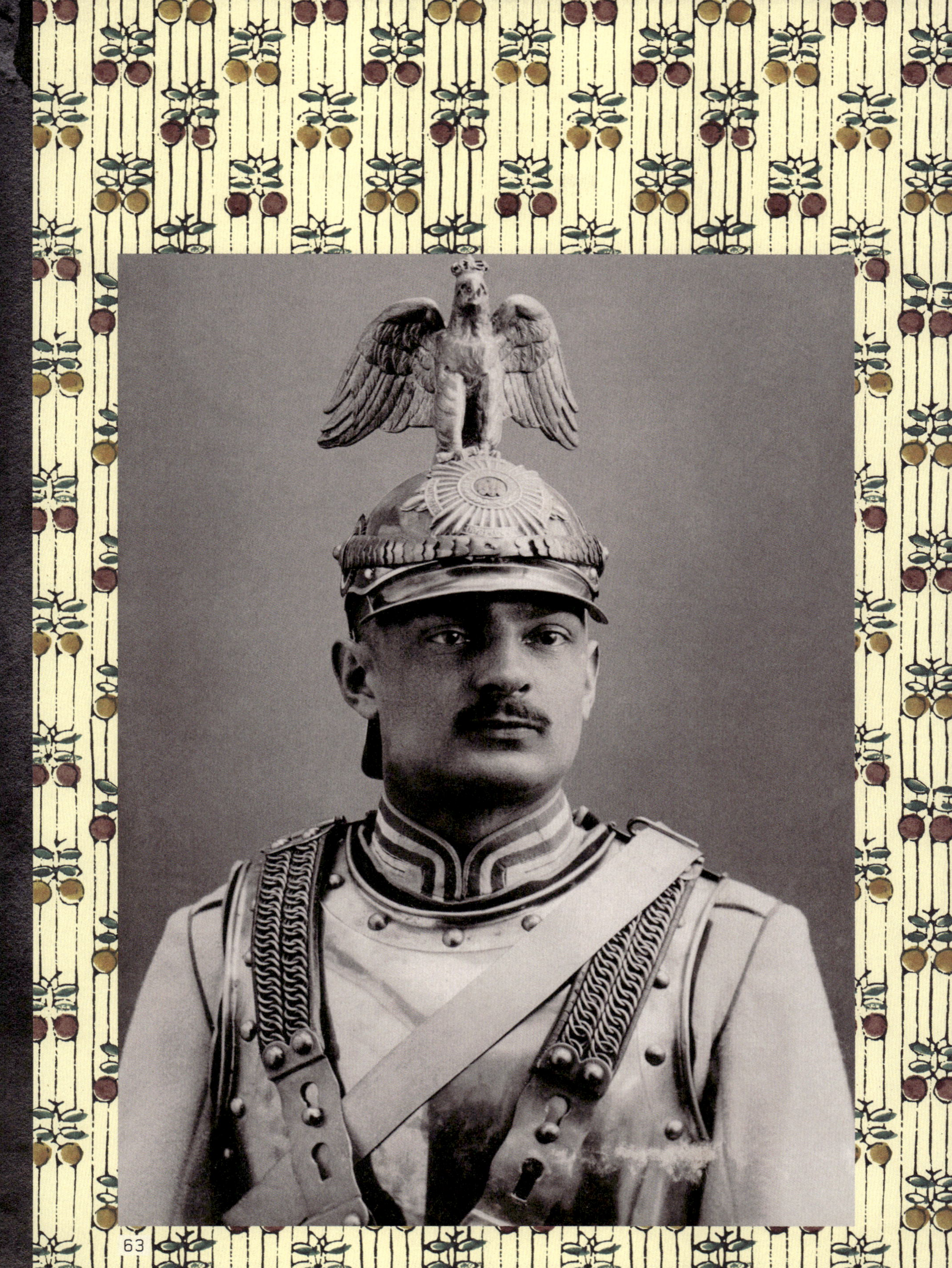

Suddenly a large flock of al-
batrosses swooped down on the
men in the sea . . .

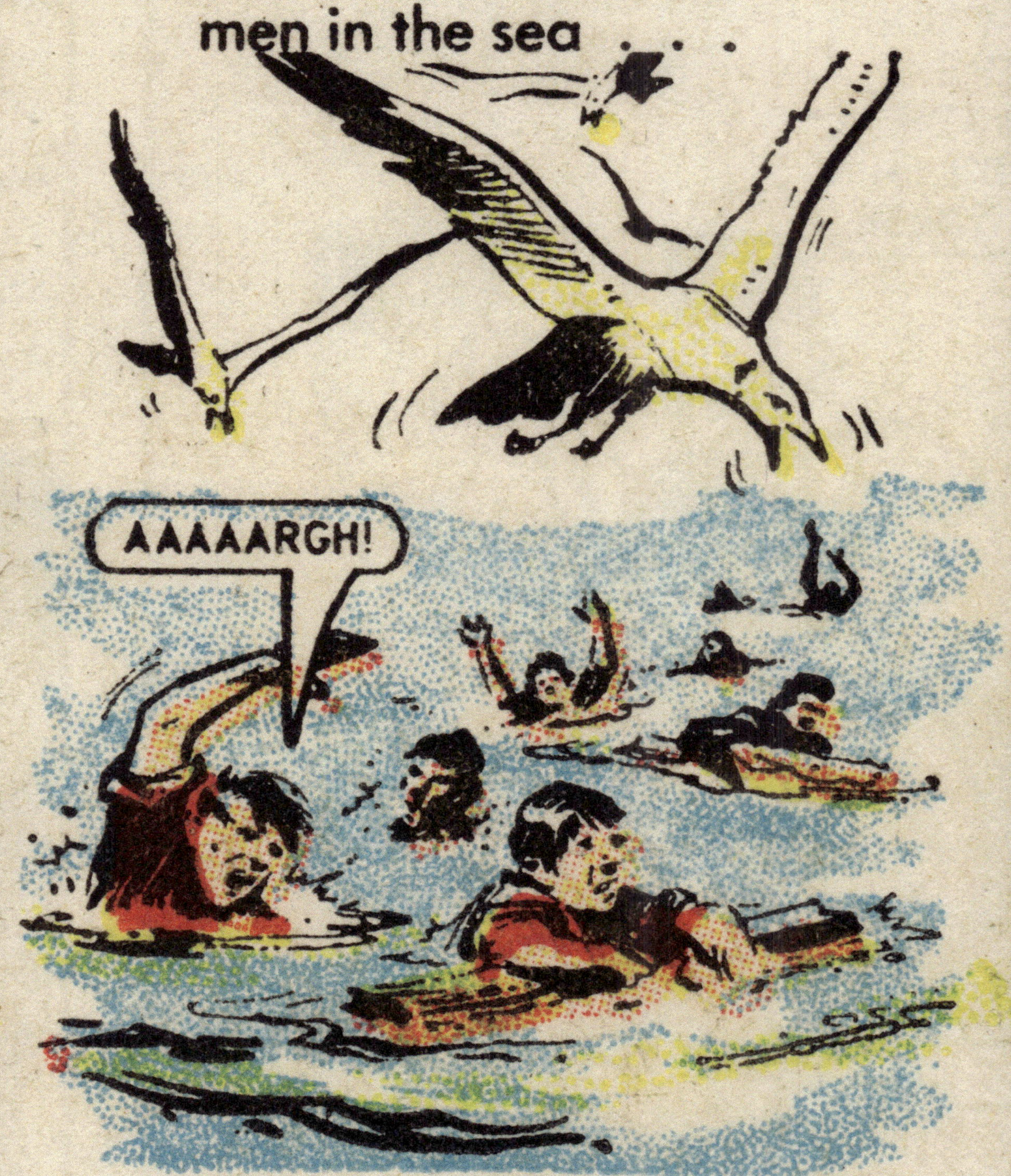

mans have a fort well guarded

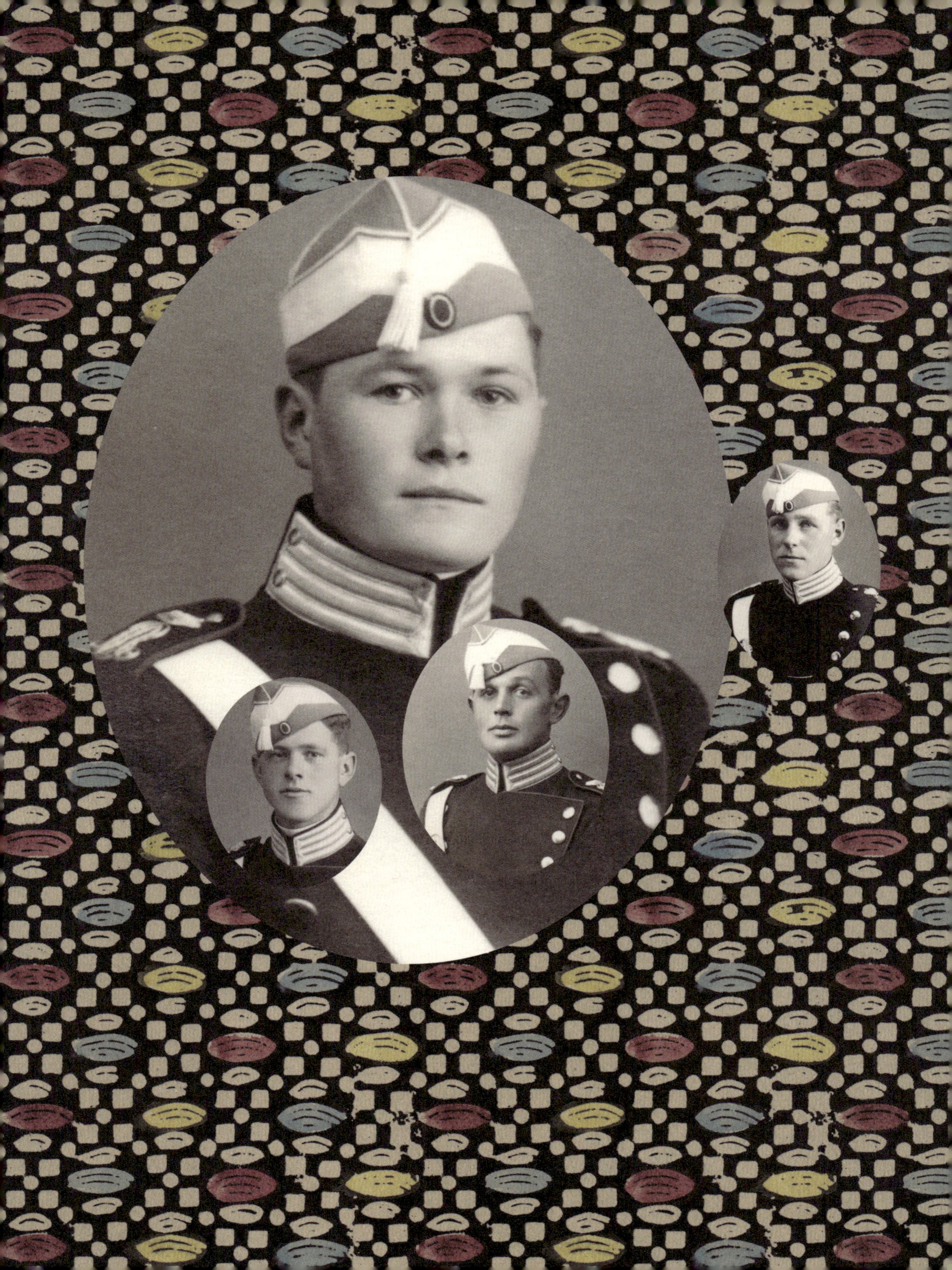

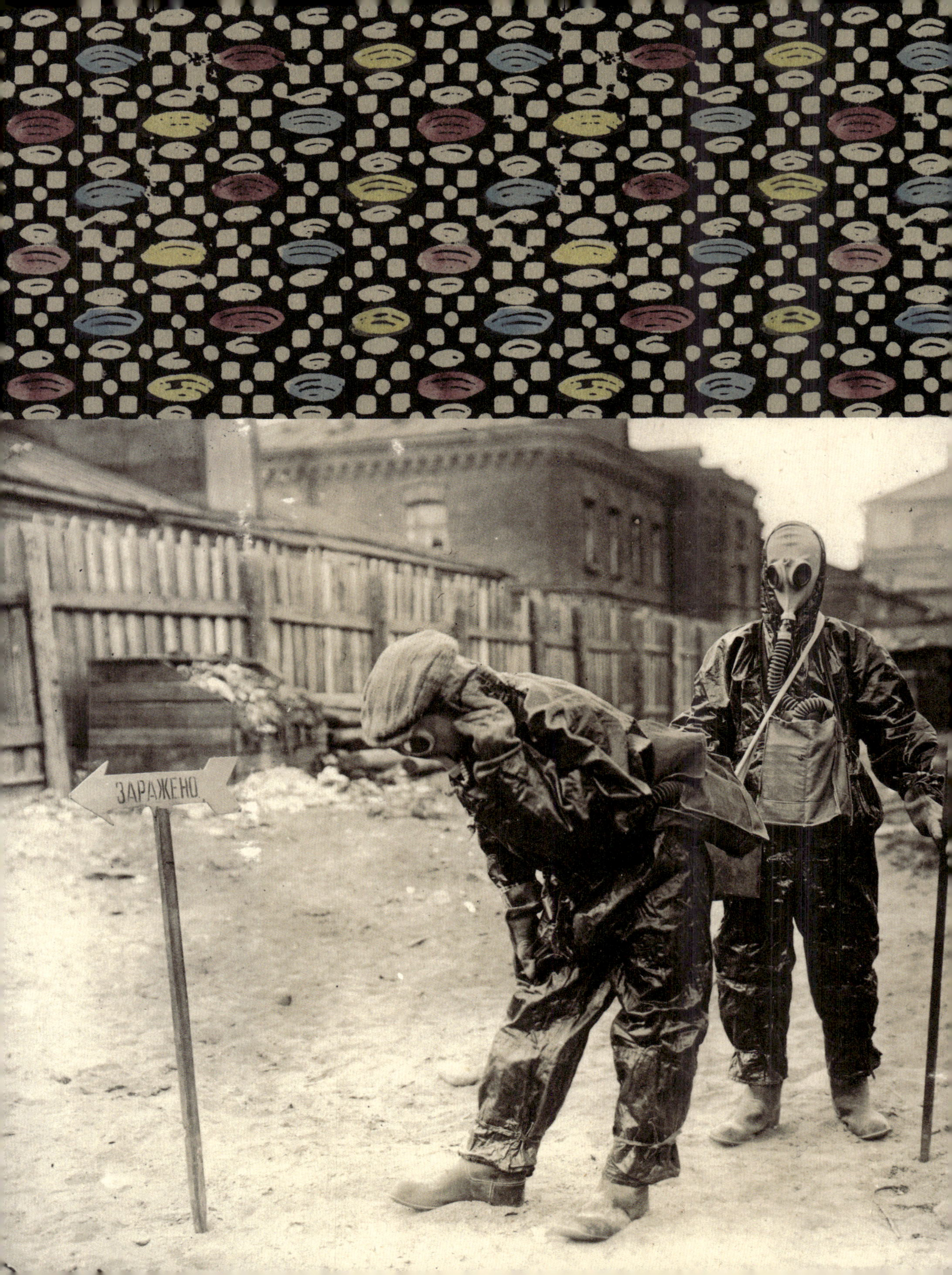
ЗАРАЖЕНО

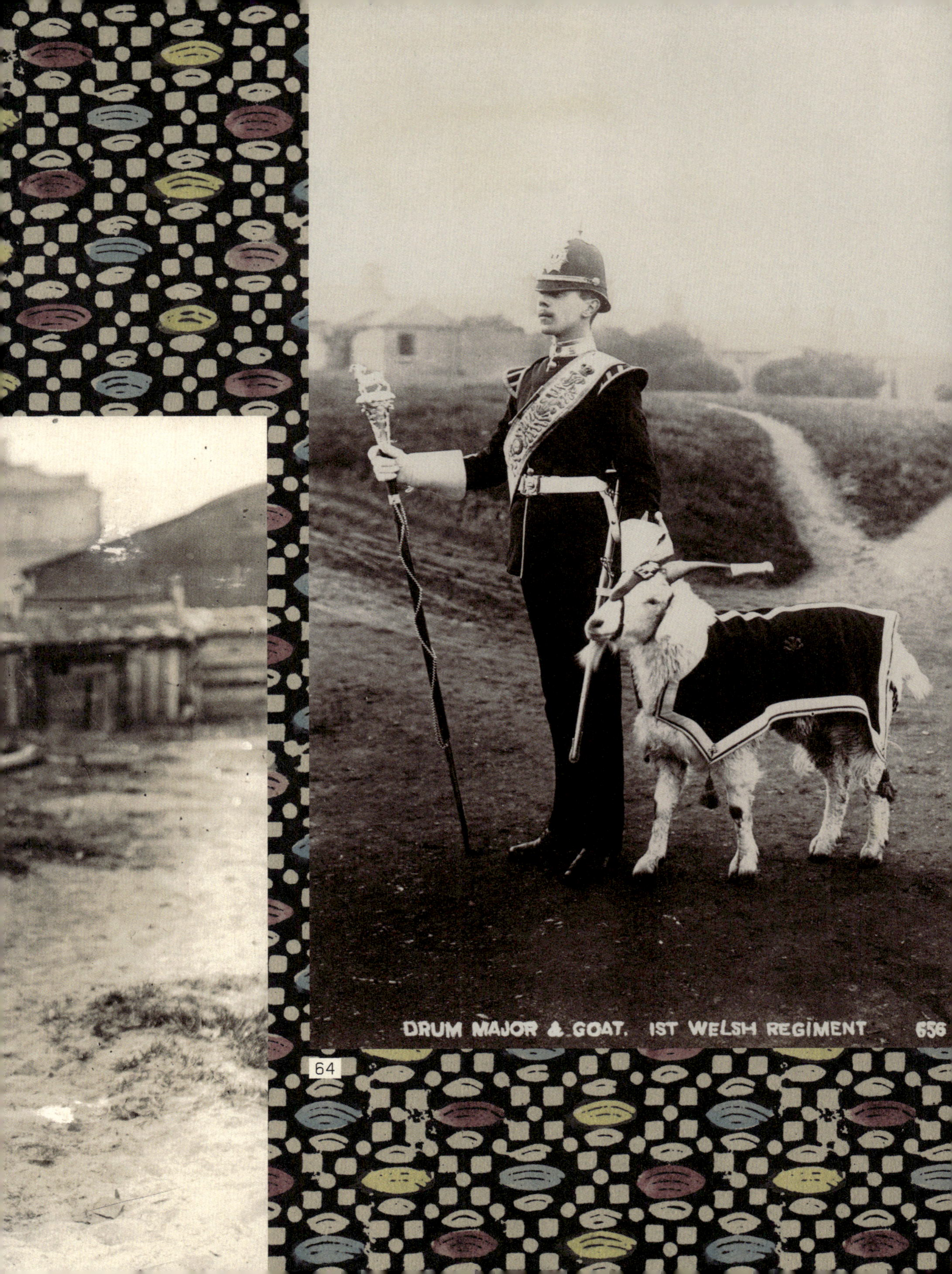
DRUM MAJOR & GOAT. 1ST WELSH REGIMENT   656

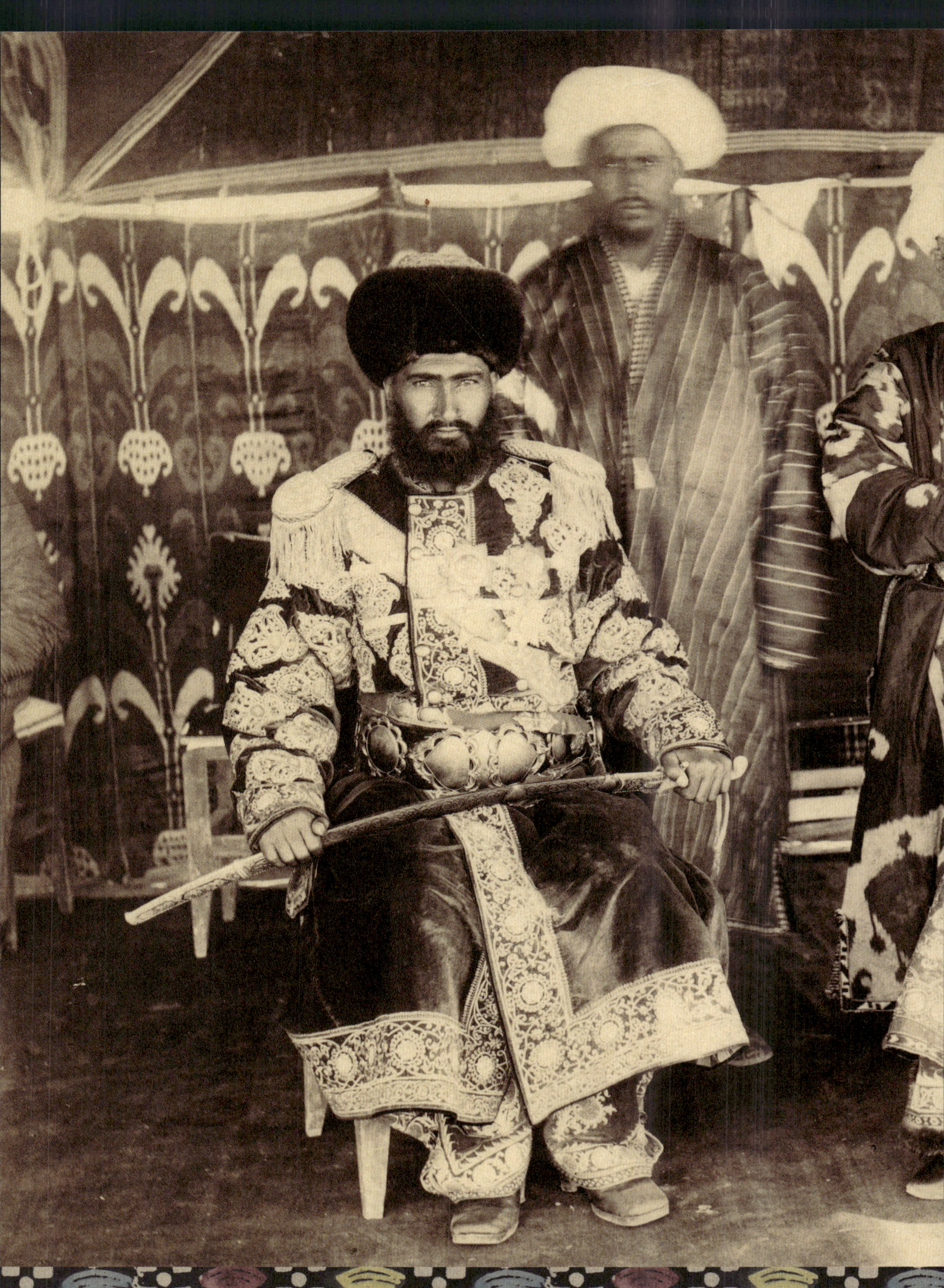

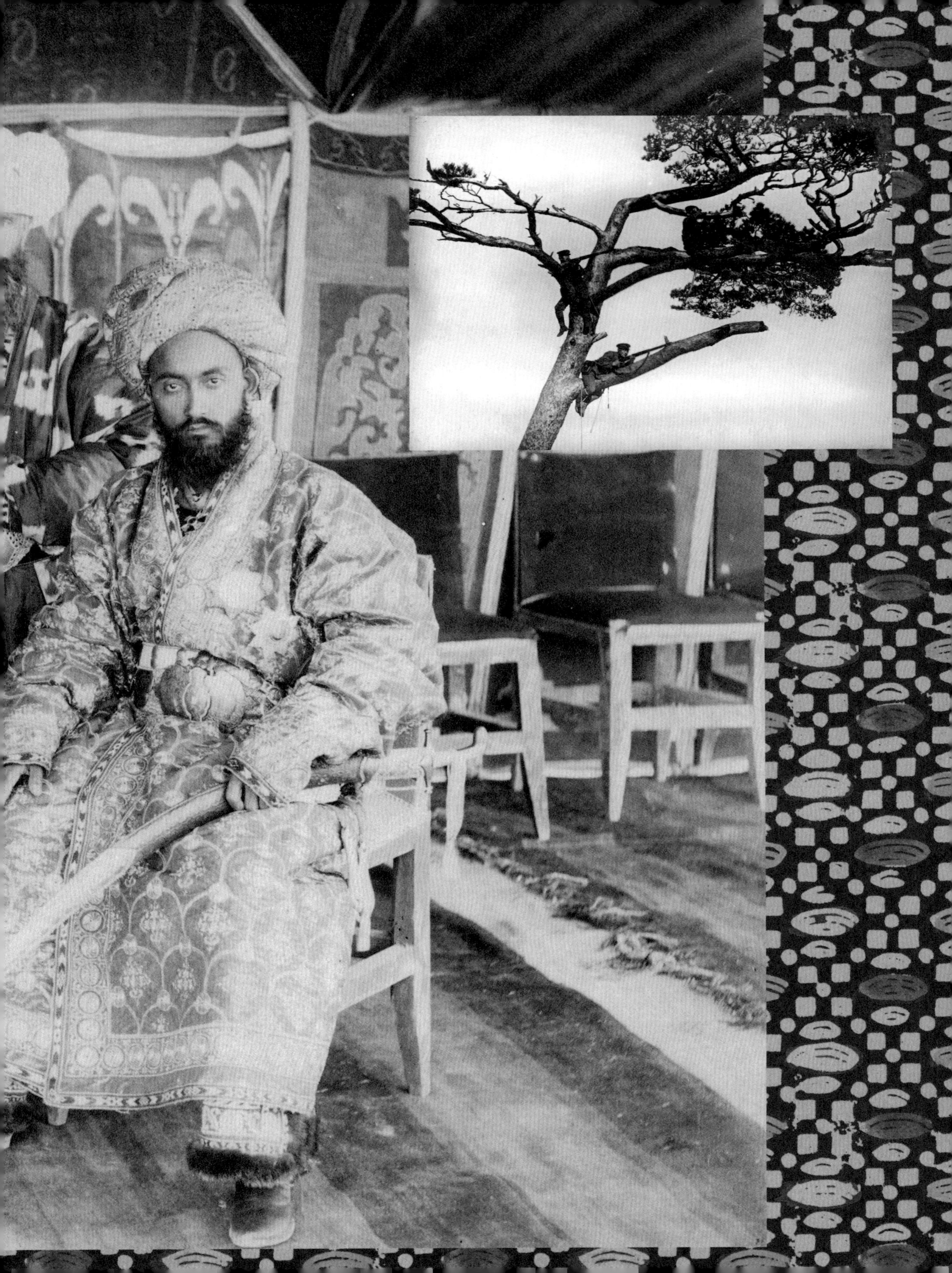

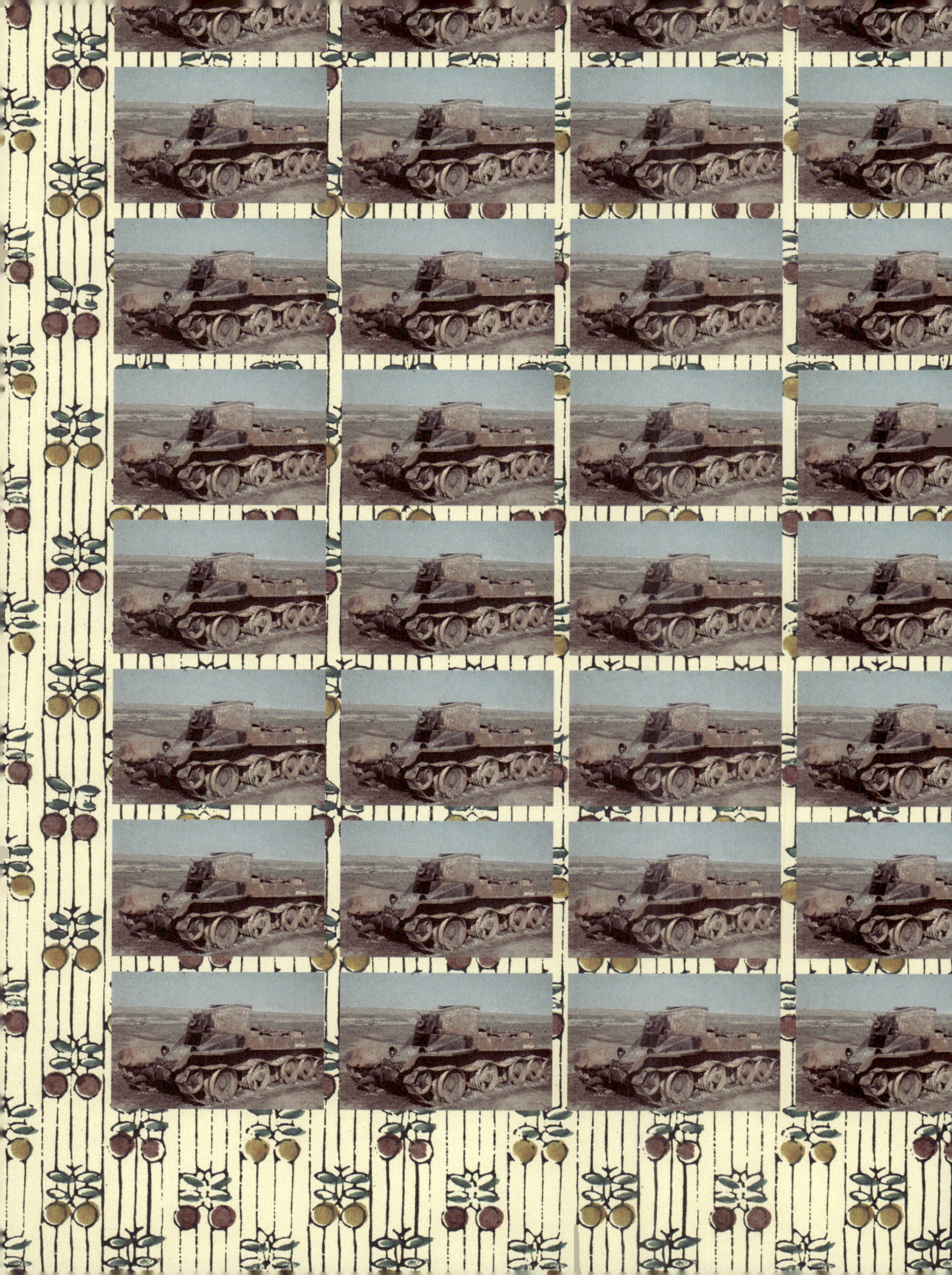

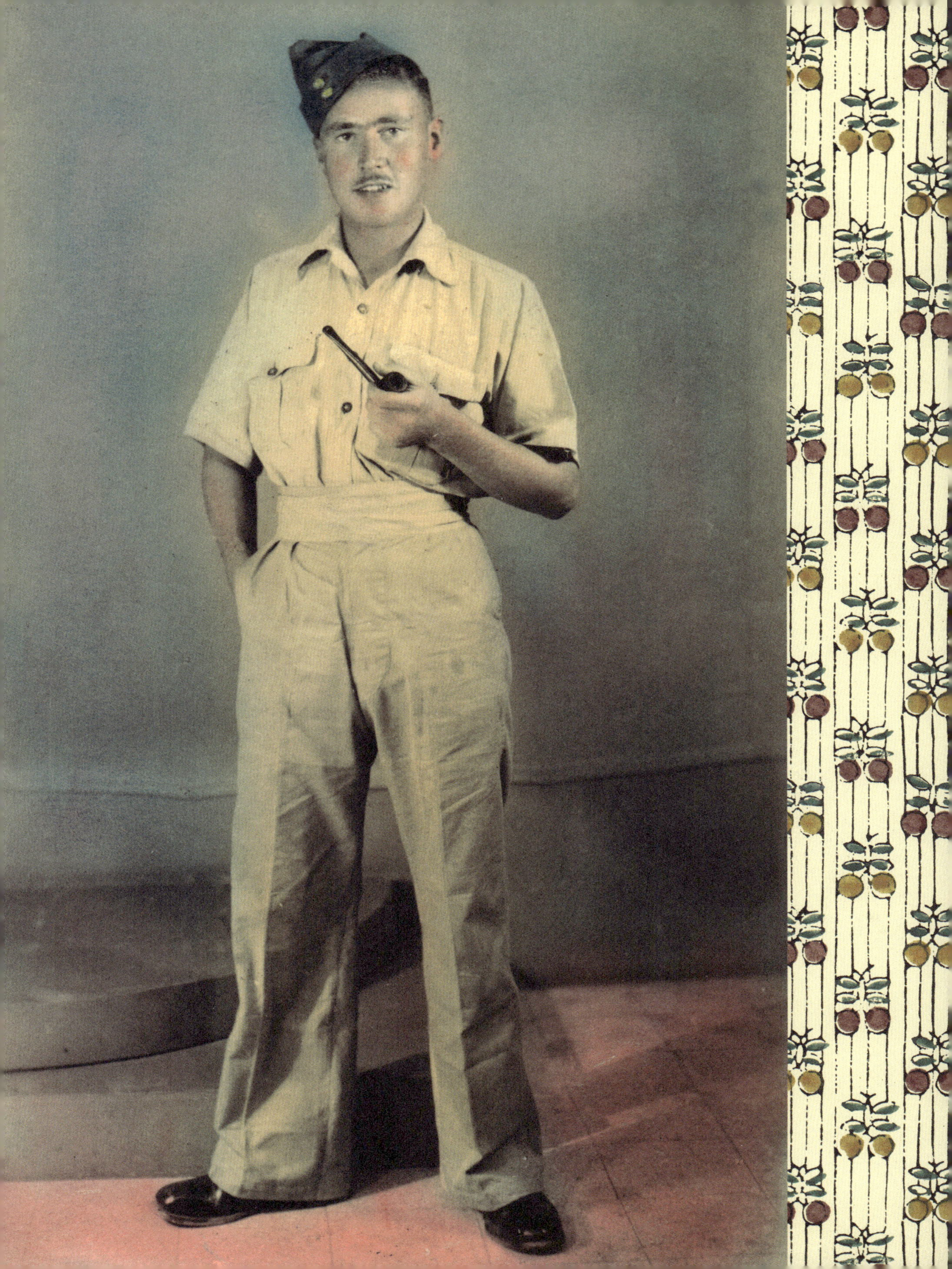

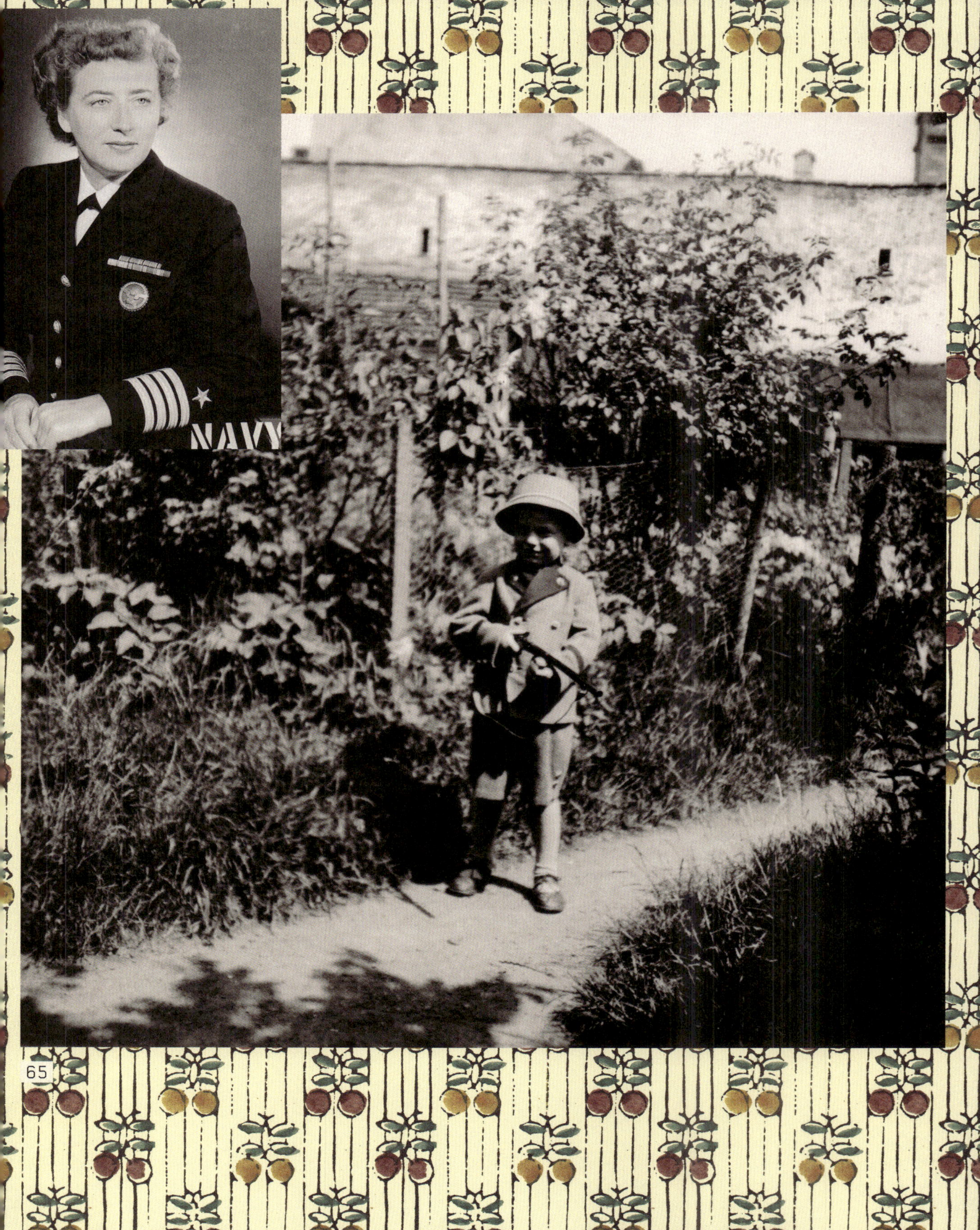

NAVY

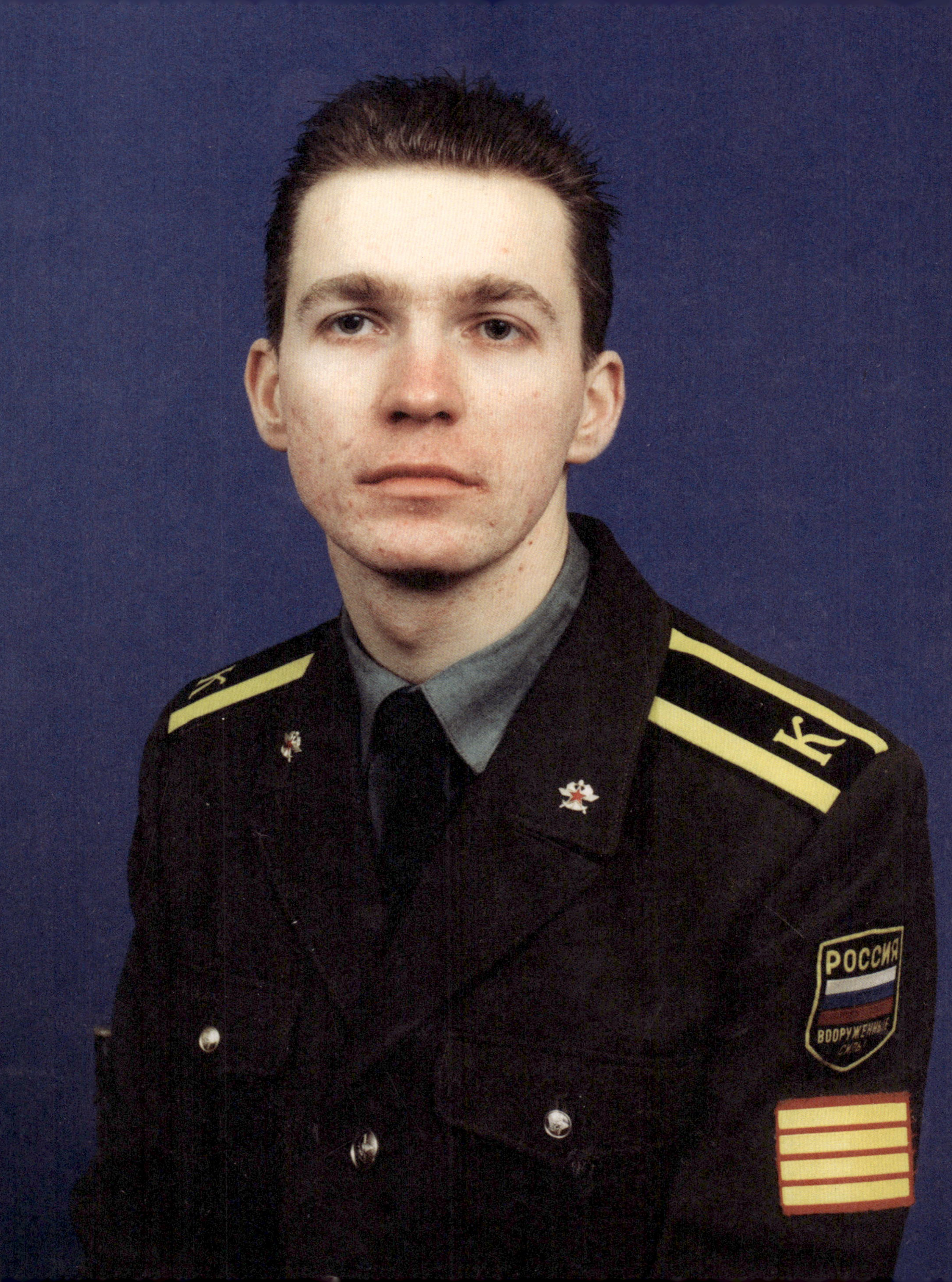

Пролетарии всех стран, соединяйтесь!

Советская Сибирь

ИЮЛЬ
2
ПОНЕДЕЛЬНИК
1934 г.
№ 148 (4418)

Орган Зап.-Сиб. Крайкома ВКП(б), Крайисполкома, Крайсовпрофа и Новосибирского Горкома ВКП(б)

На слет ударников приедут лучшие водители машин

Больше первосортных кузнецких рельсов!

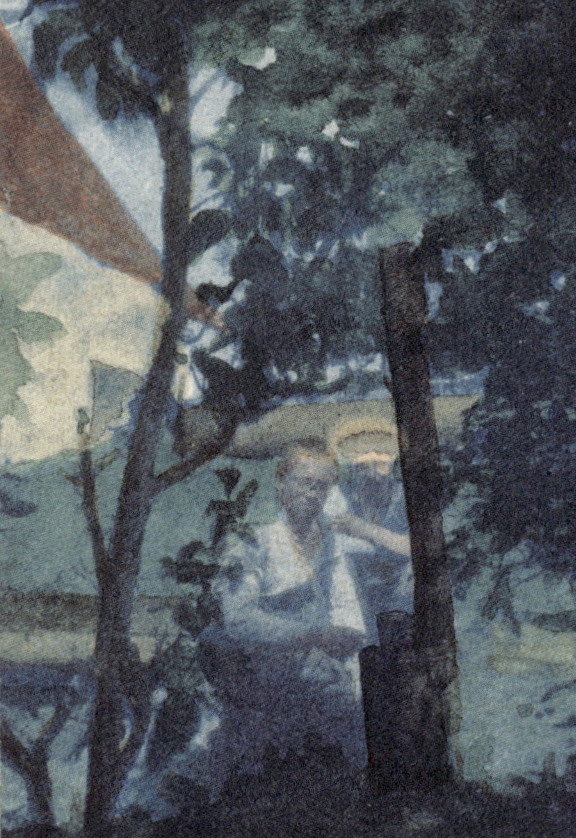

организовать равномерный ход производства не только в пределах декад...

ТРАКТОРИСТАМ—ОСОБЫЙ ПОЧЕТ

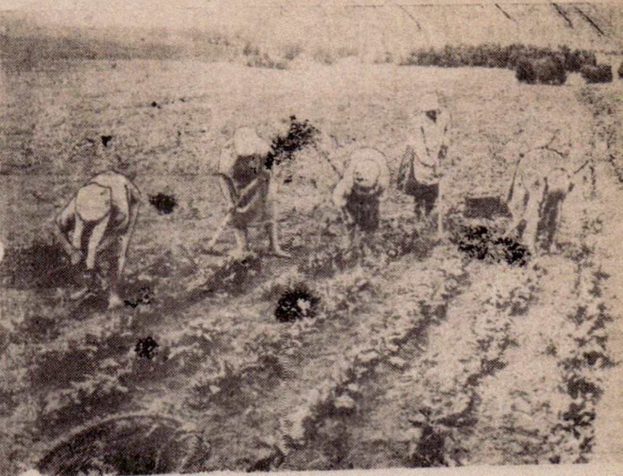

Прополка и прорывка посевов сахарной свеклы в колхозе имени Сталина, Троицкого района.

БЕСПРИЗОРНЫЕ ПЛАНТАЦИИ
(Чистюньский свеклосовхоз)

ТОПЧИХА, 30 (От нашего спецкора). В колхозах Топчихинского района «Майское утро», «Свобода» и других ожидают нынче обильный урожай сахарной свеклы. Хорошо обработанные плантации свидетельствуют о том, что колхозники много поработали, чтобы завоевать хороший урожай. В передовых колхозах района («Гигант», «Пятилетка», «Свобода», «Майское утро», им. Сталина) посевы свеклы полностью прорежены и прополоты.

Ф. ЛИТАСОВ.

Правильно определить урожай

С 1 июля совхозы и колхозы приступают к систематическому наблюдению за состоянием урожая.

ВЫРАСТИЛ СТАДО ЖЕРЕБЯТ

БРИГАДИР ФИЛИППОВ—КАНДИДАТ НА СЛЕТ

СУЗУН. — Седьмая тракторная бригада Лушниковской МТС...

С. ЛАМ.

По Советскому Союзу

НОВЫЙ РЕКОРД ВЫПЛАВКИ ЧУГУНА
— 31.986 ТОНН В СУТКИ

МОСКВА, 30. (Тасс). — Заводы черной металлургии дали новую рекордную выплавку чугуна — 31.986 тонн.

26 июня по Союзу добыто 257.742 тонны угля — 96 проц. плана.

40 судов идет в Карскую экспедицию

ЛЕНИНГРАД, 30. (Роста). — Сегодня из Ленинградского торгового порта уходит в Карско-Ленскую экспедицию ледокол «Ермак». Задача ледокола — вывести зазимовавшие суда с острова Самуила и провести Ленскую экспедицию в бухту Тикси. В нынешнем году в Карско-Ленской экспедиции будет участвовать 40 судов.

Детям—техническую игрушку

МОСКВА, 30. (Тасс). — Наркомтяжпром решил специализировать Серпуховский завод «Пресс» в производстве массовой детской технической игрушки.

СОВЕТСКИЕ МОРЯКИ СПАСЛИ АНГЛИЙСКИЙ КОРАБЛЬ

АРХАНГЕЛЬСК, 30. (Роста). — ...На помощь «Готику» вышел советский пожарный пароход «Лебедин». Он взял терпящее бедствие судно на буксир и доставил его в Архангельский порт.

«Сибиряков» спущен на воду

АРХАНГЕЛЬСК, 30. (Роста). — 28 июня спущен на воду ледокол «Сибиряков».

«Литке» вышел из Владивостока

БОРТ ЛИТКЕ, 30. (Радио). — 28 июня ледорез «Литке» вышел из Владивостокского порта в арктический рейс.

1000 мотоциклов „Л-300"

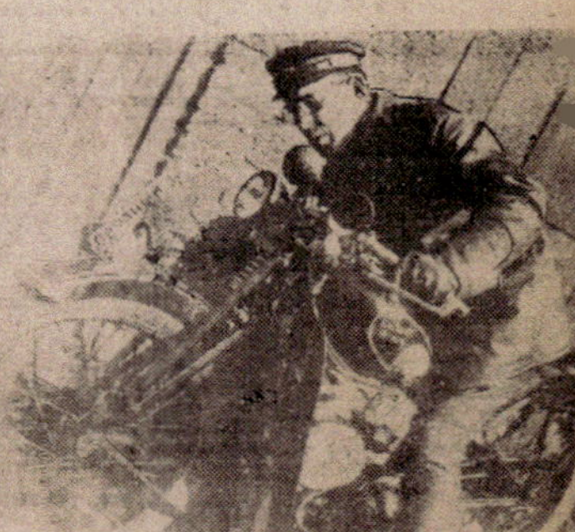

В 1934 г. завод «Красный Октябрь» (Ленинград) выпустит мотоциклов типа «Л-300». НА СНИМКЕ: Готовый мотоцикл на пробег.

Начат стройкой „Средуралмедьстрой"

МОСКВА, 30. (Тасс). —

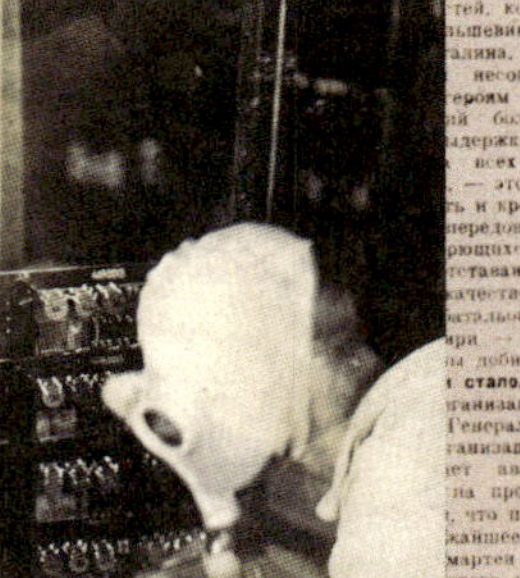

ВТОРОЙ ПЛЕНУМ КОМИССИИ ПАРТИЙНОГО КОНТРОЛЯ ПРИ ЦК ВКП(б)

26-28 июня проходил второй пленум Комиссии Партийного Контроля при ЦК ВКП(б). Были заслушаны отчеты уполномоченных комиссий по Азово-Черноморскому краю (Шаханов), Сталинградскому краю (Френкель), по Одесской области (Акулинушкин).

Раз'яснение краевого прокурора

За последнее время отмечены случаи кражи имущества колхозников, рабочих совхозов и предприятий, уходящих на полевые работы.

Краевой прокурор И. БАРКОВ.

Советская СИБИРЬ

Орган Зап.-Сиб. Крайкома ВКП(б), Крайисполкома, Крайсовпрофа и Новосибирского Горкома ВКП(б)

27 ОКТЯБРЯ СУББОТА 1934 г. № 248 (4518)

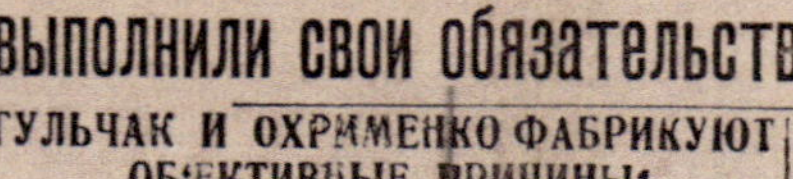

„Крайком и Крайисполком будут считать выполненным районный план хлебозаготовок при условии, если в районе все колхозы, все единоличники выполнили свои обязательства на сто процентов"

(Из речи тов. Р. И. ЭЙХЕ на совещании секретарей райкомов и начполит отделов Омске)

Решительно пресечь малейшие проявления демобилизованности

ГУЛЬЧАК И ОХРИМЕНКО ФАБРИКУЮТ „ОБ'ЕКТИВНЫЕ ПРИЧИНЫ"

КОЧЕНЕВО, 26. (Наш спецкор.). — План хлебозаготовок по Коченевскому району на 25 октября выполнен всего лишь на 43,2 процента.

В КОСИХЕ ПОПРЕЖНЕМУ ЗАНИМАЮТСЯ ГАСТРОЛЕРСТВОМ

КОСИХА, 25. (Наш спецкор.).

Взвешивание зерна перед отправкой из элеватора в колхозе «Красный Октябрь», Алейского района.

РЕЙД ПО ПРОВЕРКЕ ПРИЕМКИ И ХРАНЕНИЯ ХЛЕБА НА ЭЛЕВАТОРАХ

На Калачинском элеваторе зерно под угрозой порчи и хищений

КАЛАЧИНСК, 25.

66

ВЫВОЗКА ХЛЕБА СОВЕРШЕННО НЕ ОРГАНИЗОВАНА

ЛОКТЕВСКИЙ ЗЕРНОСОВХОЗ ВЫПОЛНИЛ ГОДОВОЙ ПЛАН ХЛЕБОСДАЧИ

25 октября план хлебосдачи. 92000 центнеров выполнили. Уборку 18000 гектаров закончили. Комбайна.

...овосибирск, Крайком партии— тов. ЭЙХЕ

Управляющий ПРОКОПЕНКО.
Партнием—БОГАЧЕНКО.
Партием—ЛЕГОРЕНКО.

установлении сроков выборов в советы по краю и о созыве краевого с'езда советов

Постановление президиума Западно-Сибирского Краевого Исполнительного Комитета

Председатель Крайисполкома ГРЯДИНСКИЙ.
И. о. секретаря АЛАГЫЗОВ.

Безоговорочно выполнить план зяблевой пахоты

КЛИМОВ.

Бригада «Советской Сибири»:
КАЗЕННИКОВ,
ЛУЦЕНКО.

...ТОВОК ПО РАИОНАМ КРАЯ

...му сектору)

	Проц. выполнения	ФАМИЛИИ	
		Секретарь райкома	Председатель рик
	81,1	Соболев	Трусевич
	80,9	Лучин	Тужилкин
	80,9	Рябцев	Кокрятский
	80,6	Курилович	Стрельцов
	80,6	Митрофанов	Гусак
	80,1	Ерзменко	Медовецкий
	80,1	Шекотов	Вадаиов
	79,9	Кулашников	Наталевич
	79,3	Колинский	Костенко
	79,2	Понуров	Крошнев
	79,0	Ужов	Курамжин
	78,7	Шемеравкин	Дудников
	78,0	Кириллов	Кротов
	78,0	Бедейц	Баранов
	76,6	Жестиков	Партов
	76,4	Хлыбов	Сафронов
	76,1	Плотников	Ведерников
	76,0	Ахремычев	Алексеев
	75,6	Селехов	Алексеев
	75,6	Никитин	Курмачев
	74,6	Еременко	Ляпшов
	74,4	Гусов	Школдин
	74,1	Тырель	Мартин
	74,0	Долганов	Шелест
	73,7	Волдин	Казаков
	70,1	Поморцев	Климек
	69,8	Алексеев	Добрыгин
	69,0	Капаев	Шахов
	67,3	Колпащиков	Акатьев
	67,3	Гладков	Борисенко
	67,2	Врид секретаря Мачт	
	67,1	Глалышев	Зайцев
	66,8	Мокин	Шишлев
	66,1	Вахрин	Толстова
	66,0	Пардеев	Кремин
	64,8	Бойленко	Вдовин
	64,3	Кохенко	Хогдав
	63,7	Зайцев В. (врих)	Маньковский
	63,4	Бакунин	Толстихин
	63,1	Гладнер	Бычков
	62,2	Корсаков	Романов
	61,8	Соболев	Губка
	61,4	Эрганов	Лысых
	60,8	Сотников	Кошеленко
	58,6	Котхин	Гухов
	46,1	Рыбаков	Лучин
	43,2	Гульчак	Охрименко
	19,1	Акимов	Рязанин
	17,3	Спих	Ехимов

...жные МТС, годовой план выполнен на	83,7%
»	95,9%
»	75,9%
»	93,6%

52. Каченский	83,6	Солтатов	Бычков
53. Б.-Истокский	83,4	Лариков	Мишин
54. Залесовский	81,7	Беттжанов	Цишин
55. Тайгинский	81,7	Масляников	Окодинов
56. Маслянинский	81,4	Лихонов	Лукошин
57. Успенский	81,4	Денисов	

The *degree and extent of the retrograde amnesia* ha[...]
many cases through the *administration of elec*[...]
thousands of instances it is found that the p[...]
the preparations. He may merely *forget the ap*[...]
or he may even *forget the entrance of the therap*[...]
which occurs five minutes before the shock i[...]

When he recovers consciousness it is by [...]
about stupidly, he makes faulty observations, p[...]
or the pillow, *perception is weak* and he is lat[...]
recollection of events immediately following the [...]

The cumulative effects of repeated seizu[...]
day consist of *gradual loss of alertness,* pauci[...]
environment and *regression.* As treatments co[...]
marked. The patient first forgets his telepho[...]
address, then affairs outside his family and [...]
information as *whether he is married.* Anybod[...]
future is a bastard, *it's the present that counts.* [...]
like making speeches to worms.

been determined in
shock convulsions. In
nt has amnesia for
cation of the electrodes
with his entourage
iven.

grees. He first *looks*
haps grasps the bed
shown to have *no*
izure.

given every other
of interest in the
nue, *amnesia becomes*
number, then his
ally such intimate
ho talks about the
voking posterity is

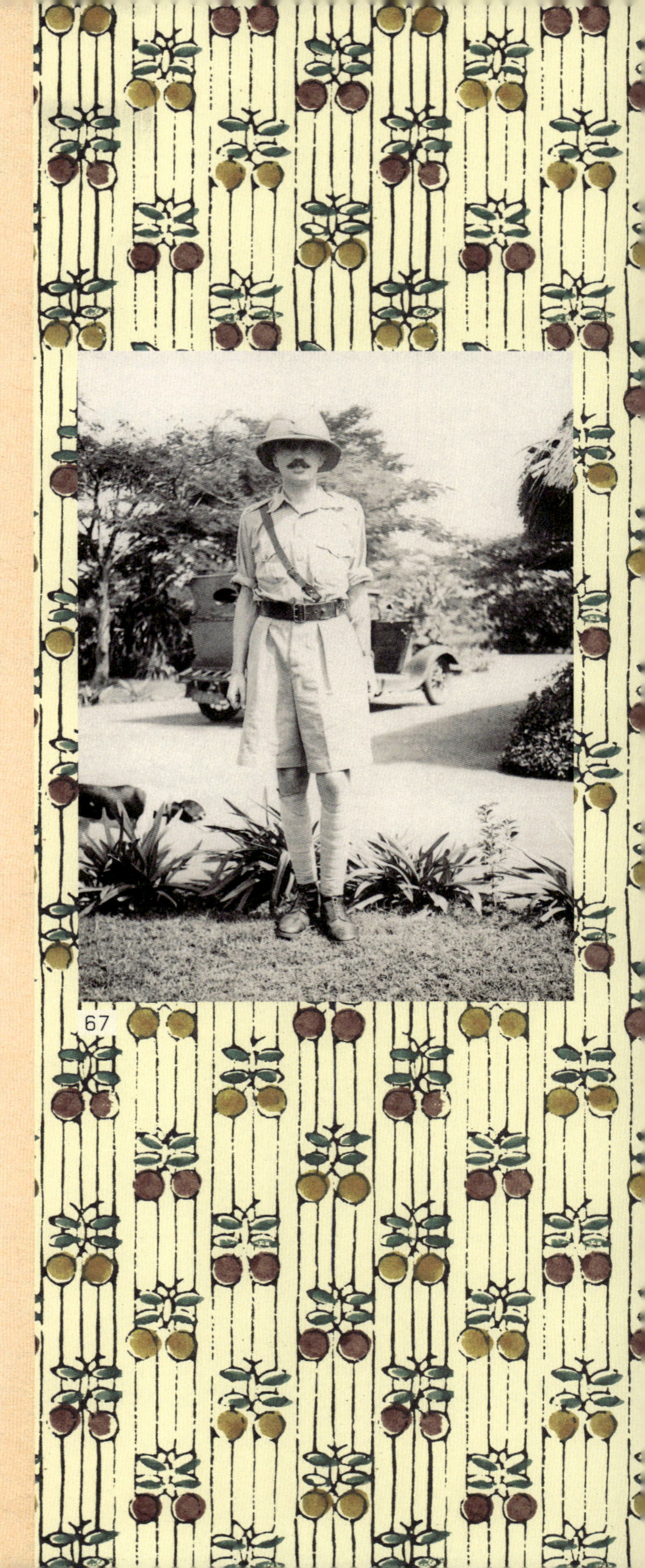

de gaz suffocants.

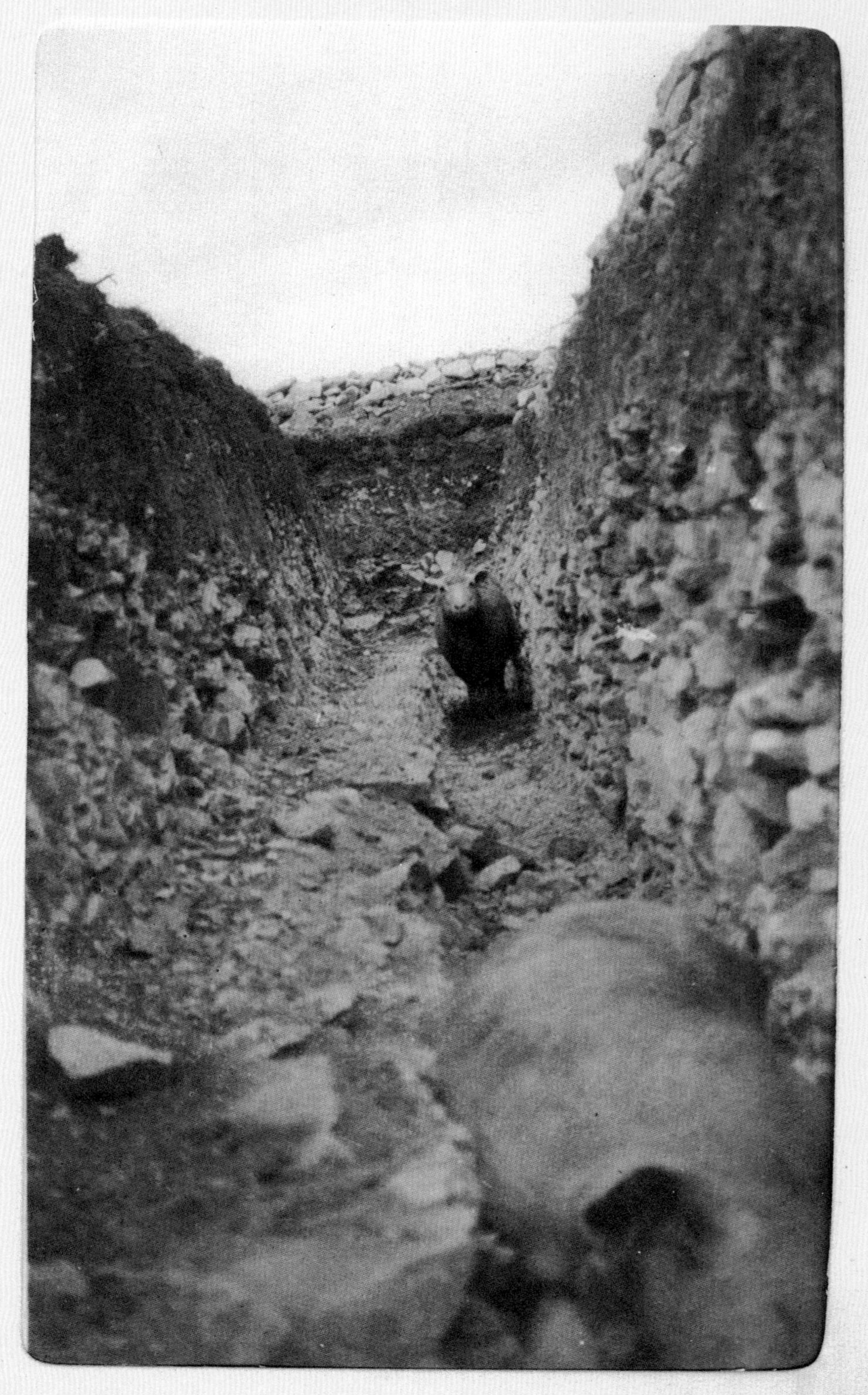

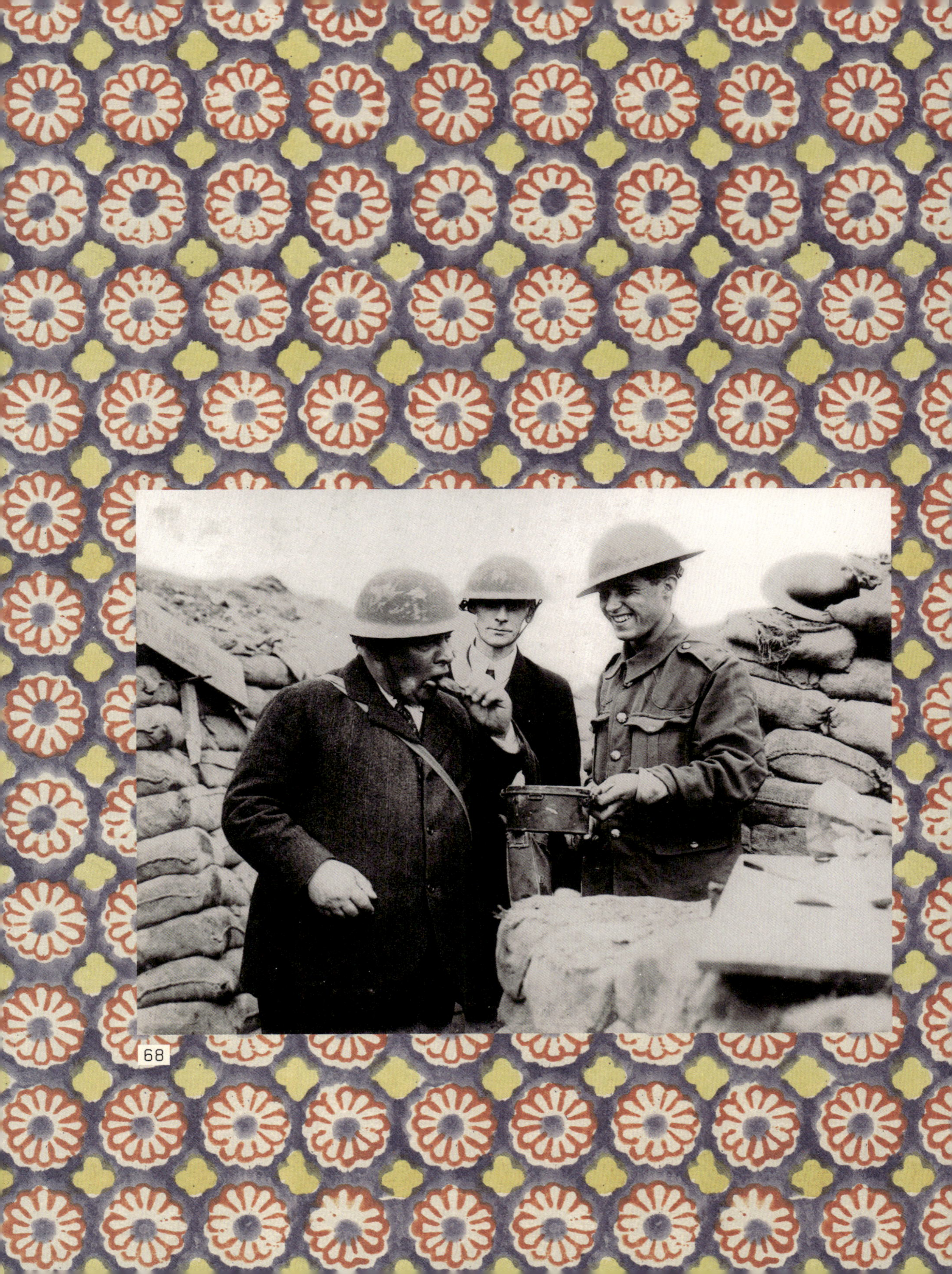

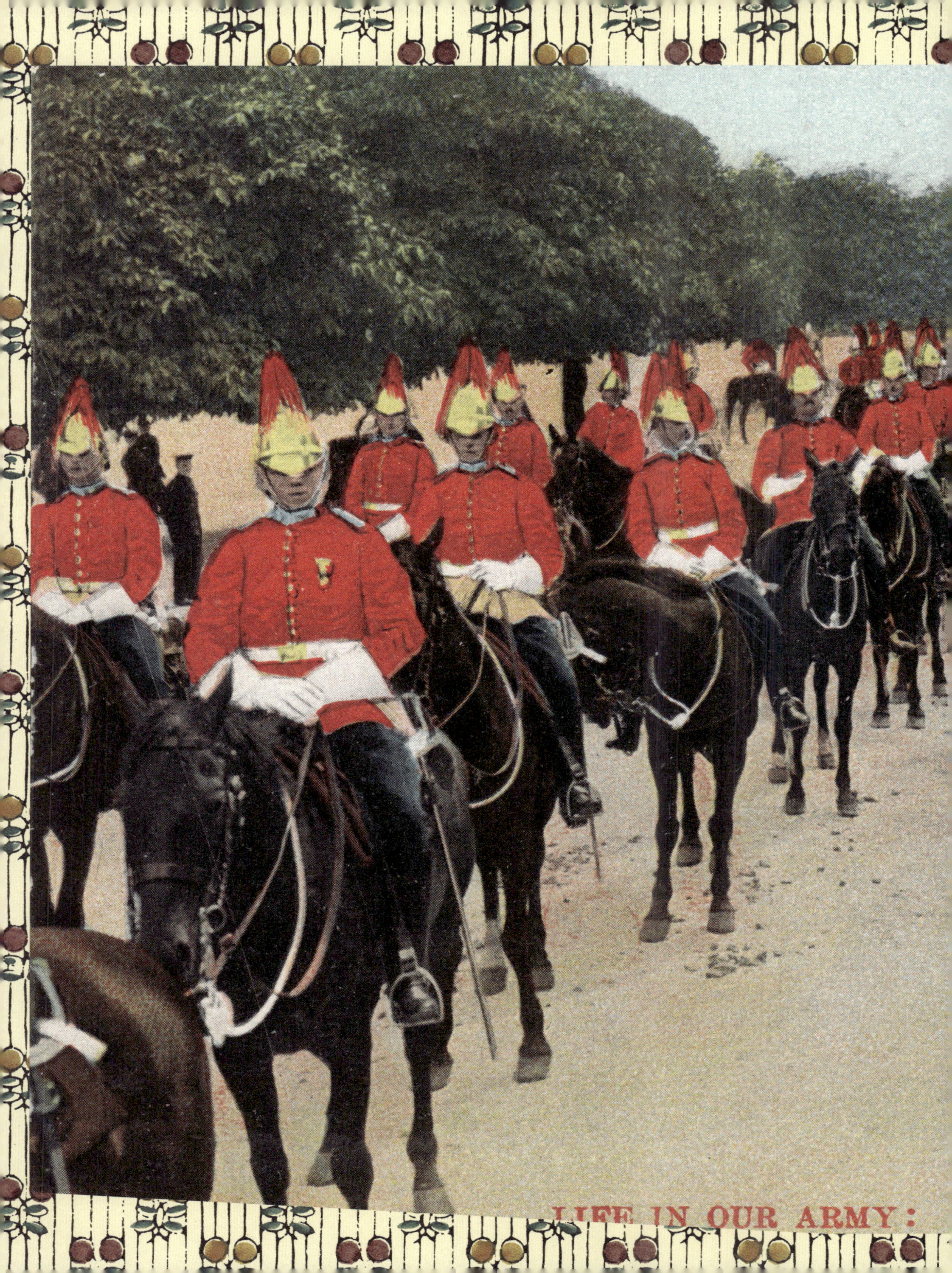

LIFE IN OUR ARMY:

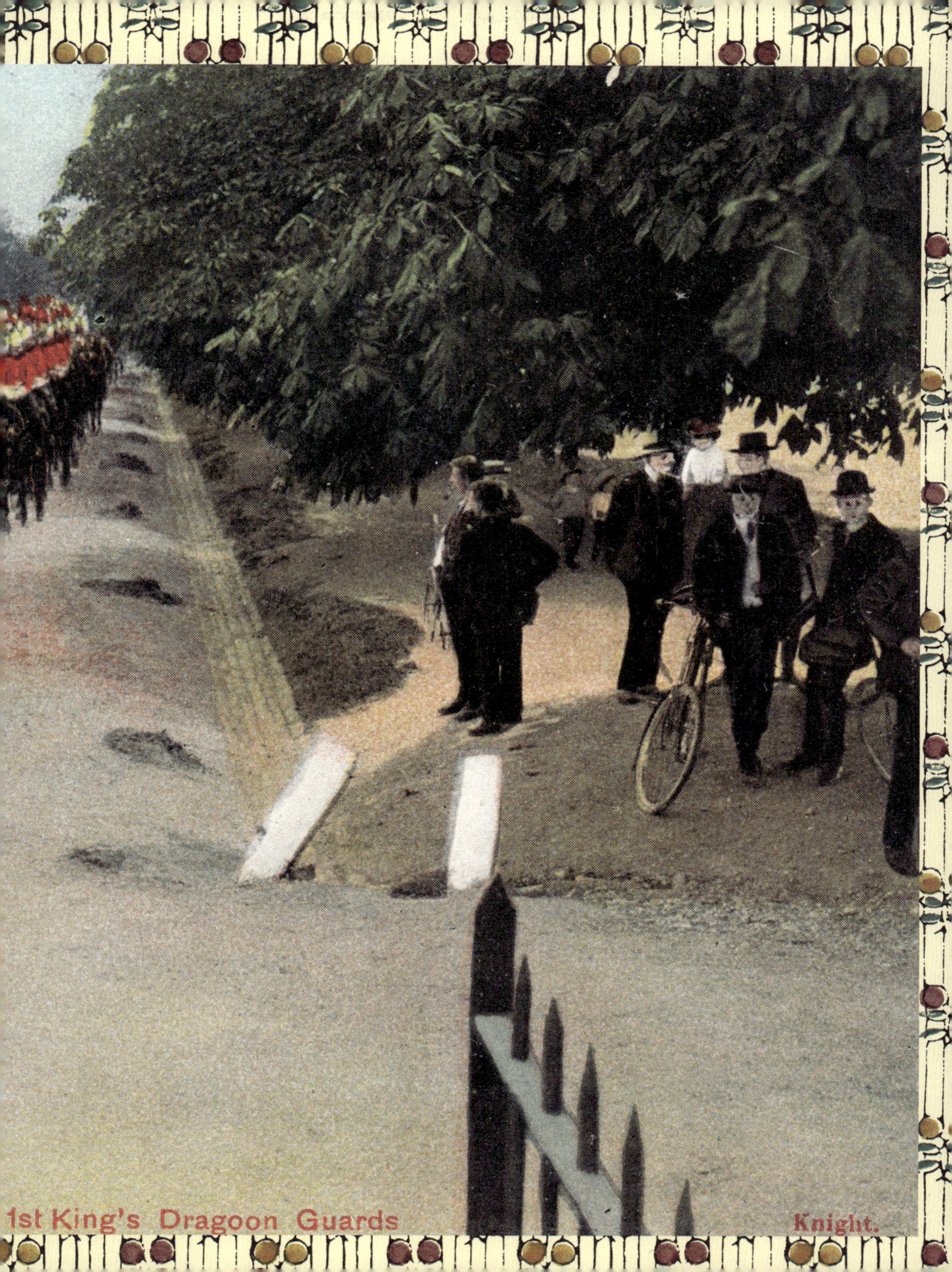

1st King's Dragoon Guards
Knight.

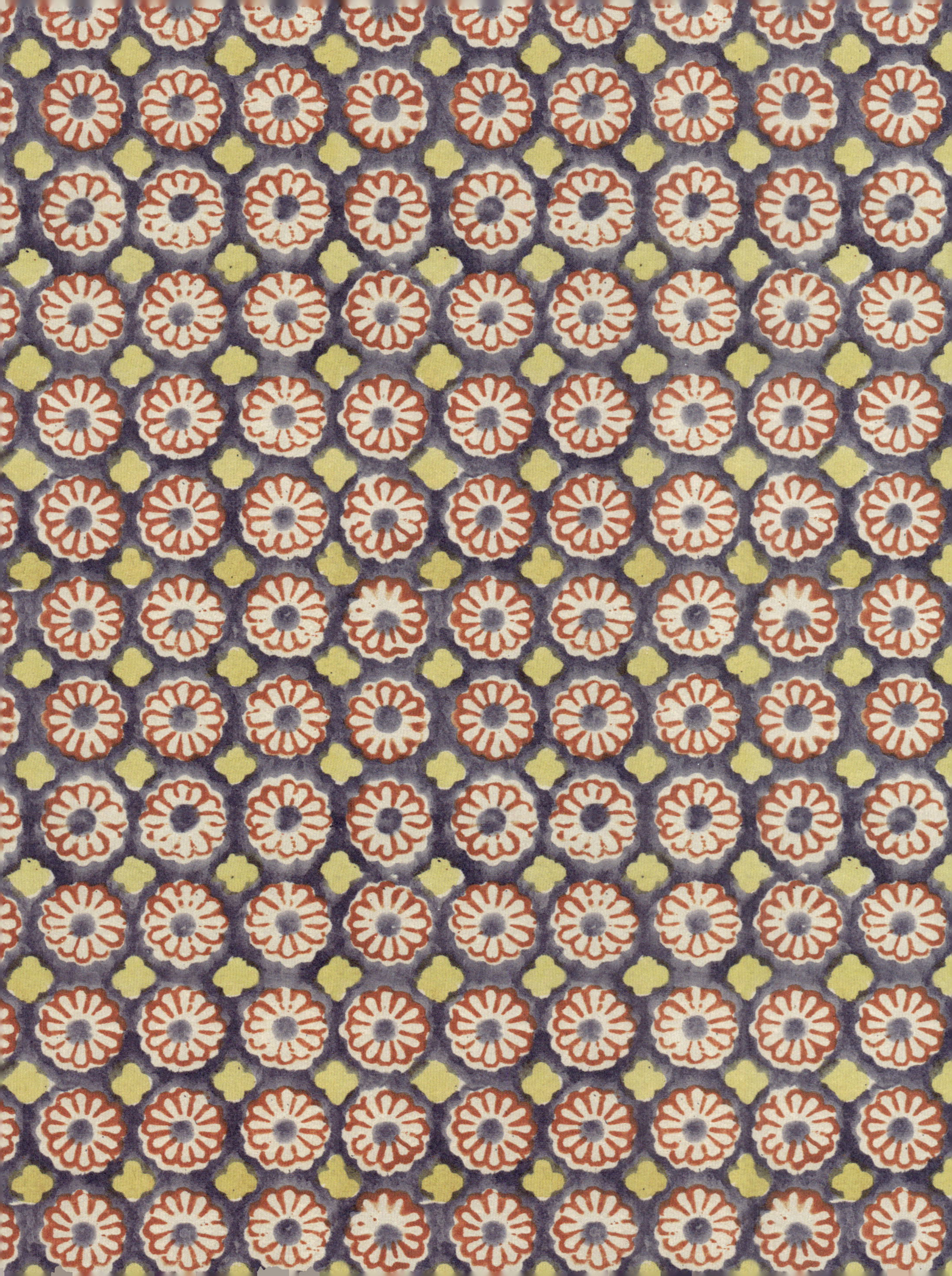

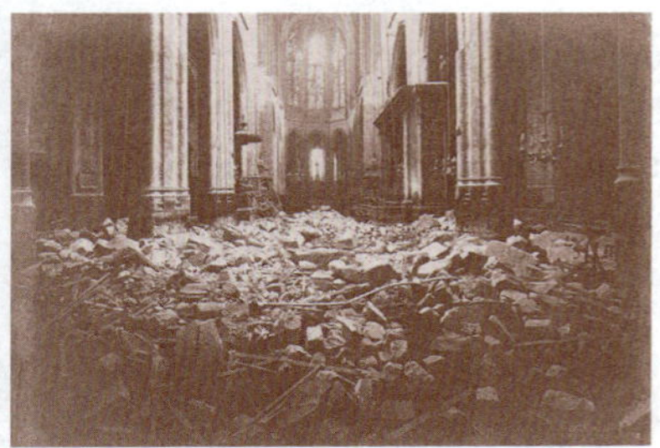

Rheims Cathedral after German bombardment, 1914
01

This photograph has had two lives. In 1914 it stood as a rebuke to German barbarism, showing the piles of debris heaped in the chancel. In this role it was widely reproduced and circulated at the time and into the 1920s, as in Pierre Anthony- Thouret's folio, *Rheims après la Guerre* (1927). The message was that not just a specific cathedral, but an entire nation – *La France* – had been desecrated by German explosives.

In 1961, its inclusion as a still in the film *La Jettee*, which tells a science-fiction history of the near future, gave it a second life. A nuclear war has destroyed all monuments and habitations above ground, and the film's viewer is shocked to see familiar sites and townscapes devastated. The Arc du Triomphe has its grand upper storey shorn off by atomic blast, and the roof of Rheims Cathedral is lost a second time. The film's director, Chris Marker, was not only triggering trauma through images, but also plucking at the French national memory of modern war as mediated by photographs.

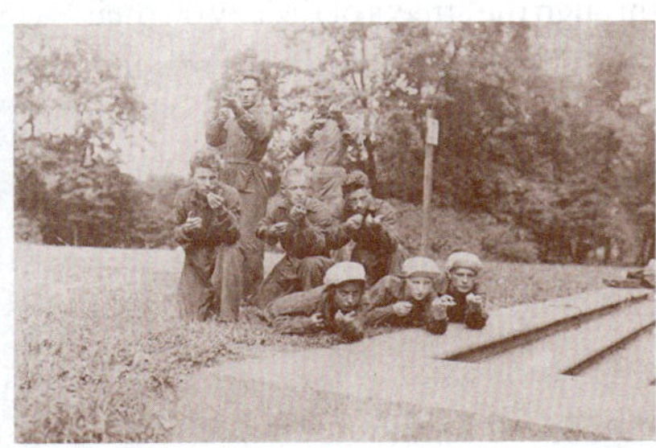

An agitprop troupe in Leningrad, 1932
02

Fearsome, faces determined, these actors are dressed in overalls and are manically mimicking the aiming of non-existent rifles. The troupe aspires to fufill the role of the 'worker-soldier' to encourage industrial workers in Leningrad. The hybrid 'worker-soldier' emerges from both Communist and Fascist imaginations by the late 1920s and early 1930s.

On the one hand it was an invention of German writer Ernst Junger, who believed a kind of ecstasy in communal industrial achievement was shared with the experiences of German assault troops (*Sturmtruppen*) during the spring offensive of 1918. On the other hand, from the Soviet Communist point of view, beginning in 1929 Stalin encouraged *udarniki* – brigades of shock workers whose sacrifice on the factory floor was intended to provide bodily examples to inspire greater productivity.

The photograph originates from an album completed in 1932 which surveyed many examples of industrial labour mobilised across the 'Chemical-Aviation-Construction Organisation of Leningrad', published by the Revolutionary War Committee. Propaganda for Stalin's first Five Year Plan of industrialisation was paramount, but it also went hand in hand with preparations for renewed war against imperialist powers and Germany in particular. Vigilance and uncompromising armed response is portrayed in this mime.

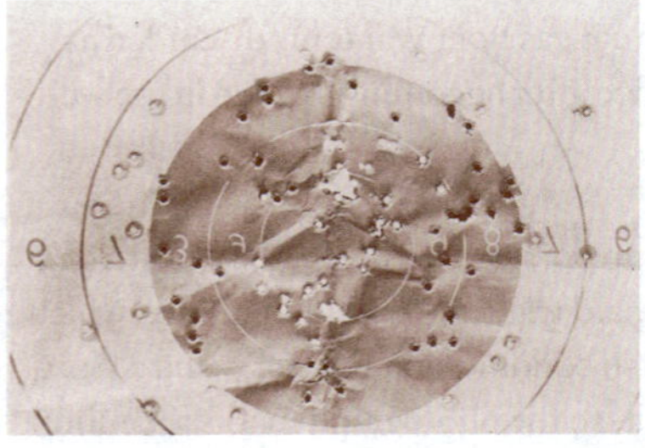

Target
03

This particular target has been taken down and roughly folded two ways. It has also been patched or re-covered in zones 8 and 9, to judge from many darkened entry holes. Zones 6 and 7 have been more or less left alone, although there are some signs that scars have been repaired with white paper. The second-phase shooter, whose entry marks show up white in zones 9 and 10, has been more successful. There are other traces of repair work, mainly on the edge between zones 7 and 8 where the edge is interrupted by small rectangles made by the shadows of patches applied on the far side of the sheet. In any period of scarcity it would be sensible to re-use a target, even if that meant patching. At the same time, the shooter has been profligate with ammunition.

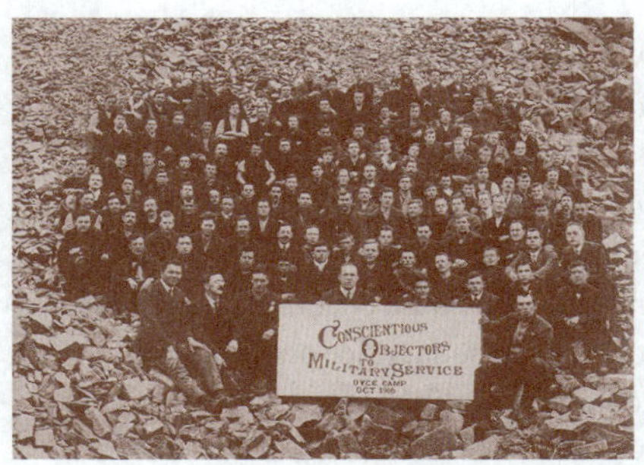

Conscientious objectors at Dyce Work Camp, Aberdeen, October 1916

04

Conscientious objectors sentenced to hard labour break granite rocks at Dyce Quarry near Aberdeen. Some look desperate; others stare down the camera gaze of the commercial photographer brought in to document them; most are blank and impassive. Recently released from jail, they are unused to the grinding conditions at Dyce Camp and many are sickly and malnourished as a Scottish winter approaches. Their only shelter comes from canvas Boer War tents discarded as unusable by the War Office after becoming sodden in the wet autumn of 1916.

A month before this group portrait was made, the death from pneumonia of one occupant triggered outside agitation which led to a review of the harsh conditions at the camp and a War Office decision to close it, so the photograph marks a sombre celebration of some sort of liberation. During the Great War 16,000 men in the UK claimed exemption from military conscription on conscientious grounds and 6,000 of them were imprisoned, 70 of whom died from disease, exposure or maltreatment.

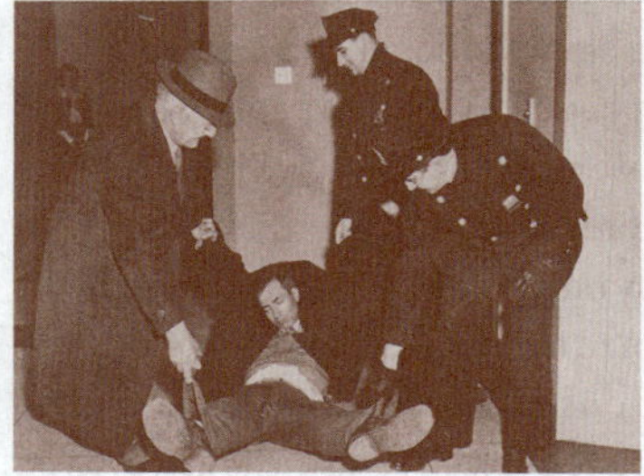

Draft dodger

05

US marshal Harry A Coxe and patrolmen Frank Klaub and Isadore Segal carry Corbitt Bishop – a recaptured fugitive from a conscientious objectors' camp – through the corridors of Philadelphia's Federal Building after he refuses to walk from the prison van to the courtroom, where he was held on $1,500 bail for return to the camp. He was later carried to a cell block after again refusing to walk the distance himself.

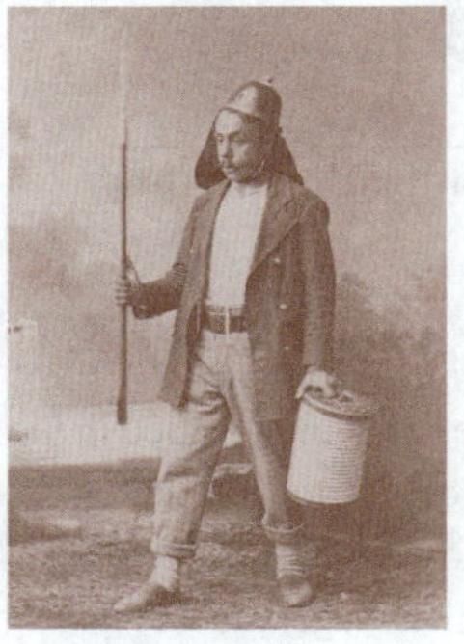

A Turkish fireman

06

He appears in a postcard from the late 1870s as an *aviseur d'incendie*, perhaps someone who guided units to the scene of the incident. There is a crescent on his official issue helmet, but otherwise he is informally got up in a spare jacket and outsize trousers. He is a good instance of the kind of urban tradesman photographed in London and Paris around this time, even if unusually disheveled and bemused. The photographer has probably moved his helmet off centre to clarify his profile. He carries what looks like a Chinese lantern and a wand in the style of a contemporary tour guide. At that time teams of firemen carried metal pumps through the streets of the city on their shoulders and would have needed direction in an emergency and through unfamiliar alleyways.

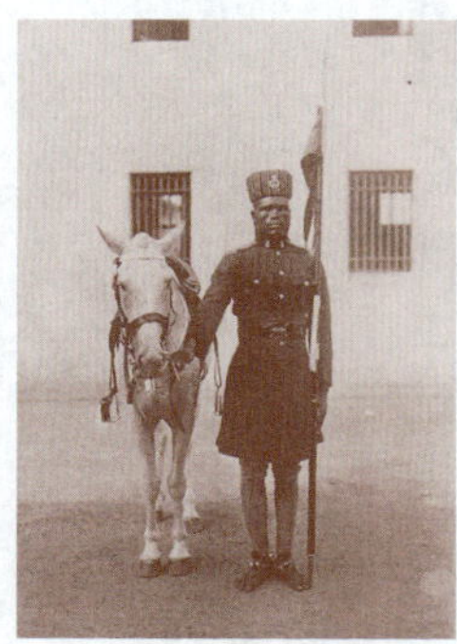

British Lancer, Accra, Gold Coast

07

This soldier belonged to the Sierra Leone Battalion of the West African Frontier Force, according to his cap badge, which shows a palm tree above a prowling lion. The emaciated horse standing quietly by his side would have had a hard time of it in West Africa because of tsetse flies and the disease nagana bringing about lethargy and weight loss. Lancers showed the flag carried in that socket attached to the stirrup on the far side of the man's horse.

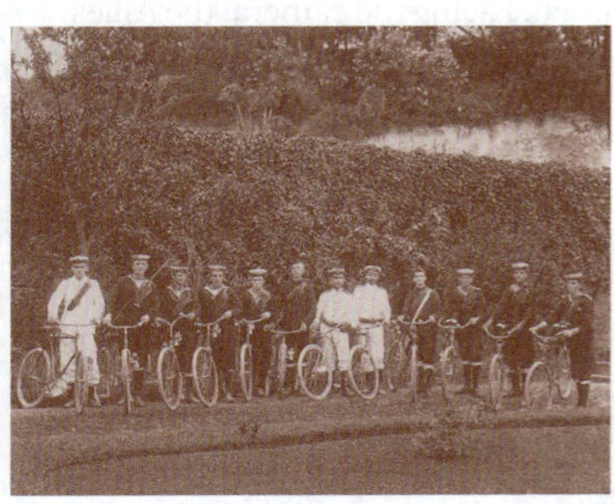

The Cycle Corps of HMS Hermes, 1900
08

HMS Hermes, a cruiser, was launched in 1898 at the Govan shipyard in Glasgow. This picture was taken when it visited Bermuda in January 1900, when the islands were used to house Boer prisoners from the war in South Africa. Armed patrols would have been necessary, and bicycles were a handy way of getting around the islands. Carbide lamps had not been long in use, and bicycle technology was beginning to develop at the same time. The two men in forage caps may have been resident guards with local knowledge. The beardless sailors may have been marines, or just from a younger generation that preferred a cleaner look.

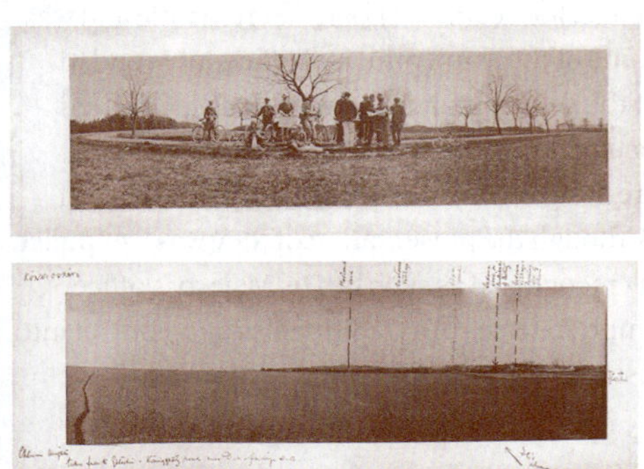

A party of English cyclists tour the battlefields of the Franco-Prussian War
09

In 1905, military antiquarians Pugh, Knox, Hase, Blundell, Moffit and Shea set off from England to survey the battlefields of the Franco-Prussian War of 1870. They stopped at the scene of the decisive Battle of Königgrätz of 3 July 1866 and photographed themselves and the battlefield using a panoramic camera, later annotating the sweeping landscape with ink-drawn pin-pointed vertical lines detailing topography in relation to military emplacements.

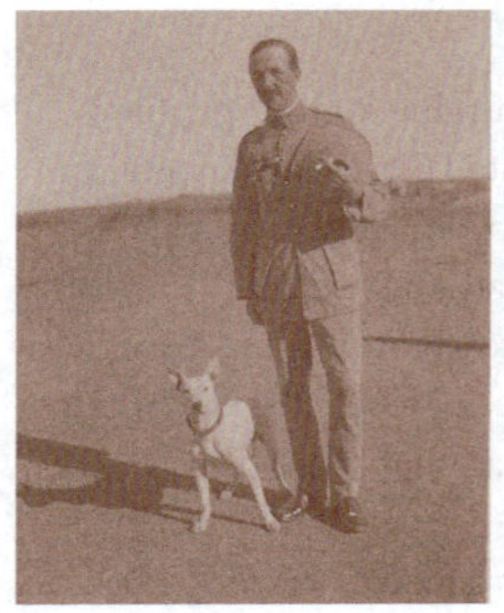

A British officer, c.1905
10

He has removed his hat to oblige the photographer – otherwise his face would have been in the shade. He is fastidiously dressed with his trousers cut and taped to fit securely onto his polished shoes. But it is a hot day in the desert nonetheless, and he has thought fit to keep a rolled towel up his sleeve to mop his brow. He holds himself elegantly and casually, relaxed but composed at the same time. His dog, too, a Cirneco dell'Etna, holds a studied pose in harmony with that of his master. It is a dog from Sicily, of ancient lineage with a reputation for hunting rabbits on volcanic terrain and for coping with a hot, dry climate – well chosen, that is to say, for desert duties. The man, whoever he is, stands as an embodiment of forethought and of *bella figura* in what looks to be a most unpromising landscape.

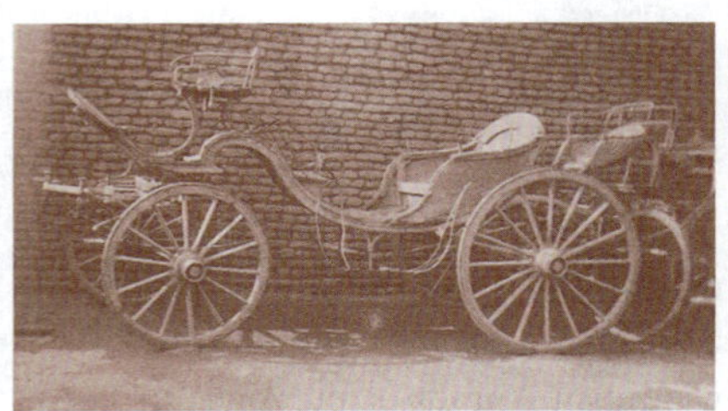

General Gordon's coach, 1885
11

Major General Charles George Gordon was killed in Khartoum on the morning of 26 June 1885. He was decapitated and his body was thrown into a well. Gordon had an international reputation as a decisive and successful leader, gained in the Crimea in the 1850s and in China in the 1860s – where he led the 'Ever Victorious Army' against the Taiping rebels. Leopold II of Belgium twice asked him to become Governor of the Congo Free State. In Africa he campaigned against the slave trade and made war and peace far and wide, from Darfur to Abyssinia.

He had been in Sudan since 1874, working for the Egyptian government. In 1884 he was appointed Governor-General and spent most of that year in Khartoum, organising its defence against insurgents led by Mohammad Ahmad. But the British government wanted him to evacuate Khartoum and leave the troublesome Sudan to its own devices. He refused, and was in effect left to his fate, resulting in a national outcry.

Hence the irony of this picture of his derelict vehicle – a Phaeton, named after the son of Helios, who borrowed his father's carriage and horses for the day, lost control and threatened to set the earth on fire. To save the situation his father destroyed him with a thunderbolt. Gordon's line managers chose a delayed and underfunded expeditionary force.

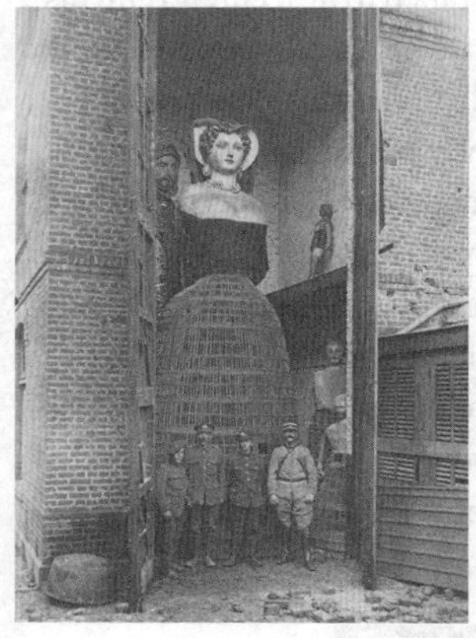

La Famille Gayant

12

It is October 1918 in the French town of Douai, and uprooted cobblestones suggest a degree of disorder. The tall doors of a storage building are wide open. A group of four Allied soldiers – one Scottish, two English and a French officer – stand awed, awkward and small in the presence of the Gayant family. The giantess behind them is Marie Cagenon, and just visible behind her is the armour-clad soldier Gelon.

These gigantic mannequin beings are guardian household deities and civic emblems, and are paraded through Douai at the beginning of July each year even today. In the context of the retreat of the German army which had occupied the town for four years, this is a premature but vital image of festivity and liberation – the return to visibility of two of the town's heroic ancestors who had presided over legends of early medieval battle. With the recapture of Douai from the Germans in the great Allied offensive of autumn 1918, a mythic narrative of overcoming evil was resumed. Facing the camera, the Allies turn their backs on the supernaturally charged ancestors of this particular French community they have just liberated.

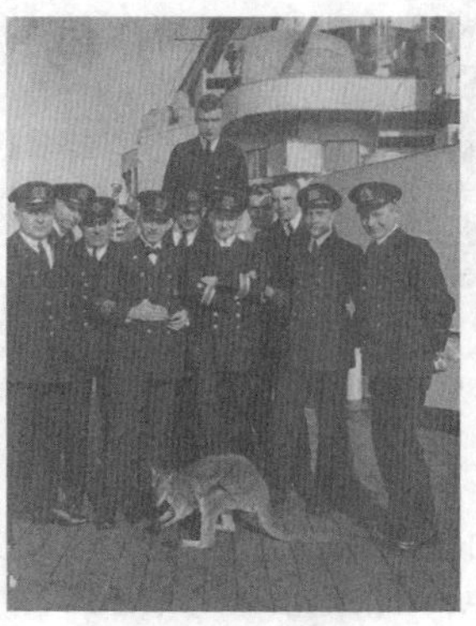

A wallaby mascot

13

Joey the Wallaby was presented to HMS Hood by the people of Fremantle in Western Australia in the spring of 1924 during a world cruise by ships of the Royal Navy. Hood, Repulse and four cruisers set off to show the flag in Africa, Asia, Australia, New Zealand and the Americas. Wherever they called they were presented with keepsakes, starting with an elephant's tusk in Sierra Leone. Joey came on board at Fremantle and was welcomed by some of the ship's principal officers. He ended up in the care of the ship's butcher and was finally deposited in a zoo at the end of the cruise. The world cruise was a publicity venture designed to enhance the Empire's sense of togetherness. Although the presentation of Joey was a populist gesture, it wasn't recognised as such by His Majesty's officers, who thought simply in terms of a traditional group portrait into which Joey had strayed by accident – best overlooked.

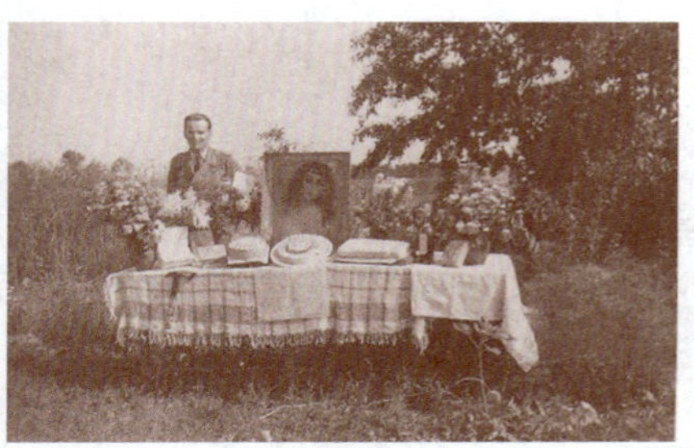

He was 30, according to the inscription on the cake in the centre of the display. The portrait of the sultry young lady who presides over the improvised feast may have been looted, for her style is from earlier in the century. The location, in high summer early in the 1940s, is in the Carpathians, for propped against the table is a ciupaga, one of the painted shepherds' axes that characterise the area and that were sold as keepsakes. The young man's colleagues probably thought of it as an appropriate gift. In summertime on the Eastern Front the going was good for invaders, but come autumn and winter the roads turned into quagmires and the excursion came to a halt.

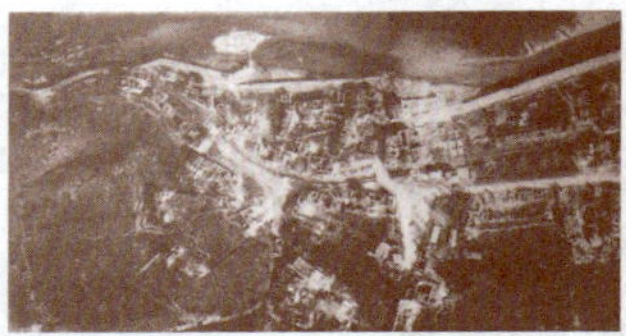 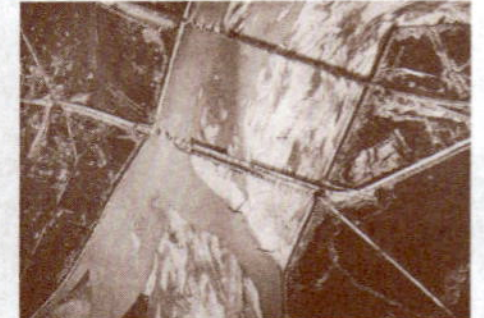

Aerial surveillance photographs from Caproni aeroplanes and battlefield surveillance photograph from the Western Front, c.1917
15

These Alpine surveillance photographs, taken by pilots and observers in Caproni observation aircraft, give an acute sense of panoramic landscape – like an enhanced relief map, they show crags, valley floors, sandbanks and broken bridges. In the Western Front battlefield photograph, the eye of a technocratic God looks down on flat, undifferentiated terrain marked by a chaotic, all-over pattern of cratering, minimal relief and the ghosts of two roads, upon which precise locational coordinates

are numbered in white ink; meanwhile, for those on the ground almost all topographical features have disappeared.

By late 1916 and the beginning of 1917, the aerial photograph had become the single most important system of visual imaging for the military. A forensic understanding of what a reconnaissance photograph disclosed was crucial to military tactics. 'The success of the advance,' wrote GR Sims in 1920, 'depended largely on the preliminary work accomplished by the aero-photographer.' But there was a vested interest in these claims on the part of the new technical cadres on the ground, because as many as 11,000 negatives a week would be made before an important advance.

Coordinated surveillance led to feedback in near real-time as photographs of a battlefield would be shuttled back to intelligence officers and commanders on the ground. Popular magazine *The Great War Illustrated* (17 September 1916, vol. 8, p.22) reported on French photo-surveillance from 'an entire fleet of photographic machines operating continually over the enemies' lines. Each piece of destruction wrought by the French guns was photographed immediately and the developed photograph was closely studied by staff officers. If the picture was not satisfactory, the observing machines went up again.'

That technocratic rationalisation of war through the means of surveillance imaging would grow apace in the 20th and 21st centuries, resulting in true real-time observation within command and control centres by the beginning of the 1990s.

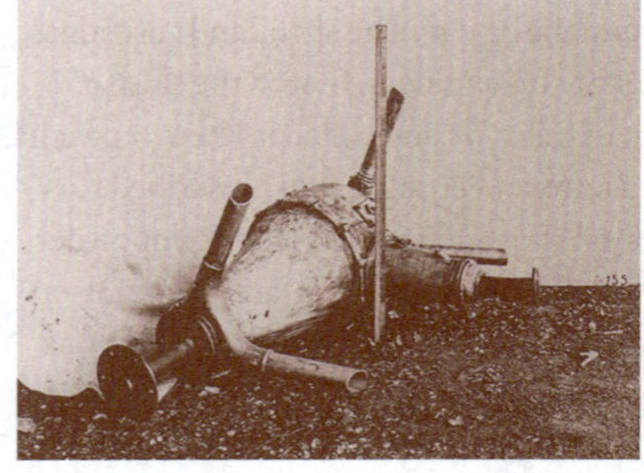

Fragment of a Zeppelin brought down over London, 1916
16

A bloated carcass, this trophy from the air war – a composite of European metal parts given a new symbolic life as an inert enemy – is being measured and displayed. The appearance of the Zeppelin, caught by searchlights as it nosed slowly through the night over London, was as an unnameable nightmare

– a thing full of droning menace, an apocalyptic sign in the sky.
But this steel fragment suggests the pathos of a horse or cow
in rigor mortis, or an African tribal fetish.

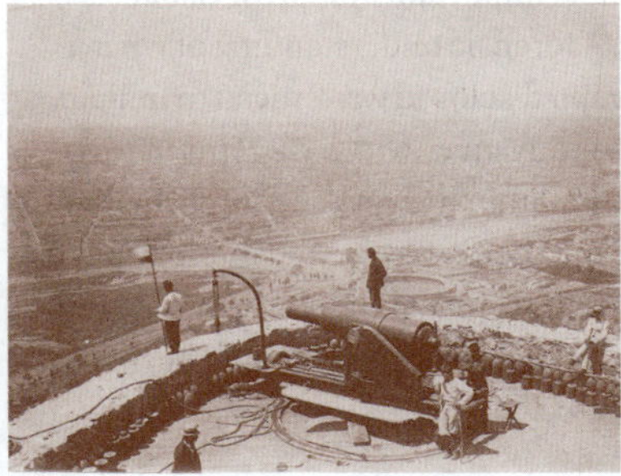

Siege gun
17

Rifled siege guns came into use in the late 1850s. The British
opted for improvements after the debacle of the Crimean War
and asked William Armstrong to develop an effective siege gun.
He came up with a breech loading gun, of the kind on show
here. Shells were sheathed in lead to allow them to grip the
spiral rifling in the barrel. Soft metal also formed a seal so that
there was effective use of the explosive charge. The American
equivalent, used by both sides in the Civil War, was known as
the Parrott rifle, after its inventor RP Parrott.

The gun in this installation seems to be manned by French
troops overlooking an unknown city – possibly in Mexico,
where the French were active between 1860 and 1867. Such a
gun would have been able to command every part of the city,
especially the bullring and the bridge. The shells and cartridges
close at hand suggest a state of readiness. In 1871 the British
introduced a 35-ton gun of this type and called it The Woolwich
Infant. John Ruskin, in a letter of February 1871, described it as
being 'fed with 700-pound shot and 130 pounds of gunpowder
at one mouthful; not at all like the Wapping infants, starving on
a half-chance meal a day'. Ruskin saw such imposing weapons
as emblems of the age.

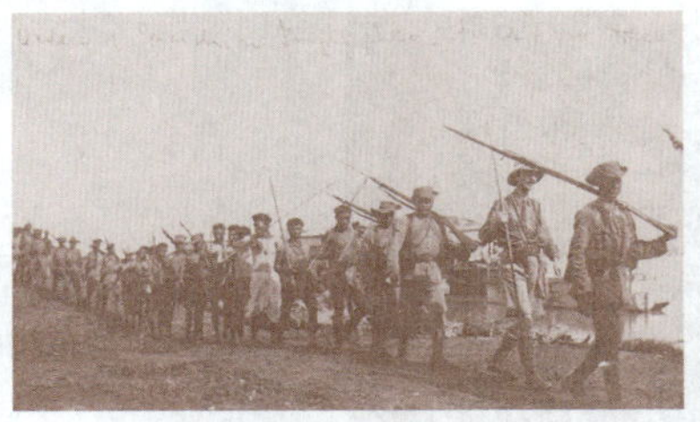

Abor Field Force, 1911
18

Written obscurely in crayon across the sky a caption: Order of
March in Jungle, Abor Field Force Dec 19. As the crayon didn't
register consistently on the shiny surface of the print, the
caption is hard to read and open to debate. The gangly white
man in a pith helmet looks as if he is dressed in an American
outfit in anticipation of Groucho Marx's Captain Spaulding
in *Animal Crackers* (1930). He carries a spear, as do the half-
dozen or so indigenous people in the column, some of them
looking askance at the camera. The uniformed remainder carry
Martini-Henry rifles with fixed bayonets – which would have
made walking in line like this a tricky business.

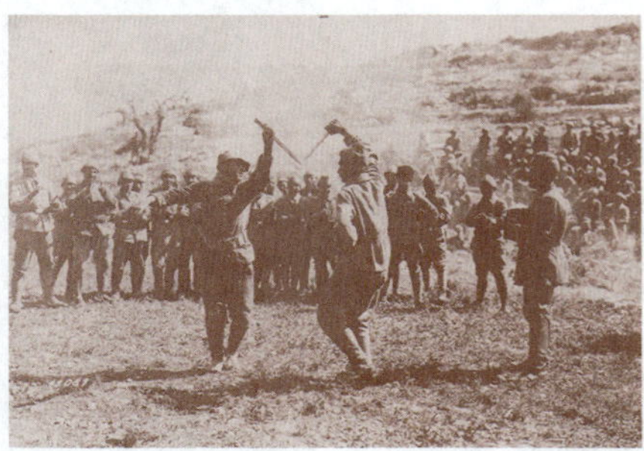

Sword dancing
19

They look like men of the Ottoman Army entertaining
themselves somewhere on an Eastern Front during the war
of 1914–1918. The two men in the foreground are dancing with
bayonets – their blood channels clearly visible. Infantrymen,
by then, wouldn't have had access to swords. Onlookers clap
and gesture in time to the music, played on a hurdy-gurdy.
Ottoman soldiers wore short tunics, somewhat in the style of
their Italian contemporaries. More distinctively, they had fabric
sun helmets called kabalaks, as they do here. One man, just
to the right of centre, wears a fez. The majority wear puttees,
although the musician has leggings. Ottoman soldiers would
have been recruited from many parts of the Near East in
addition to Turkey.

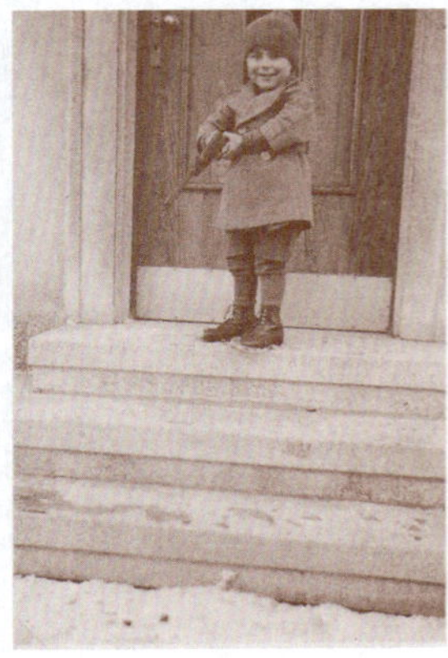

A child on steps
20

He may be three or four years old, playing with a long-barrelled pistol – which he has to hold with both hands, for it is heavy. It is just the sort of substantial thing that a little boy would want to have to hand, irrespective of its function in the real world. Here the child and his gun take their places in a durable still life of tangible matter. The door, for example, with its heavy pine grain and internal frame, has been enhanced by a metal plate to guard against kicking and scratching – against children and dogs, perhaps. The household steps are carefully undercut to shed water, and the doorframe has a serrated edging, asking to be touched. The boy's hat sits tightly on his head and he is very securely encased in boots, socks, double trousers and a sturdy coat.

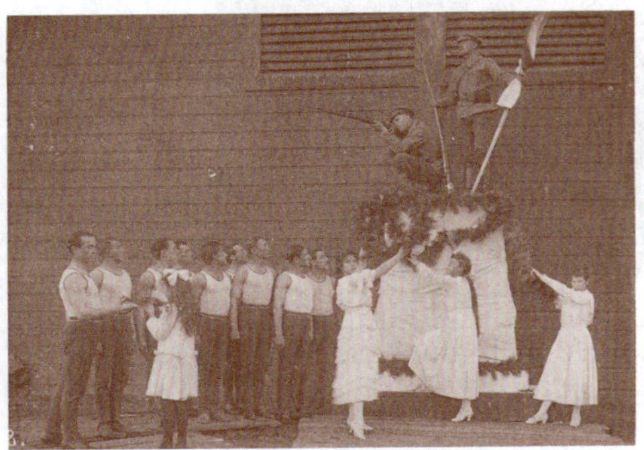

The Czech Legion in Chelyabinsk, second half of March 1918
21

A victory celebration after the Battle of Bakhmach in the Ukraine. Garlanded with branches of fir, a makeshift plinth is topped off with actual – rather than sculptural – riflemen of the 6th Hanacky and 7th Tatransky Rifle Regiments of the Czech Legion. This is a festive ceremony to mark the successful fighting retreat of the Czech Legion, which held at bay a much larger force of two German divisions. White-dressed maidens are showing off the *tableau vivant* of the resolute legionnaires, while athletic Czech colleagues, dressed for gymnastics, raise their gazes up to the riflemen. The successful rearguard action at Bakhmach enabled the Legion to take trains to Chelyabinsk to recuperate and celebrate before continuing on to Vladivostok and homeward shipping.

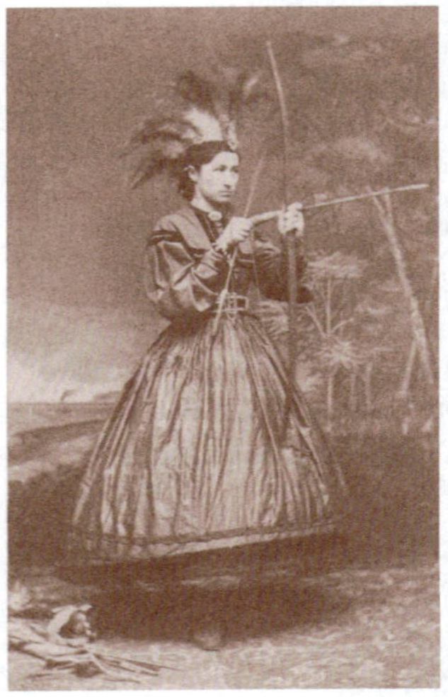

An Amazon
22

She wears a hooped dress characteristic of the 1850s–1860s, and stands in what might be meant as a tropical landscape at the edge of the sea. A small steamer makes a smudge of smoke on the horizon, which would be anachronistic in the context of Amazons – but it was probably the only suitable backdrop available. She is a North American Amazon, as indicated by the feathered headdress, and she may refer to Cesare Pugni's quite famous ballet of the 1840s and 1850s, *La Guerre des Femmes, ou Les Amazones du neuvième siècle*, put on at the Bolshoi in 1852 and performed in London in 1848 as *Les Amazons*. The ballet features Columbus returning from the Americas and stopping by at an island managed by women – from which he is extracted with difficulty by his crew, who are anxious to return home. The ballet starred Mlle Adelina Plunkett, a Belgian dancer and one of the celebrities of the era.

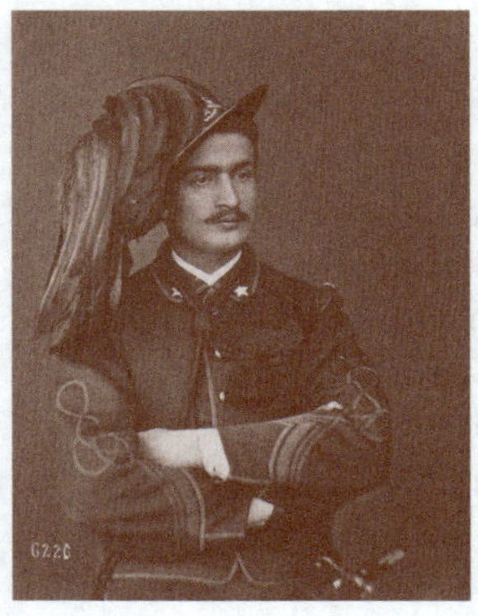

An Italian soldier
23

He is *uno bersagliere*, a crack soldier from a commando unit noted for its lavish costumes and vigorous conduct. In the 19th century *bersaglieri* dressed in blue with red trimmings and wore round hats decorated with black capercaillie feathers. The capercaillie, a creature of pine forests, is noted for its extravagant mating displays. In some habitats it has been hunted to extinction.

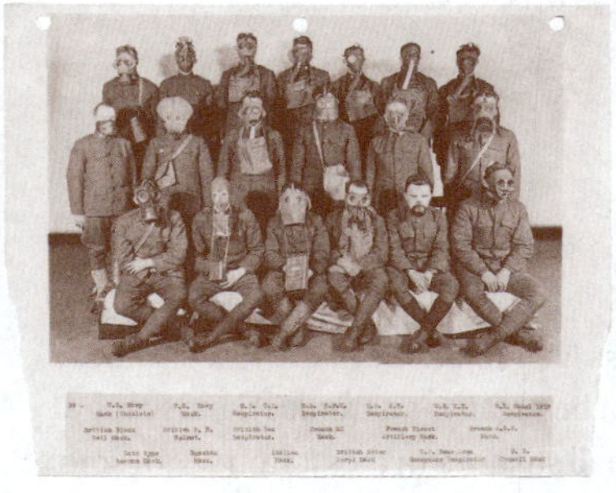

US military's comparative tests of international examples of gas masks, c.1920
24

In the quest to develop effective respirators and gas masks for the US Army, examples of Allied and Central Powers equipment were collected for exhaustive tests. A month before the US entered the Great War in 1917, the Army Medical Department commissioned the Surgeon General to authorise research and the manufacture of 1,000,000 gas masks. The war ended with the momentum to systematically develop ever more technically efficient masks and respirators still intact.

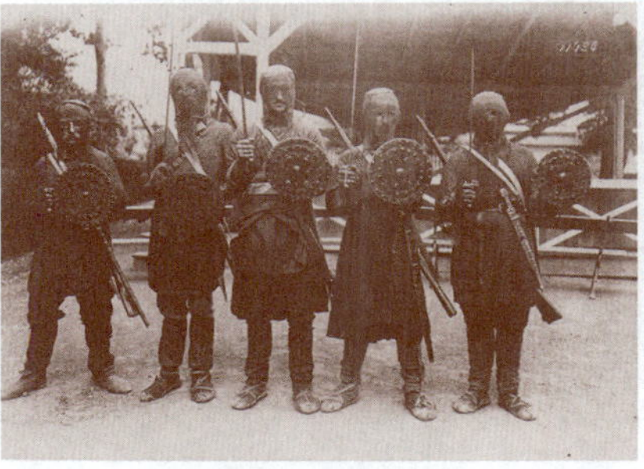

Khevsurian Warriors, Georgia c.1910
25

Western travellers, writers, artists and photographers could be forgiven for their mis-recognition of the Khevsurian warriors as they encountered them in the 19th and very early 20th century. Dressed in chainmail and carrying broadswords, their garments decorated by crosses and icons, they appeared as distant, fusty apparitions of the long-gone Crusaders surviving in an afterlife, like the re-vivified effigies of warriors in Steven Spielberg's *Indiana Jones and the Last Crusade* (1990). Guided by tribal revenge codes, they were, however, no more atavistic than their apparently advanced French contemporaries with their own dreams of revenge against Prussia, biding their time for *La Revanche!*

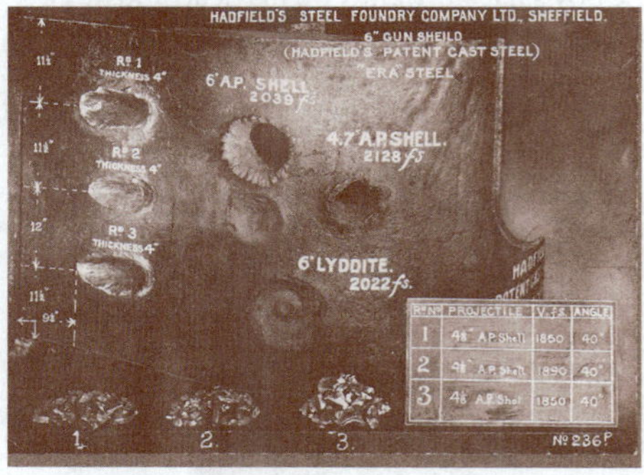

Impact tests on a 6-inch gun shield, Hadfield's Steel Foundry, Sheffield
26

Culture was re-set and re-imagined by metals technology in the course of the 19th century. Retiring from his career as an innovatory mechanical engineer, James Nasmyth collaborated with James Carpenter on the physics of *The Moon: Considered as a Planet, a World and a Satellite* (1874). Nasmyth constructed hyperrealistic plaster models of the moon's cratered surface which were photographed for illustrations for the monograph using the new reprographic technology of the Woodburytype.

The photographs invited a scientific gaze which could speculate on the formation of the lunar craters as products of volcanism or devastating meteorite impact.

Morphologies of fantastic forms – catastrophic changes that threw up weird and traumatic shapes – depended on velocities and the physics of solids. But this dark military-industrial test photograph from the Great War, which measured the results of various shells shot at the same angle onto a cast steel gun shield, evokes Nasmyth's simulation of the cratering of the lunar surface. A variety of British army explosive rounds were itemised in white ink 'after attack', tabulated and the information measured and diagrammatised.

As a barrier, as a metaphorical defensive skin, scarred and pitted, the patent cast steel shield was to protect one of the most powerful and versatile weapons: the BL 6-inch Mk VII naval gun. This piece of ordnance was also used on land as artillery to bombard 'targets in depth' preparatory to high-casualty ground advances such as that on the Somme in the summer of 1916.

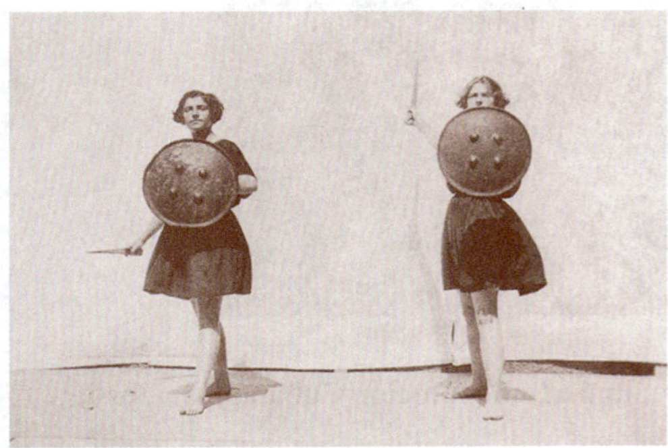

Two armed young women from Bedford Physical Training College, c.1915
27

Photography enables time travel – and what is uncanny in this photograph is the impression that a moment from the deep lost past of Archaic Greece has been restored in all its severe weirdness and is materially present in the bodies on display. Two young women, standing with shields up and short swords ready, plausibly stand in for a couple of Amazons. The photographer convinces the viewer of the veracity of the scene, possibly by the overlit realisation of their outlined bobbed hair.

Placed before the white canvas sheeting, they are on stage. The contemporary vogue for making Greek drama authentic, present and disturbing was the aim of the leading English theorist of the Greek stage, Gilbert Murray. As the world passed into the bloodiest conflict in history, Murray, informed by the ungentle anthropology of James Frazer, continued to re-stage the Classics as ritual spectacles of violence, stirring primal and mythical memories of threat, dismemberment and catastrophe.

At Bedford College they were tutored in a new version of women's bodies – a gymnastic one, cutting up the spaces around and before them with their limbs. The college had been established in 1903 by Margaret Stansfield, who imported Swedish gymnastic techniques into education in the UK. The abrasions on these young women's shields rhyme with the tearing, destructive strategems of the militant Suffragettes. If the implacable vitality of the Amazons had returned, it was now in the service of contemporary female emancipation.

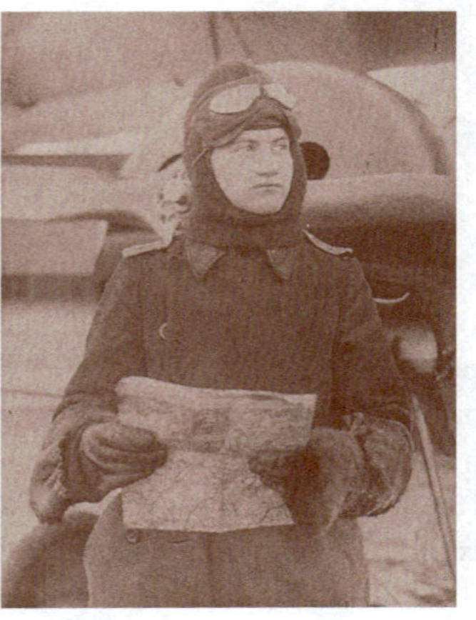

Lt Eberhard von Stapenhorst, winter 1917–1918
28

While massive machine slaughter and abject horror characterised the attritional experience of the deadlocked Western Front, a beatific spirituality informed the faces and bearing of the heroes of the air above the trenches. Lt von Stapenhorst appears to be already translated into a version of Christian ascension. He stands on frozen earth at his airfield in northern France holding a map in his fur gloves which projects roads and rail that he has seen below him; he isn't earthbound and his gaze turns to his left and beyond, above him.

This celestial orientation recalls the narratives assigned to the French pilot Guynemer – on his disappearance, French schoolchildren were advised that he had flown up to heaven. Lt von Stapenhorst is impossibly baby-faced, yet he is nevertheless a killer, attacking defenceless Allied observation balloons. He possesses the most advanced vehicle available to the Central Powers to take him on his ascensional trajectory: the ultra-manoeuvrable Fokker Dr 1 triplane. Here he has the guise of a technological hero-cum-saint; he belongs to the fellowship of aces in von Richthofen's *Luftstreikräfte* Jasta 11 squadron.

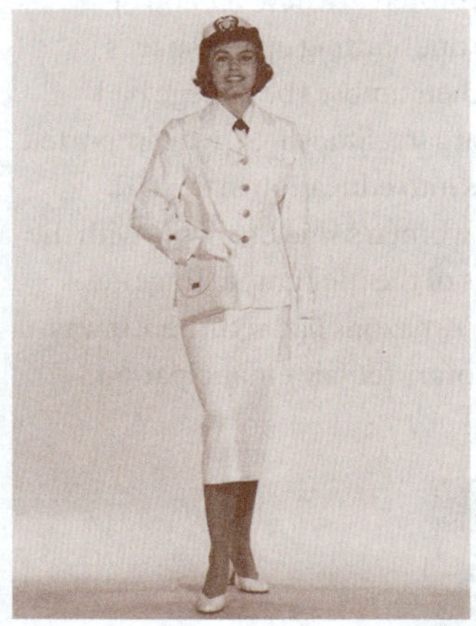

US Navy uniform, 1950s
29

Reciting the innovations engendered by technologies of destruction has been the habit of generations of cultural historians. War has ever been a fulcrum for the inventions of frippery. Fashion, music and the arts have also been invigorated by tumultuous conflicts. This US Navy creation radiates a postwar optimism.

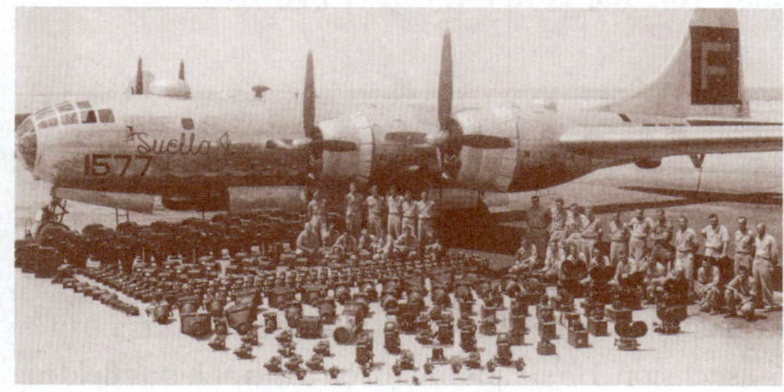

USAAF technical personnel gathered before Super-fortress 44-61577, preparing for Operation Crossroads
30

A near-vertical tropical sun burnishes a polished aluminium B29. Sitting on Kwajalein Island's airstrip in the Pacific is an important military aeroplane known as camera aircraft Suella J, and it is surrounded by arrays of film and still cameras and their operators, drawn up in a rectilinear diamond. Suella J

was dedicated to filming the detonations of atomic weapons under and above Bikini Atoll in July 1946. The cameras are on ornamental martial display like lances, pikes and swords in an armoury or museum, and the test explosions were themselves to be a set piece media spectacle as much as elements in a complex experiment in weaponry.

Less than a year after the atomic bombing of Hiroshima and Nagasaki, Bikini Atoll was to be the site of the fourth and fifth nuclear explosions. On the airstrip to carry out the bomb dropping, the radiological tests and the official filming, and also to carry press representatives and radio broadcasters, together with Suella J were Dave's Dream, Sweet 'N Lola, The Belle of Bikini, Mary Lou, The Angelic Pig and Over Exposed. The B29s were customised with graphic lettering which named them, as had been the practice with US bombers in the Second World War. Suella J uses the decor of faux-dude ranch cowboy/Hollywood script as a font.

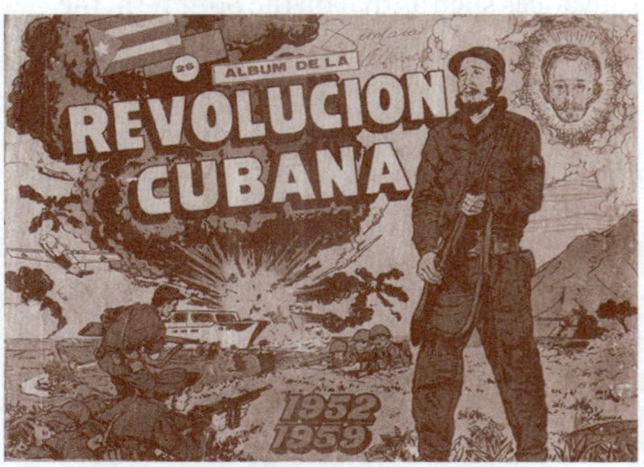

Front cover, album La Revolución Cubana 1952–1959, c.1961
31

The heroic pop cover of a trading cards album promoted by Felices, a Cuban fruit canning manufacturer. The cards and the album, tracing the history of Castro's guerrilla struggle, were aimed specifically at the children of post-revolutionary Cuba. A circuit of exemplary heroes and a reiteration of the history of Cuba's first liberation at the end of the 19th century are established on the cover. To the top right, removed from the present and gazing posthumously from a cloud, is Jose Marti, the leading figure in the Cuban War of Independence, martyred more than 60 years earlier; while to his side, planted in the present, is Fidel Castro, a superhuman figure wearing battle fatigues and carrying a carbine. He rallies his soldiers, who advance towards newly entrenched Yanquis on the Cuban shore, while behind an invading boat has been hit and is exploding.

Given this iconography, the scenario may be as much a
reference to the failed US-sponsored Bay of Pigs invasion as
to Castro's own 1956 landing from the Granma, which was
an attempt to follow the route of Marti's insurgent forces
from Playitas in April 1895. The Cuban graphic artists who
composed the album's cover were using the visual language
of US war comics, a language about to be parasitised by
Roy Lichtenstein.

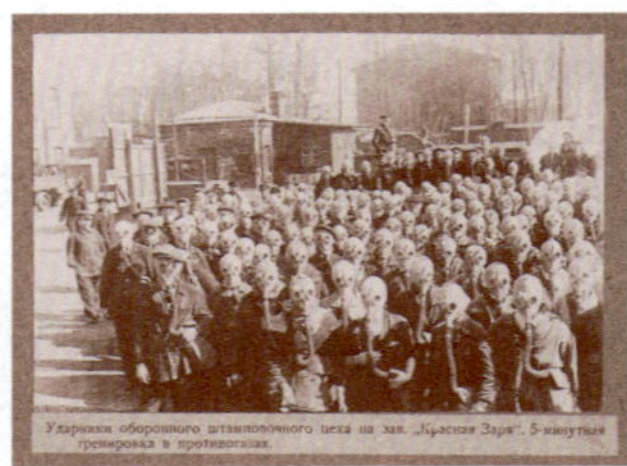

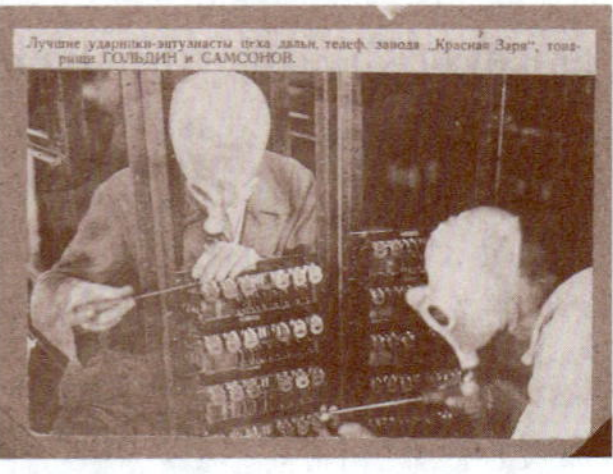

**Leningrad's industrial and technical workers and
students rehearse a gas attack**

33

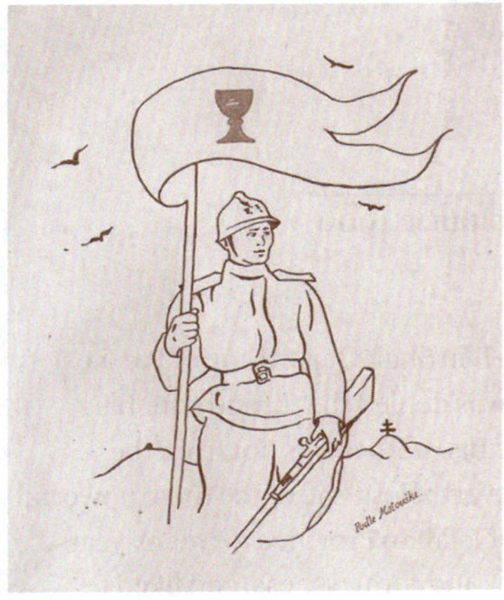

**Rifleman of the Czech Legion carrying a banner with the
symbol of the Grail, 1936**

32

In the afterlife of hermetic signs and symbols, the Holy Grail
is perhaps the most persistent. One strand in Czech culture
suggests the presence of the Grail at the church of Žd'ár nad
Sázavou. Blood-red, it stands on the banner held by a soldier
in a line design at the beginning of a presentational album of
photographs recording the epic of the Czech Legion during
the Great War. The Legion fought to wrest Bohemia and
Moravia from the Austro-Hungarian Empire, joining the
Imperial Russian Army, but following the Bolshevik Revolution
they evacuated home via Siberia and Vladivostock, fighting
Trotsky's Red Army when it attempted to disarm them.

This sequence was soon identified with the foundational
narrative of military epics of the long march home: Xenophon's
Anabasis. The presence of the Grail compounds the aspects
of legend and redemption. A substantial fighting force, the
Legion totalled nearly 70,000 including Jaroslav Hasek, author
of *The Good Soldier Svejk*. The album re-writes the Russian
Civil War as a cavalcade – like a Trans-Siberian rail journey,
with pet bears and frozen corpses and western European
interventionists – soldiers like them, thousands of miles from
home and waiting in train depots.

There are imaginary and fantastic histories as well as actual
ones. The horror of chemical warfare – such as the 'black
smoke' used by Martians in Wells's *The War of the Worlds* (1897)
– was realised in the combats of the Great War.

The protective countermeasure of masks laid down a graphic
symbol of a ghoulish future, suggesting humanity's evolution
into alien beings. In the first image, in a yard outside a
Leningrad factory this depersonalisation has been offset by
a handful of workers choosing to wear their cloth caps over
the top of the mask, asserting some measure of their former
individuated selves. In the second image, at the city's telephone
exchange, student enthusiasm is channelled into maintaining
equipment. From 1932, this photo-reportage of abject and
forbidding alien bodies which are uncannily discovered inside
a security-sensitive technical environment forecasts the
paranoid visions of the Roswell Incident of 1947, recreated
as filmed phantasms in the hoax alien autopsy videos that
circulated in 2006–2007.

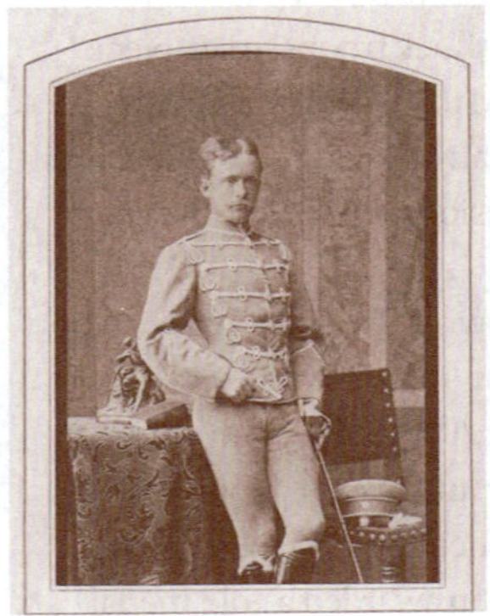

A German hussar

34

He was a German hussar, photographed in a Dresden studio
in the 1870s. The original hussars were Hungarian horsemen,

many of whom quit their homeland to join foreign armies where they served as outriders, raiders and scouts. Eventually the British, French and Germans set up their own hussar units, all of which had a reputation for reckless behaviour. Their uniforms were based on Hungarian originals, featuring jackets ornamented by braid – originally attached to secure bone toggles at a time when buttons were in short supply. The racing colours of the British royal family are based on hussar originals. Hussars appear in Franz von Suppé's operetta of 1866, *Light Cavalry*, in the company of a ballet troupe.

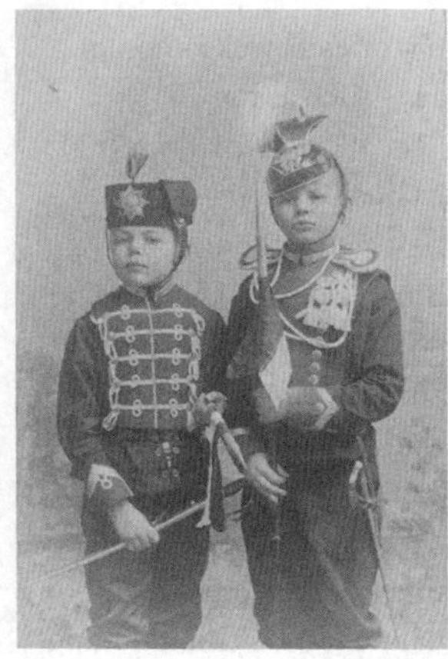

Boy soldiers
35

The Napoleonic wars left an enduring mark on the European imagination. Napoleon's armies were recruited widely and even exotically, sometimes from Eastern Europe – and dressed splendidly. Lancers often came from Poland and made important contributions as shock troops in set-piece battles. Mounted troops continued to be held in high esteem, especially in court circles in Germany. Warriors on horseback made a brilliant and heroic impression on parade.

These two youngsters, from the town of Iserlohn, present themselves as a lancer and a hussar – although the hussar, too, appears to be carrying a lance. They were pictured not long before the Great War by Paul Müsse, a reputable photographer established at Hagener Strasse 2 in Iserlohn, in the west of Germany. He had been awarded a gold medal at Arnsberg in 1903 and a silver at Bremen in 1907. In 1920 he photographed Iserlohn's famous Iron Cross monument, raised in 1816 in honour of Prussia's decisive role in the Battle of Liepzig in 1813 – a huge event where hussars and lancers added to their reputation.

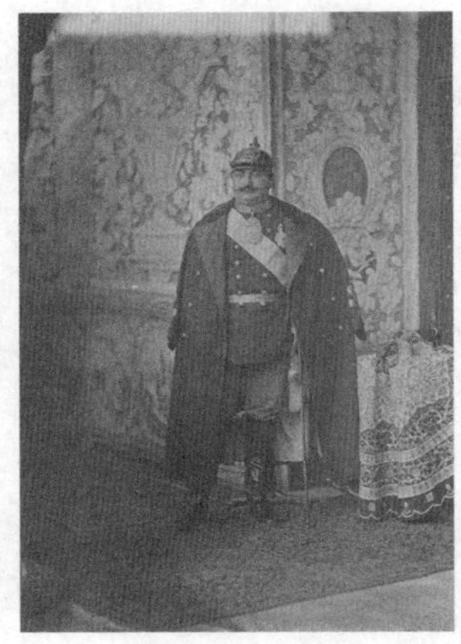

Mass'oud Mirza Zell-e Soltan, c.1900
36

The eldest son of Nasser al-Din Shah Qajar (King of Persia 1848–1896), Zell-e Soltan was denied the throne after his father's assassination since his mother was not from the correct dynasty, but was nevertheless one of the most powerful men of his day. Governor of Isfahan Province for many years, he was famed for his cruelty and ruthlessness, and liked to arrive at his palace on horseback with a brass band to announce his entry. Here he wears a German-style pickelhaube with the emblem of Persia – the lion with the sword. His many honours included:

    2nd class of Order of the Lion and the Sun of Persia
    1st class of Order of the Lion and the Sun of Persia
    2nd class of Neshan-e-Aqdas of Persia
    Knight of the Order of the Star of India
    Knight of the Order of the Black Eagle of Prussia
    Knight of the Order of the Red Eagle of Prussia
    Knight of the Order of the White Eagle of Russia
    Grand Cross of the Legion d'honneur of France
    Exalted Order of Honour of Turkey.

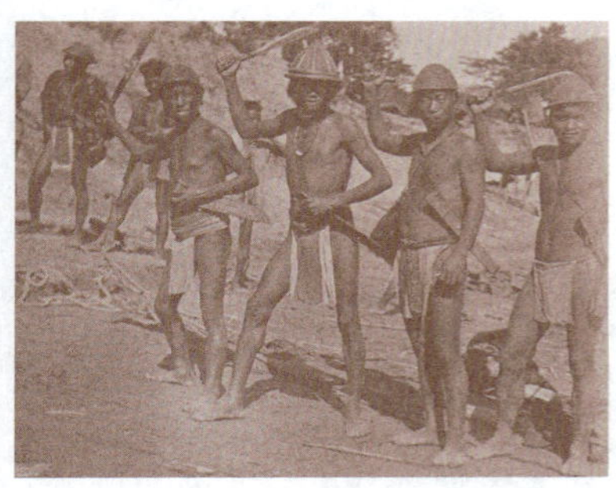

The men of Orchid Island

37

They lived on Orchid Island to the south east of Taiwan, and their descendants still do, even though the island is used as a deposit for Taiwan's atomic waste. Anthropologists today might call them Austronesians. Locally they are known as Yami or Tao. They have a reputation as boat builders and they used to live to a large extent on flying fish, which they caught and dried. Their artefacts are noteworthy, especially helmets of the kind worn by the central figure here. They are made of rattan woven over a coconut fibre material and they were used to deflect cudgel blows in warfare. Knives also featured in Yami culture – talismanic daggers and these longer blades which served as weapons and as tools. The photographer must have asked them to pose in a threatening manner, although not all of them have risen to the challenge, for they were probably just going about their business – there are ropes in the background, perhaps put out to dry. They may not all have been used to the requirements of photographers, although the man in the middle seems to have been quick to see what was expected.

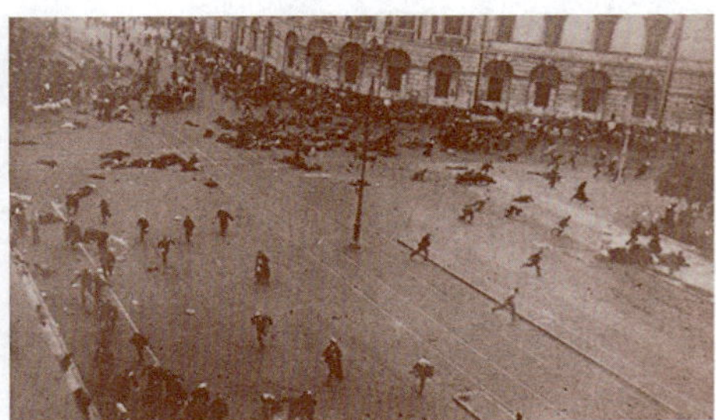

An incident during the July events at Nevsky Prospekt, 9 July 1917

38

A fascinating image of mediated violence and an archetype of the visual imagination of the terrible 20th century in its recording of the turmoil of metropolitan insurrection. Karl Karlovich Bulla, the photographer who took and made this

picture of Bolshevik protesters being machine-gunned by cadets loyal to the Menshevik government directly under his commercial studio, managed to sell hundreds, if not thousands, of copies of this photograph. It took on a special and 'official' existence when it was widely published as an emblem of the Soviet Revolution in the history book *Proletarskaia revoltsiia v obrazakh I kartinkh* in 1926.

From the beginning its graphic aspects compelled viewers' attraction and close study as a fascinating souvenir of an episode during the hinge of history. This print was collected and put into an album by an unknown member of the Czech Brigade, probably a year or more after the event had taken place, while he was in Russia fighting against the newly established Communist government. The written caption, 'The crowd surprised by fire from Bolshevik armoured cars', betrays the anti-Bolshevik sympathies of the album's compiler: according to his narrative the historical victims of the massacre are repositioned as the aggressors.

Within a few years the image had acquired a vast visibility that was internationally influential. Soviet director Sergei Eisenstein would use it to recreate the shootings for his film *October*, directing his camera from a slightly different angle but from the same building Bulla had used. Francis Bacon owned at least two versions of the Bulla photograph. Perhaps it was its power to go beyond conventional renderings of the human – to be bafflingly unintelligible, strange and primal – that moved him. Bacon's critic John Russell writes of 'the famous photograph of July 1917... [which] shows the people of Petrograd in every variety of bizarre posture as they run for shelter, throw themselves flat across the Nevsky Prospect, and in general abdicate the sedate procedures of everyday life in the street.' He adds: 'It is true that this photograph had in its day a real pioneer significance, and that Bacon prizes it for the strange kinship between this panic-stricken populace and the distortions of cave painting.'

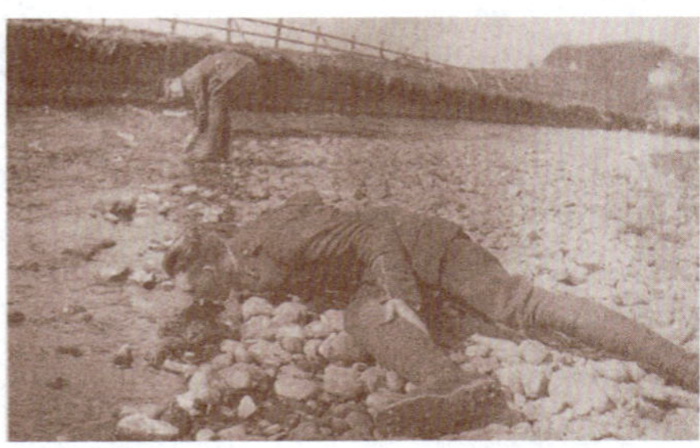

British officers, World War I

39

God advised Gideon in his struggle with the Midianites and Amalekites, who were 'like grasshoppers for multitude' (Judges VII). At the same time, God was wary of Gideon and his Israelites, for he knew that a comprehensive victory would lead to insufferable self-importance. There had already been a lot of trouble with backsliding, forgetfulness and general lack of piety. His advice to Gideon was to reduce the size of his army. 'Ask for volunteers to stand down, and if that fails – as it will – set the remainder a test. Tell them to go to a nearby stream and to drink from it. Some will go down on their hands and knees to drink and others will lift water in their cupped hands and lap like dogs. Select the second lot to make up your army.' Only 300 came through the test from the many thousands who made up the original army. God's idea was that with such a handful of men everyone would see the inevitable victory as a miracle – God's doing, in other words.

Gideon attacked by night, and things turned out as predicted, 'and all the host ran, and cried, and fled'. Anyone who has ever drunk from a stream will have wondered how exactly Gideon's aptitude test was carried out and why it took the form it did.

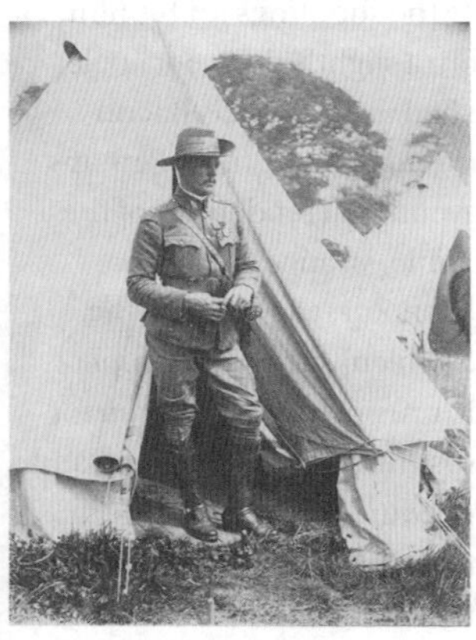

Farrier-Major William James Hardham VC
40

Hardham was in the 4th New Zealand Contingent attached to the British Army in South Africa. On 28 January 1901 his section was attacked by Boer guerrilla fighters and forced to retreat. One of Hardham's men, Trooper McCrae, was wounded and his horse killed. Hardham rode out to him under Boer fire, dismounted and gave him his horse. He then ran by his side, still under enemy fire, until he had seen him out of danger. For this act of courage he was awarded the Victoria Cross in July 1902. In this picture he wears the medal, as well as unusual speckled epaulettes which distinguished New Zealand forces from Australians, who wore identical outfits at the time.

The Victoria Cross, introduced in 1856–1857 at the end of the Crimean War, gave rise to a culture of gallantry. For the awards to be made records had to be kept and exploits recounted.

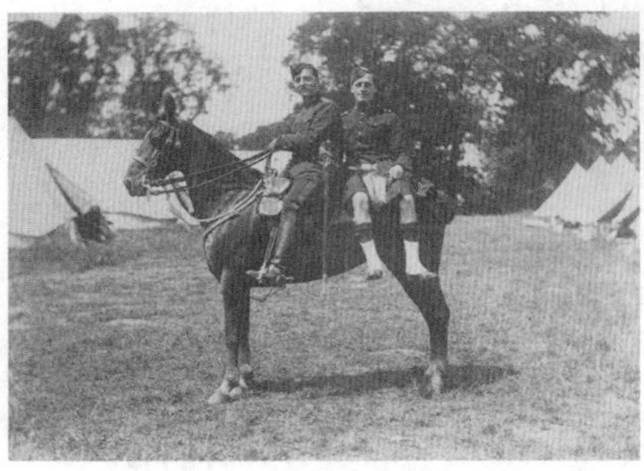

Two men on a horse
41

The Scottish soldier holds what looks like straw rope in his left hand, maybe for security's sake. How on earth did he get up there unaided, for it is a substantial animal? Perhaps there was a scheme afoot to send pictures home to show entertaining times in camp – with a loading ramp offstage. The soldier was also there by grace of the cavalryman's expertise, for the horse holds its position not out of good nature but because of its training. That piece of ironwork, for example, is a Liverpool bit, a curb bit used to provide leverage in the horse's mouth, and in widespread use in the cavalry. The halter tie rope, cunningly wrapped, is another sign of expertise in horse management.

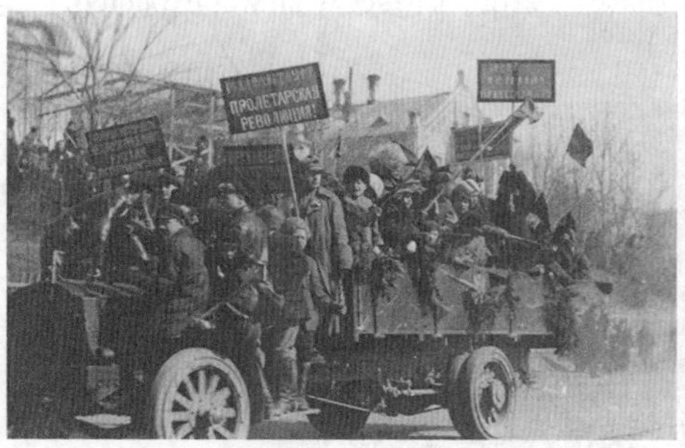

A Bolshevik truck carrying armed volunteers and Red militia, winter 1918–1919
42

They travelled in militarised civilian trucks at headlong speed and dealt ruthlessly with any obstructions – this was a primary secret of their messianic insurgency – and by June and July they had overrun key cities. The shock of ISIL/IS/ISIS's advance across Syria and Iraq in the summer of 2014 was partly a disbelief at their rapidity and the lack of any kind of dynamic response from their opponents. Blitzkreig was rewritten for postmodern times.

One of the most striking technical factors that made itself felt from the beginning of the Great War was the pressing into service of motor transport to shift substantial numbers of infantry to the front line – by buses and taxis if necessary, as with the French at the close of the first week in September 1914 bringing reservists up from Paris to the Battle of the Marne. The flexible mobility of the motor changed the nature of war and time.

The fur-wearing, heavy-coated civil war insurgents in this photograph, a year into the Bolshevik seizure of power in Russia, are crammed into a goods truck with drop sides. They cling to the running boards and mudguards, but they are crucially transported by their own messianism and their adherence to the released energies of Bolshevism. The drama of announcing by brandished banner and flag their conviction and their cause at speed (the lettering of the central sign in the photograph declares the proletarian revolution) would be repeated in the black flags of ISIL/IS/ISIS borne aloft in their flying columns across the Syrian and Iraqi deserts. Similarly, the faces and expressions of the Bolsheviks are transfigured in the apocalyptic moment.

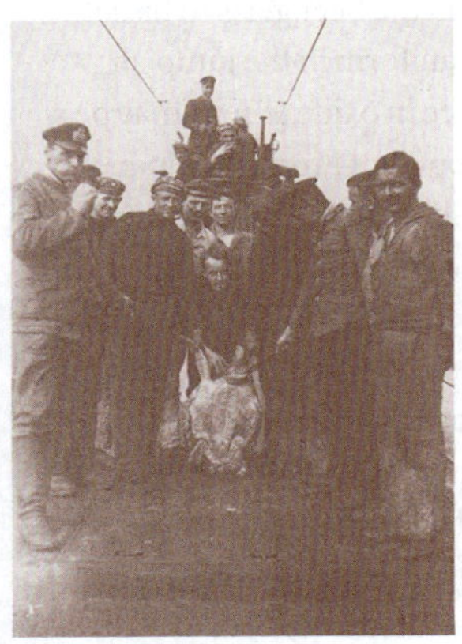

U-boat diet

43

German submarines operated in the Mediterranean and in the Caribbean, where they were refuelled by special ocean-going submarine tankers. The crews lived on rye bread and hard sausage, and drank water provided by the ship's condensers. Fresh turtle would have made a very welcome addition to their diet. It must have been a lucky event, worth recording. Many of

the crews were eaten in their turn by seagulls, who had a liking for human eyes. For a good account of life under the ocean wave during the Second World War see Wolfgang Ott's *Sharks and Little Fish* (1957). Ott claimed to have been in U-372.

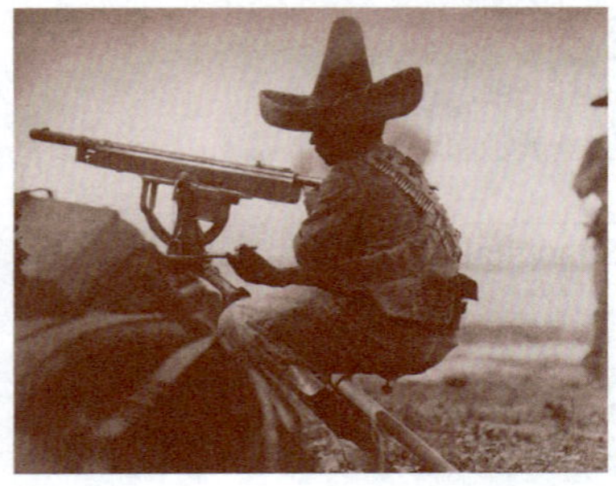

A machine gunner in the forces of Emiliano Zapata or Pancho Villa, Mexico, c.1914

44

The schematic silhouette, the contrast of dramatically hatted figure and a plain ground, the conjunction of projecting automatic weapon and peasant male body, stands at the beginning of the iconography of 20th century heroic insurgent action genres. The Mexican Revolution of 1911–1919 was spearheaded by warlords Zapata and Villa: both seized on the revolution in rapid-firing – mostly US – weaponry at the close of the 19th century to give their troops advantage. This bandolier-festooned soldier, squatting on the seat of his standard tripod-mounted M1895 Colt-Browning, is wisely raising the gun's barrel – it had a tendency to shoot low and spatter the ground in front of its target, earning the soubriquet of 'the potato digger'. Relatively portable, belt-fed with 7mm Mauser bullets and air-cooled, its gas-operated repeating mechanism could fire 400 rounds a minute: the Latin-American world discovered at the same time as the European one that wartime slaughter could be mechanised and automated.

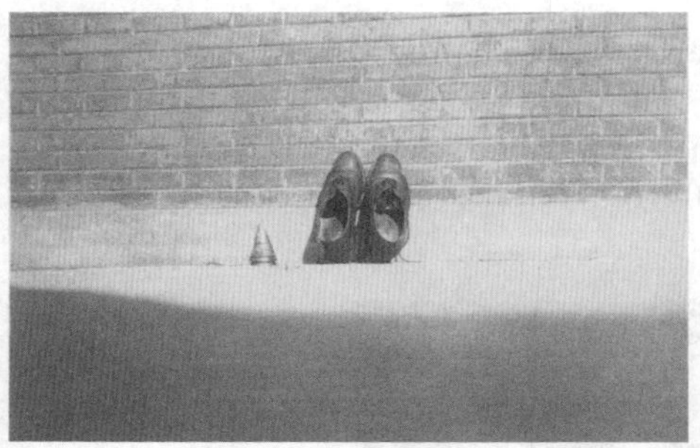

Shoes and a shell cap, Shanghai
45

WH Auden and Christopher Isherwood went to China early in 1938. They had been commissioned to write a travel book and opted for China, then under attack by the Japanese. The book, called *Journey to a War*, was published in 1939, with a text largely by Isherwood and photographs by Auden. Both reporters took a dispassionate approach to whatever it was that came their way. In one sonnet an embassy event is described with attention to lawns, cultured flowers and 'the conversation of the highly trained'. The text goes on: 'The gardeners watched them pass and priced their shoes.'

Isherwood's own Chinese shoes, which were too small, caused him great distress on the road from Hong Kong to Macao. Isherwood invoked small things and everyday experience. On 29 April in Hankow they witnessed a Japanese air raid: 'Presently a shell burst close to one of the Japanese bombers; it flared against the blue like a struck match.' Auden, known as Au Dung on his visiting cards, introduced his cast of characters as representatives. Robert Capa, for instance, who was with them in China, is simply introduced as Press Photographer. They saw themselves to some degree as mere recording machines who remarked on events without choosing to explain or to take sides.

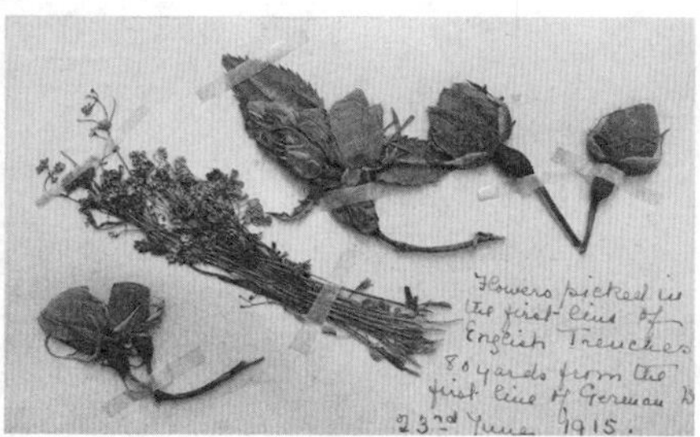

Flowers picked in no man's land, Western Front, 23 June 1915
46

It was an unusually warm spring and early summer in 1915. In the disturbed, shelled soil between the new trench systems, seeds had germinated and were growing in clusters.

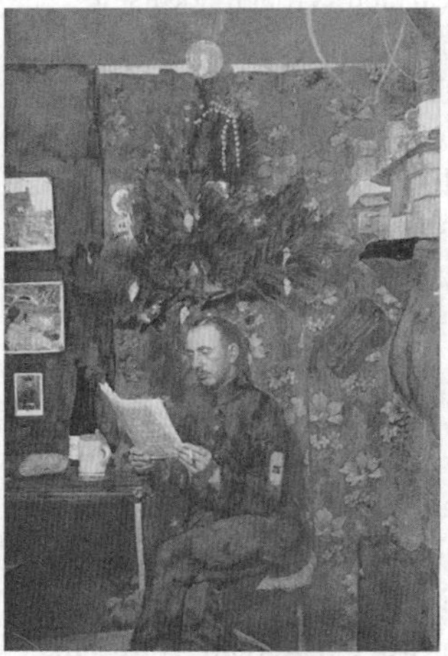

Sebastian Geiger at ease
47

In 1914 some Germans, such as Sebastian Geiger who is shown here, looked forward to encounters with French art and culture – represented here by extravagant floral wallpaper. He reflects on Franco-German differences embodied in the *Steinkrug* close to his right hand and the beer glass to his left. He has overpainted his own plain uniform in the lumpish greys of Manet or Cézanne. The tree in oxide greens may be a German motif in contrast to that opulent French wallpaper, but it too has been handled in the loose style of Manet and some other Impressionists. On the wall in that little gallery he appears simply as a German soldier under a quintessentially French scene, of the kind very much admired by the great Max Liebermann. In the remaining image German troops walk through a French townscape. He may only have been no. 286 but he amused himself to good effect in a subtle arrangement that refers back to Manet's portrait of Emile Zola (1868) but which would also have been appreciated in 1914.

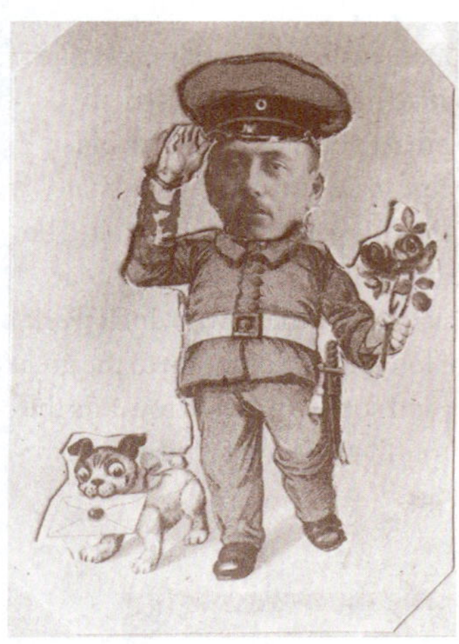

**Unknown Czech artilleryman, photomontage
self-caricature c.1915**
48

Comic caricature drove key elements in the visual cultures
of the Great War. This Czech soldier incorporated a portrait
photograph of himself into a chromolithograph caricature
of a soldier of the Central Powers, a grave-faced and squat
mannequin walking forward, saluting and holding a bouquet
of flowers, accompanied by an equally squat comic dog with a
sealed envelope in its mouth. Presumably in the act of greeting
a beloved or family member, his melancholy face exudes an air
of stone-faced inexpressivity rather than presenting an image
of the bearer of festivity.

In this respect, the photomontage anticipates that embodiment
of the anti-heroic characterised as a sort of martial blankness:
The Good Soldier Svejk. Although finally published as a comic
novel in 1923, Jaroslev Hasek had first outlined Svejk as 'The
Idiot of the Company' in 1911, in a contribution to graphic artist
Josef Lada's satirical journal *Caricatures*. Lada developed a
collaboration with Hasek through his drawings of the simpleton
Svejk for that 1923 publication.

This photomontage soldier steps out to greet the world
with festive kitsch props – flowers, a pug dog – which are
in themselves prefabricated graphic signs that parallel
Svejk's verbal clichés in the face of authority. An unbearable
pathos stems from a tension between the heavily codified
sentimentality of the comic bearing of the soldier and his
voided deadpan facial expression, a pathos so bleak it veers
towards nihilism.

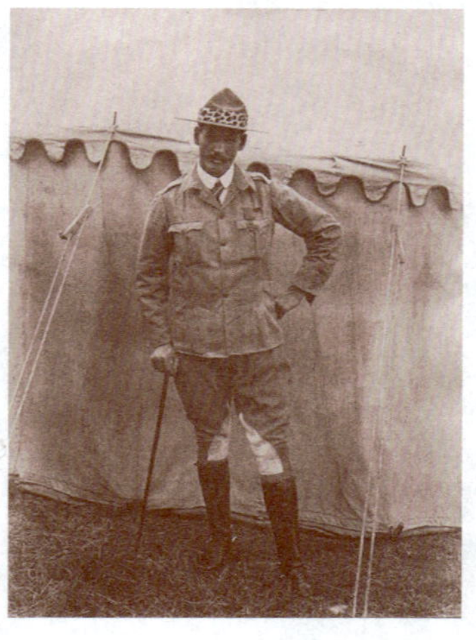

Corporal John James Clements VC
49

On 24 February 1900, Corporal Clements was badly wounded
near to the settlement of Strijdenburg in South Africa. He
was up against five Boers, who called out to him to surrender.
Although shot through the lungs, Clements charged them,
wounded three with his pistol and got them all to surrender.
With the aid of two other companions he took them in. For this
he was awarded the Victoria Cross. At the time he was serving
with Rimington's Guides, a crack unit of light horsemen whose
job it was to carry out night actions and to take prisoners for
questioning. The unit, set up by Major MF Rimington, was
recruited from South Africans able to speak Afrikaans and
indigenous languages. They were popularly known as the
Catch-'em-Alive-Os and as the Night Cats, and sometimes as
Rimington's Tigers on account of their leopardskin hatbands.
The South African or Boer War of 1899–1902 was notable for
skirmishing and for acts of heroism.

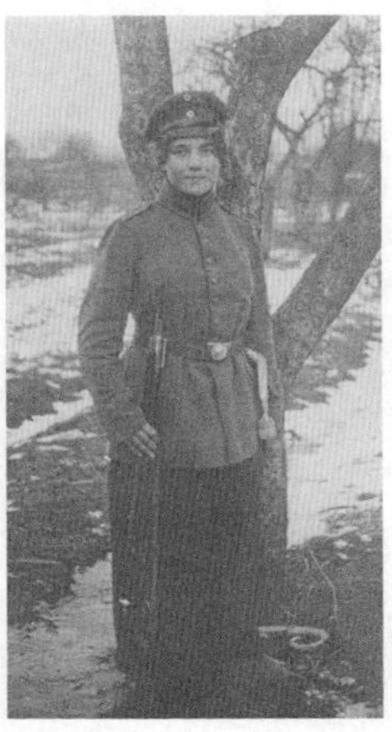

She wears a German officer's *Schirmmütze* (peaked cap). Caps like this, with the chinstrap fitted over the peak, date from 1914–15. The great air ace von Richthofen sometimes appears in such a cap, stylishly crumpled. Her coat, with flashes on the collar and eight buttons (one hidden by the belt buckle) is also a German model. It is late winter, or at least a period of thaw, to judge from the state of the ground. She is dressing up, perhaps for a suitor who owns the camera and the rifle – which she is holding dangerously close to her right breast. She might be at an event, for she also holds a tasselled cap and has put down an odd serpentine crook at the base of the tree. Is she Eve in the Garden, tempting a young military Adam in an army of occupation?

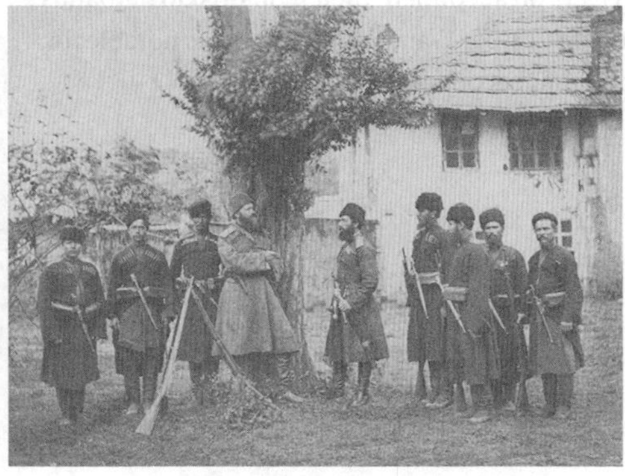

There were several different types of Cossack, but these appear to come from the Kuban grouping – named after a river and region between the Black Sea and the Sea of Azov. They are armed with single-shot Berdan rifles that were standard issue to the Russian army between 1870 and 1891. They carried paper cartridges in elaborate breast pockets, and bayonets in scabbards attached to their belts. In this instance, two small units have met to confer and to feature in a group portrait. The soldiers attached to the more imposing man in the grey coat make an orderly row, in contrast to the others, who don't work in unison. Two in the group of four pay no attention to the great event, and look with curiosity and some suspicion towards the camera. They are a disorderly outfit who have failed even to replenish their stock of cartridges.

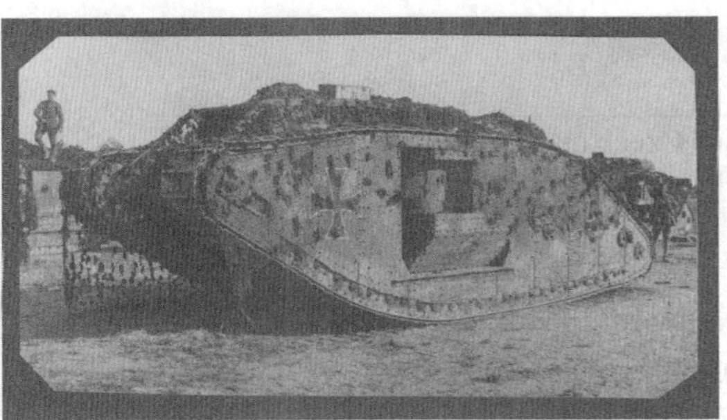

This British Mark IV female tank was captured in December 1917 and Germanised by the addition of Iron Crosses at the front and back of the side armour. The chalk inscription '1918' and the light dress of the men indicates that the vehicle was probably photographed in the spring of that year, and close to the front line – as the camouflage netting served to hide the tank from air reconnaissance.

British tanks were produced and used in male, female and hermaphrodite versions. The male tanks were equipped with two 6-pounder guns (in sponsons to the left and right of the vehicle respectively) and three .303 Lewis machine-guns (two in the sponsons and one at the front). The female tanks were armed with five .303 Lewis machine-guns in sponsons, while the hermaphrodites had a gun and a machine-gun in one sponson and two machine-guns in the opposite sponson, together with a machine-gun at the front.

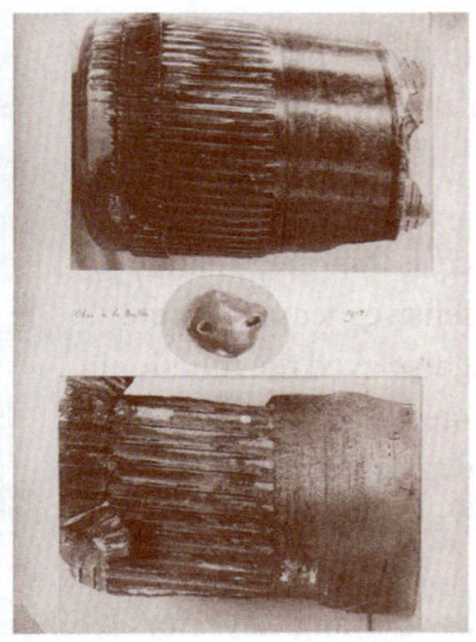

Fragments of shell casing fired from Big Bertha

53

Photography displays the fascinating sheen and patterning of discarded military technologies and turns them into battered, archaic, enigmatic fetishes which could pass for archaeological fragments like Roman drainpipes. These German shell casings were collected by a Frenchman in 1918 and had been fired from a large howitzer designed by Krupp's Fritz Rausenberger – the *Wunderwaffe* (wonder-weapon) *Dicke Bertha* (Big Bertha). These French photographs of a vanquished enemy technology, tamed but still spectacular with a forbidden allure, resemble crime scene documentation. The embellishment of the residues of killing technologies in their own afterlife has included their domestication and customising as umbrella stands or, more often, as souvenirs for the mantlepieces of the victors.

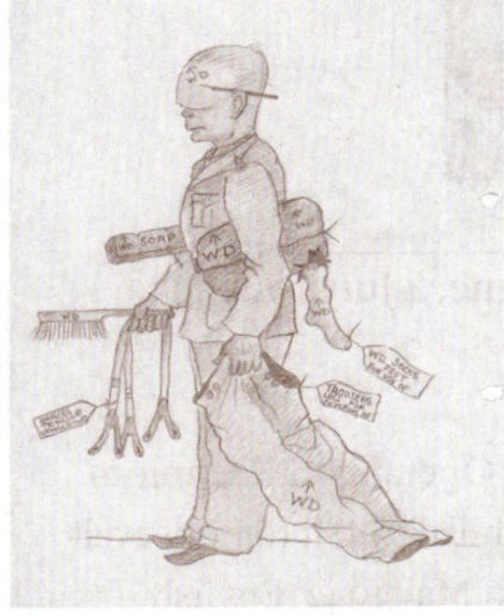

Colour pencil drawing of a British soldier, c.1943

54

Like millions of others in National Service (for which every able-bodied male between the ages of 18 and 41 had to register in 1939) this man's body belongs to the War Department of the British state. A subdued, absurd officer, he trails his uniform and other pieces of kit and clothing accessories. This tattered spectacle positions him as a modernised variant of the irregular soldiers and bandits in Jacques Callot's 17th century engravings – protagonists who are walking piles of rags.

The torn brown paper parcel under his arm, held together by string, scatters socks tagged with the War Department's monogram. Even his forehead bears that stamp of state possession, next to the pencil with which he has been drawn. A huge bureaucracy directed the lives and deaths of such conscripted soldiers: they had entered an over-administered universe which was to become the chief topic of English imaginative literature dealing with the Second World War – including the not-so-secret narratives of Evelyn Waugh and Anthony Powell in their serio-comic accounts of wartime experience.

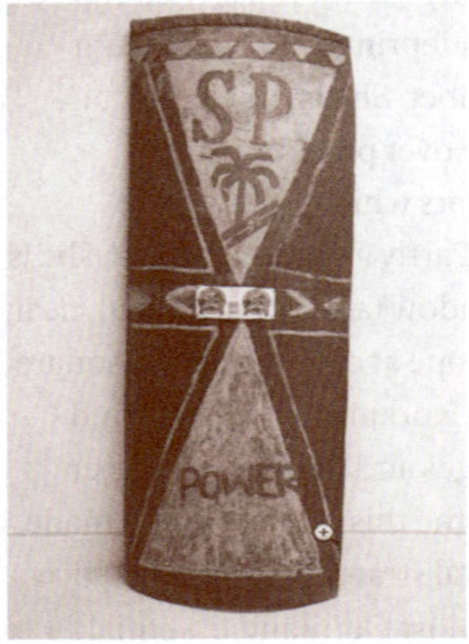

New Guinea Highlands Shield

55

The association between beer and fighting is not just an occidental phenomenon. In the Western Highlands of New Guinea getting drunk and perpetuating the endless cycle of revenge skirmishes is part of the regular fabric of life. Some groups and clans identify themselves with reference to a particular brand of beer – in this shield, South Pacific lager is the stated preference. The shield was most likely made in the Wahgi Valley sometime in the early 1990s. Most of the shields would have a feather ornament stuck on the top, just as the humans do.

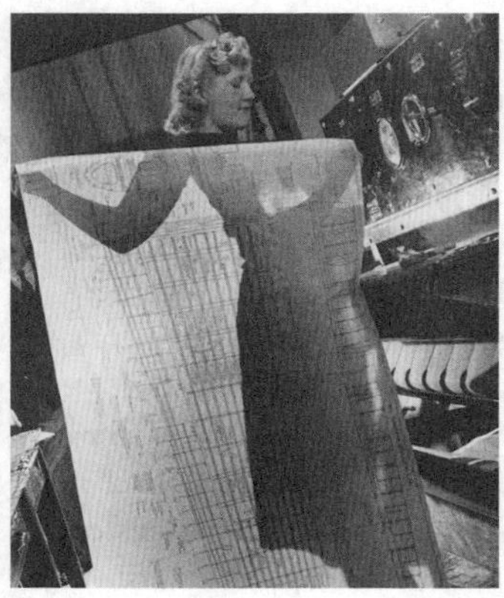

Worker in the drawing office of Avro Co, Yeadon, Yorkshire, c.1942

56

She is the embodiment of modernity – a fashionably coiffured young Yorkshire woman holds a blueprint overlay of a wing section for an Avro Lancaster bomber. She is a mechanical bride, her body cast as a silhouette over precisely drawn versions of the metal struts and spars which would give a structure to actual aircraft wings. Partly a shadow herself, she is in the Avro aircraft company's 'shadow factory' at Yeadon, near Leeds – the largest building in Europe at over 1.5 million square feet. She has 17,500 colleagues, all working in concentrated shifts, under a roof which has hedges and fields on its upper side to act as camouflage. By the time this photograph is made, the Avro 'shadow factory' was a vital strategic asset for British Bomber Command's offensive against Germany, essential to the bombing of engineering plants at Frankfurt and Cologne, but vulnerable to Nazi raids.

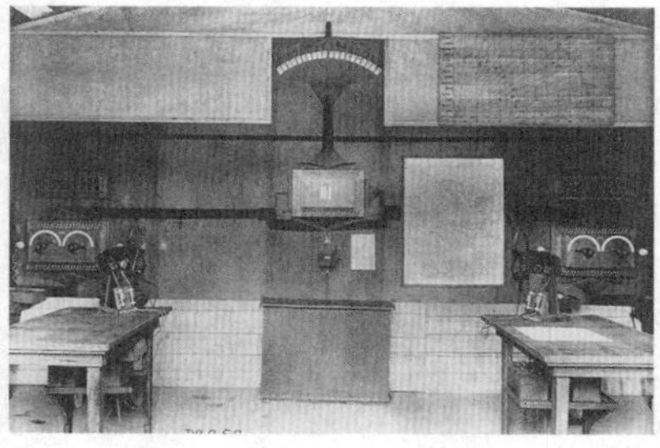

Room, Defence of Paris headquarters, c.1917

57

The disembodied freedom of wireless would change everything as the Great War progressed, but this photograph displays the moment just before that transformation. The room is temporarily empty of human bodies and is populated by assertive circuitry, ducts and the symmetries of electromechanical warfare, which are drawn out across wooden walls.

Control and response centres, such as this one in Paris monitoring and co-ordinating defensive measures, were entirely new types of building that displayed the functioning hearts of the modern industrial state at war. Such command systems held armies together, directed their movements and predicted targets; but they were all too often inadequate.

On the top right hand of the photograph, angled vectors are described on a wall diagram, mirroring the decorative fountain of numbered wiring that rises rigidly towards the roof. In the wake of the war, ex-serviceman and Cologne Dadaist Max Ernst would mimic such electromechanical diagrammatic forms as figurations of the postwar absurd; so too would Marcel Duchamp. By the 1920s, electromechanical hardware took on totemic presence and could become threateningly anthropomorphic, for example, the *Moloch-Maschin* which is crucifying its human operator who works feedback controls in Fritz Lang's *Metropolis* (1927).

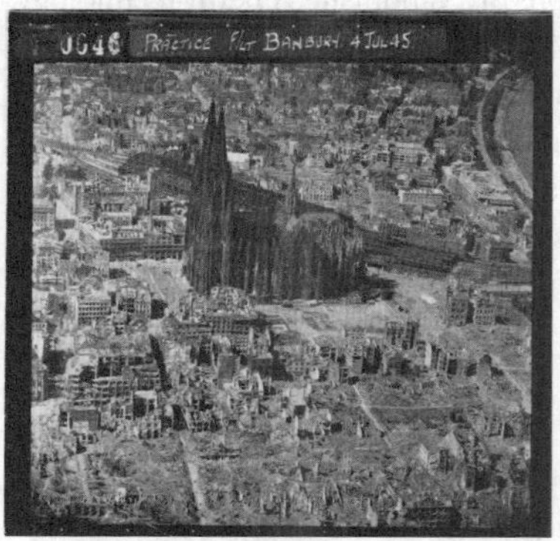

The cathedral and ruins of Cologne, 4 July 1945

58

A thousand British planes mounted Operation Millennium – the first 'mass air attack', as Churchill called it to Roosevelt – on Cologne during the night of 30–31 May 1942. English poet WH Auden had visited Cologne before, in May 1929, but in 1945 he arrived at the city in US military uniform, sent to the defeated Germany by the US Army Air Force's Strategic Bombing Survey to assess the effects of the Allies' aerial bombardment.

On 4 July 1945, the same summer Auden surveyed the ruins, Flight Lieutenant Banbury flew a Mosquito photo-reconnaissance plane over the city, documenting its vistas of ruins as a practice flight. Photograph plate number 0646 was centred on the cathedral – the May 1942 bombing of which Nazi newsreels had called the work of terrorists and barbarians. In Banbury's photograph the streets of Cologne have already been cleared of debris and wreckage by *die Trümmerfrauen* (the rubble women) who, in the absence of menfolk, were set to work to clean up the ruins.

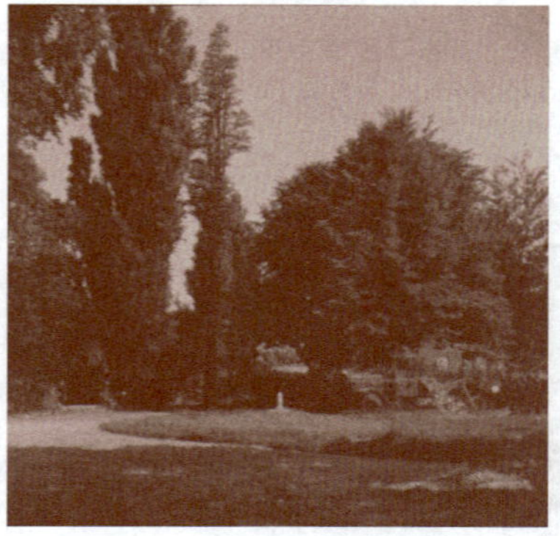

German armoured vehicle camouflaged in French parkland, c.1940
60

Death was motorised during the fall of France, and here a heavily camouflaged Wehrmacht truck, strewn with netting and foliage, sits temporarily in summer sunlight in the driveway of a French country house by a centred ornamental urn with flowers. A picture taken by the Agfacolor process, whose softness renders the coloured world into a powdery, pictorial spectacle.

In the hands of the *Propagandakompanie* photographers, Agfacolor gave a peculiar life to the Nazi conquest of Europe. It managed to harmonise landscapes of combat – of flame and destruction – into a particular melancholic genre-dream of Western art: the elegiac, where tragedy exists but is mitigated by aestheticised natural scenography, in this case a rococo park. Those dusty, settled, luminous atmospheres and auras of turn-of-the-century Autochrome colour process were carried forward in the meanings conferred on things pictured by Agfacolor. Colour, here, is atomised.

Even as the photo was being made, Agfacolor was being pressed into service for the Nazi film industry, which at first went back on the kitsch lost world of the 18th century in movies such as *Die Goldene Stadt* (1941). As unparalleled horror and violence fell across Europe, such idylls carried powerful countervailing sentiments. The operetta might still be staged, but sinister reminders kept intruding at the edges of vision, as the Opel Blitz 3 or Vomag 8LR truck does here. Like the peaceful woodland glade where Christian Diestl is gunned down at the conclusion to Irwin Shaw's epic novel of the Second World War, *The Young Lions* (1948), this is a deadly pastoral.

Forty years later, this conjunction of Nazi military vehicle and the rococo classical landscape would function as a template for Scottish artist Ian Hamilton Finlay when he presented a blunt

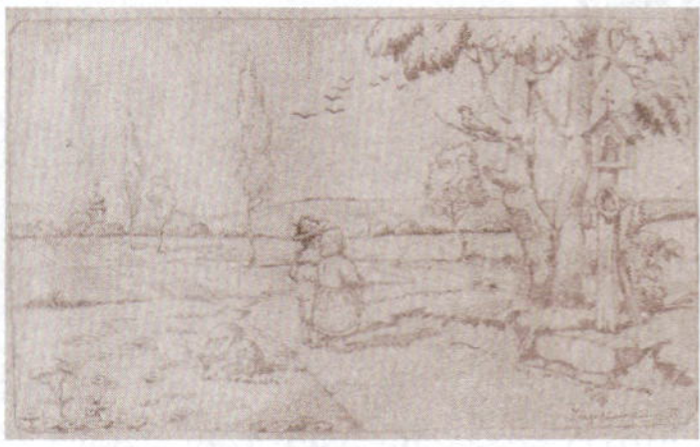

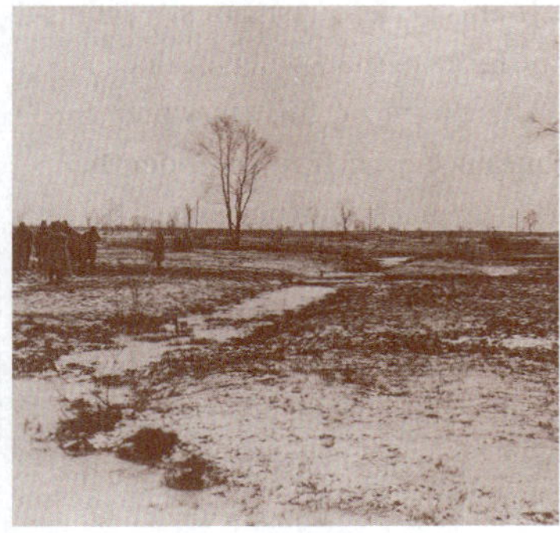

Idyllic kitsch landscape drawing contrasted with a photograph of bleak wartime countryside, c.1916
59

Landscapes of fable, children's stories and fought-over wasteland. In the drawing, as in a sentimental scene from a storybook, a country path curves right and a small chubby boy and girl (like Hansel and Gretel, they appear to eat too much) halt to admire a leafy tree and a wayside shrine with a flight of birds in attendance. The gingerbread cottage shouldn't be too far; but in the layout of this Czech album, the horror of the wicked witch's sinister interior is displaced into a photograph of a blighted and desolate landscape, muddied and damaged by war.

line-drawn composition showing a Panzer tank juxtaposed with idyllic scenery, titled *Et in Arcadia Ego*. Death, too, is in Arcadia.

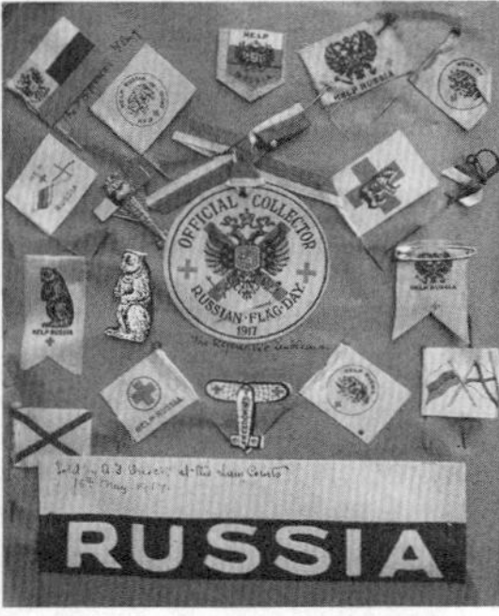

Russian Flag Day: a page from Mrs Ida Florence Orrock's Flag Day album, 1916–1922
61

Intended to be pinned to the body, these miniature emblems lent a sense of affiliation with the national community of Britain and its allies during the Great War to those who bought, wore or collected them. Ida Florence Orrock was an indefatigable nurse from the London General Hospital who sold the badges on London's pavements for the benefit of an extensive range of wartime charities.

When laid out in the pages of Orrock's album, the favours and flags take on a complex heraldic form. In their decorative aspect and sentiment, the vivid and dense graphic popular culture of the late 19th and 20th centuries is assembled in a patterned way that anticipates Peter Blake's English vernacular pop. While Blake has, since the 1950s, figured his paintings in an imperial twilight and negotiated the challenge and stimulus of US culture, something of the earlier confidence of European supremacy is redolent in these pages. Despite this, there are occasional reminders of national catastrophe and the limits of British power – one of which is a page devoted to the Mesopotamian campaign of General Townshend, which met with a final humiliating defeat at the hands of the Ottoman Turks in April 1916.

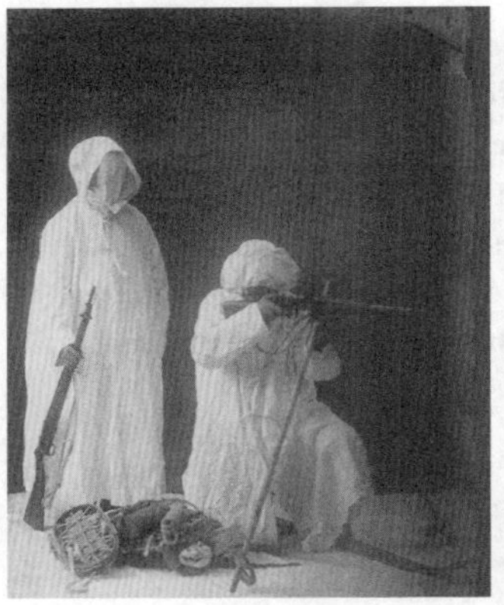

Turkish sniper ski troops, Caucasus, c.1917
62

Camouflage shifts the body into spaces where entirely other meanings become possible. In this eerie, quasi-priestly picture, a white gauze mask covers the faces of marksmen under their white hoods and caps. This phantom guise is winter camouflage for Turkish mountain snipers trained under the guidance of Austrian officers – against snow they aim to be invisible men. Sharp-shoooters of the Ottoman Empire, their long white military smocks are appropriations of commercially produced Turkish hunters' capes. These ghostly apparitions are adapted, improvised, but all is functional – even their ski poles, lashed together, form a tripod mount for their Martini-Henry rifles.

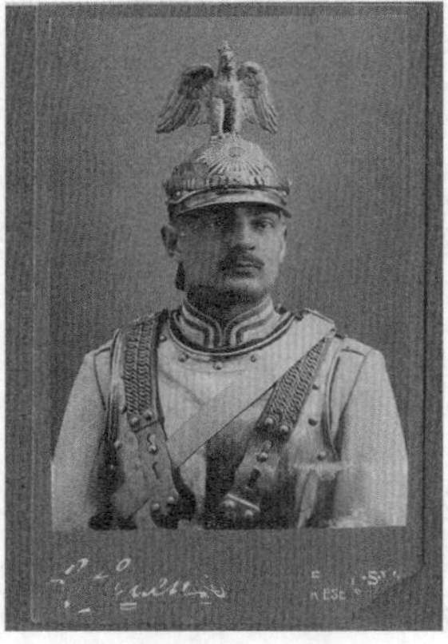

Prussian trooper, c.1890
63

This Prussian trooper wears the uniform of the Garde du Corps – with cuirassier's breastplate and distinctive brass helmet topped by a white metal eagle. Below the eagle, the helmet's central sunburst carries the motto *Suum Cuique* (To Each His

Own). The Garde du Corps was the elite of the Prussian army, founded during the reign of Frederick the Great. As with the elite regiments of many countries in the 19th century, the cost of purchasing and maintaining uniforms and of participation in social events often led to financial difficulties.

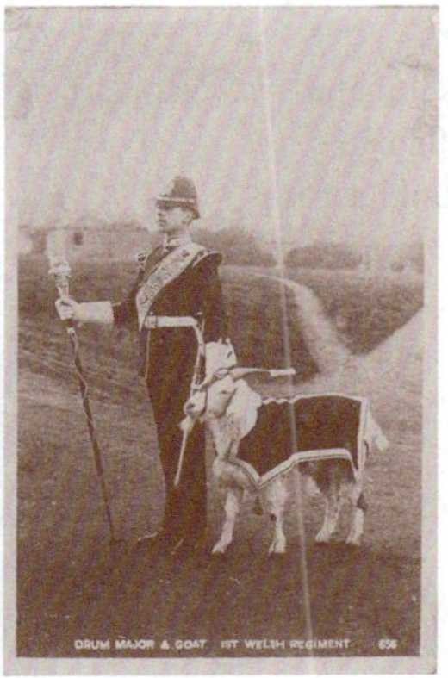

Drum Major and goat, 1st Welsh Regiment
64

Goats run wild in the mountains of Wales. They became associated with the Welsh Regiment, however, at the battle of Bunker Hill in 1775 when a wild goat joined the ranks. Subsequently goats were recruited from a herd donated to Queen Victoria by the Shah of Persia in 1837. The officer in charge was a 'Goat Major', and the animals could be relied on to act inappropriately in public – 'acting the goat'. The Irish Guards have a wolfhound as their mascot, and the American Marines a bulldog.

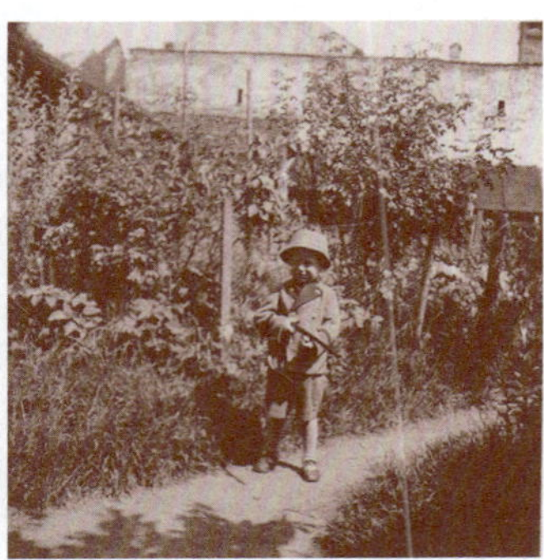

A child on a path
65

The young boy, perhaps five years old, holds a makeshift rifle with a carrying strap. A sun hat shaped like an inverted bowl

keeps him in the shade and gives him something of the air of a white hunter in an imagined rainforest. With his hat and jacket he looks the part, and he has the stance to perfection. He must have learned it from his elders as they shot birds in the locality. Shooting entails getting ready, waiting and watching until game comes into view, and then acting quickly and decisively. Shooting of this sort teaches a watchful way of life as the subject assesses the outlook, in this case an adult with a camera shooting in his or her turn according to an agenda that a five-year-old has still to understand.

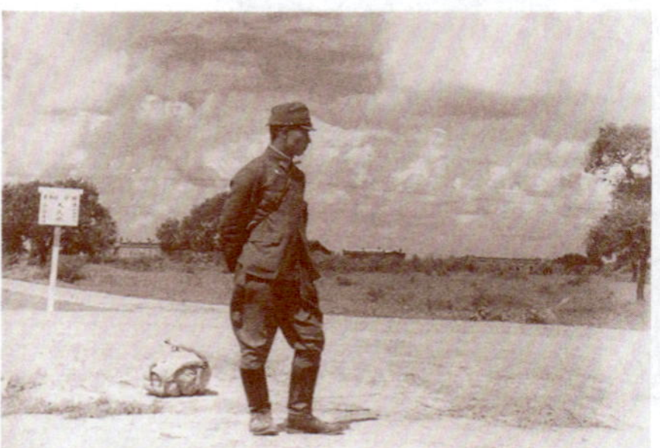

Roadside scene with an unknown soldier from the Imperial Japanese Army
66

More than 1,000 miles from his home, a Japanese soldier stands in open country in Manchuria at some time in the late 1930s, waiting for transport in alien land annexed by Japan for colonisation.

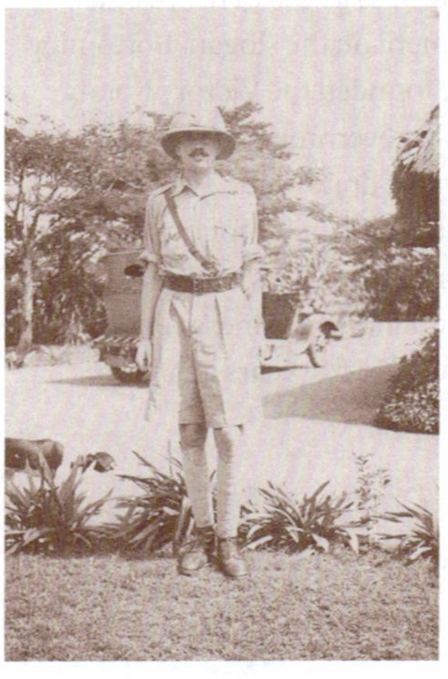

British army officer, Kenya, 1930s
67

British adaptation to tropical life involved a lot more than simply replicating the manners and mores of the Home Counties. The large moustache was borrowed from Indian culture as a necessary emblem of masculinity. The shorts are a pragmatic consequence of prevalent British theories of hygiene and airiness, while the puttees – another gift from India – are by this time already an anachronism soon to be phased out altogether.

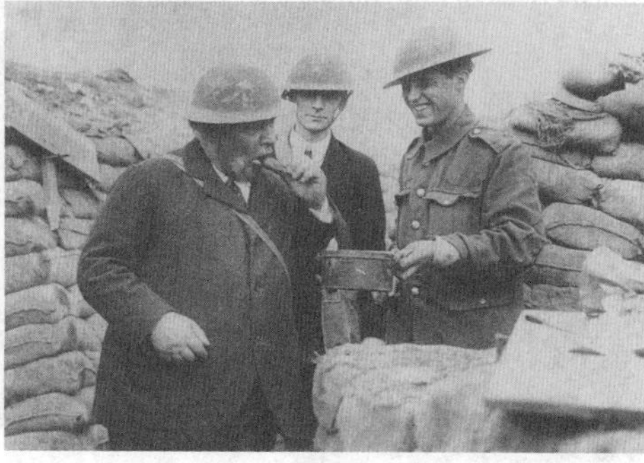

Horatio Bottomley
68

Whenever a country is engaged in all-out war, there are always enthusiasts who assign themselves the task of encouraging the public to demonstrate their patriotism by enlisting. Horatio Bottomley was one such, and during the First World War he made hundreds of speeches urging the destruction of what he called 'the unnatural freaks' – by which he meant the Germans.

In 1917 Bottomley toured the Front as a man of the people. In 1918 he was elected to Parliament on the slogan 'Bottomley, Brains and Business'. In 1919 he founded the Victory Bonds Club – a scheme in which he sold government Victory Bonds with the promise of an annual raffle draw funded through interest. In 1922 he was tried at the Old Bailey for fraud, the prosecution accusing him of using the Bonds Club funds to feed his lavish lifestyle and outlandish business ventures. He was found guilty and sentenced to five years in prison. He died in poverty in 1933.

AMC² No. 11
A GUIDE FOR THE PROTECTION
OF THE PUBLIC IN PEACETIME

Published to coincide with the exhibition *Conflict, Time, Photography* at Tate Modern, 2014

Edited by David Alan Mellor and Archive of Modern Conflict
© Archive of Modern Conflict 2014

Designed by
Melanie Mues

Printed by
Trifolio, Verona

ISSN 2048-4135

Previous issues of AMC² available at amcbooks.com